THE
WAR
BEFORE

SAFIYA BUKHARI

THE WAR BEFORE

The True Life Story of Becoming a Black Panther, Keeping the Faith in Prison & Fighting for Those Left Behind

EDITED, WITH AN INTRODUCTION
BY LAURA WHITEHORN
FOREWORD BY ANGELA Y. DAVIS
AFTERWORD BY MUMIA ABU-JAMAL

THE FEMINIST PRESS
AT THE CITY UNIVERSITY OF NEW YORK
NEW YORK CITY

Published in 2010 by the Feminist Press
at the City University of New York
The Graduate Center
365 Fifth Avenue, Suite 5406
New York, NY 10016
Feministpress.org

Cover design by Faith Hutchinson
Text design by Drew Stevens

First printing February 2010

Library of Congress Cataloging-in-Publication Data

Bukhari, Safiya, 1950-2003.
    The war before : the true life story of becoming a Black Panther, keeping the faith
in prison, & fighting for those left behind / by Safiya Bukhari ; edited, with an
introduction by Laura Whitehorn, preface by Wonda Jones, foreword by Angela Y.
Davis, and afterword by Mumia Abu-Jamal.
        p. cm.
    ISBN 978-1-55861-610-3
1. Bukhari, Safiya, 1950-2003. 2. Bukhari, Safiya, 1950-2003—Archives. 3. Black
Panther Party—Biography. 4. African American women political activists—Biography. 5. African American women—Biography. 6. Women prisoners—
Virginia—Biography. 7. African Americans—Civil rights—History—Sources.
8. Civil rights movements—United States—History—Sources. 9. Social justice—
United States—History—Sources. 10. United States—Race relations—History—
Sources. I. Whitehorn, Laura. II. Title.
    E185.97.B897A3 2009
    973'.04960730092—dc22
    [B]

                                                                                    2009033074

"And that is why . . . the youth were so important,
for they would prove to the ancestors that it had not been
foolish to fight for the right to be free, to be human."

—Toni Cade Bambara, *The Sea Birds Are Still Alive*

Contents

Preface

Not until my mother passed did I realize how important she was—how hard she worked, how many people admired her and looked up to her. It took me years to understand that although she wasn't around for me when I wanted her to be, the things she was doing instead of raising me made life a little safer for my daughter and other kids. If my mother and the rest of the Panthers hadn't done their work, we wouldn't have seen the gains made in Black civil and human rights. For instance, I think of sickle-cell anemia testing. Although common today, testing for sickle-cell anemia was virtually nonexistent until the Panthers set up programs to go door to door testing for the disease. The Party founded health clinics and organized hospitals in some cities to cooperate with the testing and to hold blood drives.

I got to know my mother when I began to understand her political life and work. That's why I wanted to publish her words. To let her speak so you could understand that too.

For much of my childhood, my mother was in prison. When I was eleven years old—a few years before my mother was released—I found out a lot about her. Until then, I thought my grandparents were my parents—even though I'd been visiting my mother in prison. Finally, an uncle told me the truth, and I began to come to terms with the new facts of my life.

I learned that if it hadn't been for my godmother, Safiya's sorority sister, Wonda (my namesake), I probably would have become a child of the system shortly after I was born. But my godmother called my grandmother, and she came to get me from the Panther headquarters just a few hours before the police raided those headquarters.

I was lucky. I've talked with a lot of Panther cubs who weren't as fortunate. They were hit with police sticks or had the cops put guns to their faces when they were discovered at a raid of Panther offices. I was lucky in that way. But in another, I was less lucky. They grew up with their parents, and I didn't. I lost my father in March of 1971. Robert Webb, a member of the Black Panther Party, was found dead on a street in New York City. Police never investigated nor was anyone ever charged with the murder. Then, for years after, my mother was on the run or in prison, and my grandparents and other family members raised me.

With all that, I didn't have the worst childhood. In fact, it felt like an ordinary life to me. At home, all I heard about was the church, and heaven and hell. I never heard about the Panthers.

My mother came home from prison when I was fourteen and in the midst of teenage rebellion. I didn't want any part of her or her life. I gave her hell. I gave Ashanti Alston hell, too. Ashanti had married Safiya in 1985 and helped raise me.

Despite all this, we developed a good relationship in time. She worked at it. When I got pregnant, my mother supported me. The first time she heard my daughter's heartbeat, she cried. She said, "I can be here for her childhood like I wasn't for yours." All the attention she hadn't been able to give to me, she poured into my baby Shylis. That's when I understood that my mother did regret not having been there as a parent for me. And that's when I forgave her.

Tragically, my mother died at the young age of fifty-three. After I got over the fury at her death—at the people who'd known she was in bad health but hadn't helped her slow down and heal—I began to step back and look at it all. I saw that we all make choices in life. She wanted to fight for all the people, to make sure that everyone, including me, had a better future. So she made a choice, sacrificing being a mother to be an activist. I'm not going to say I wouldn't have loved for her to have been there for me when I was a child, but she wanted more in life.

When I first read these essays and speeches, I felt she was alive again. I could feel her power, see her hands moving, hear her voice full of determination. I realize that her legacy is living on. If it wasn't for the speeches of Malcolm X and Dr. King, some kids wouldn't know who they were or what they stood for. Or why they made the choices they did. My mother's writings do that for me, too. I have learned from her that anyone who wants to make a change has to make choices. Those who are most serious about change often make the biggest sacrifices. No matter how I felt as a child, I respect her decisions now.

So finally the two parts of my mother—the mother and the activist—are coming together. After she died I started a foundation to help the families of political prisoners. The Safiya Bukhari-Albert Nuh Washington Foundation provides funds for those families to visit their loved ones. This is my way of carrying on the work my mother began.

Thank you for reading this book, for getting to know my mother, and supporting her at the same time.

Rest in peace, Black warrior queen. We love you.

Wonda Jones
New York City
2009

Foreword

Anyone who has worked on campaigns, directly or tangentially, to free political prisoners here in the United States recognizes Safiya Bukhari as a legendary figure. Although many of us may not have known her personally, we were nevertheless aware that her name was synonymous with the political prisoner movement. This collection of her speeches and writings reveals Safiya Bukhari to be one of the very best examples of dedication to radical change and to revolutionary social justice. Her words compel us to recognize how much unacknowledged labor dwells inside and behind social justice movements. Reaching across racial, cultural, national, and generational boundaries, *The War Before* speaks to many different communities about the significance of organizing. Hopefully it will teach us respect and reverence for the organizer, who so often remains the unknown and unacknowledged figure behind progressive mass movements.

We are all very fortunate that Safiya's daughter, Wonda Jones, realized how important it was to compile a collection of her writings and speeches, even though Safiya herself did not produce them for publication, and that Laura Whitehorn—whose friendship with Safiya began during her own political imprisonment—agreed to edit and introduce these writings. It is a great privilege to observe the trajectory of an activist who refused to surrender, no matter how bleak the prospects for freedom. Safiya refused to surrender during the Clinton years, which were among the most difficult for political prisoners, as well as during the early Bush years. Had she not suffered a premature death in the summer of 2003, undoubtedly she would be just as intensely involved today in all the causes she supported during previous decades.

Longtime radical activists are often asked about the source of strength that impels them to remain committed over years and decades, and to continue to struggle, even when the prospects for success are negligible. The assumption is that somehow within one's own psyche there is a reservoir of spiritual strength that drives one forward. I myself usually try to explain that in my case, it is not so much about the individual but rather about her bonds of solidarity within communities of struggle. But such abstract explanations rarely elucidate how political collectivities striving for radical change can provide the kind of sustenance that enables human beings to remake themselves so that their individual consciousness is always in dialogue with a collective consciousness. Safiya Bukhari's writings reveal in concrete terms the inner workings of this dialectic.

The story of how Safiya became radicalized is not that unusual. What is truly phenomenal about the way she narrates her life across several decades is that she is able to forge such a powerful connection to the political and spiritual communities she joins, represents, and defends. She becomes a member of the Black Panther Party and the Black Liberation Army, becomes a citizen of the Republic of New Afrika, and an officer in its Provisional Government. Deeply spiritual, she decides to become a Muslim. She refashions her own life in accordance with the needs of these communities, and in the process, helps to ameliorate and transform them. Her momentous achievement was to build and persuade others to join campaigns to defend political prisoners, who were not necessarily members of her organizations, but were dedicated to radical goals of social justice.

Those of us who reached political maturity during the sixties and seventies recognize in Safiya's writings the many markers that structure the history we experienced during our youth—a history which is almost always relegated to the margins of official accounts. We recognize such markers as the founding of the Black Panther Party in 1966, the assassination of Chicago Panthers Fred Hampton and Mark Clark in 1969, the arrest and eventual escape from prison of Assata Shakur, the development of an international campaign to free Mumia Abu-Jamal, the frame-up and imprisonment of Geronimo ji Jaga Pratt in 1970, and his release in 1997. In connection with his and other cases, we learned about the reach of COINTELPRO—the FBI's counterintelligence program that was designed to destroy the Black Panther Party and other radical formations of that era. We also learn that Safiya went to prison in 1975, escaped, was recaptured, and finally released on parole in 1983.

People of my generation tend to reflect on that era with a certain measure of nostalgia, which is not only about our youth but also about a prevailing sense of solidarity and a widespread belief that we were in the process of making a revolution. New organizations emerged and the university began to be transformed in response to demands for Black, Latina/o, Native American, Asian American, and women's studies programs. We felt connected to the decolonization and revolutionary processes in Africa, Asia, and Latin America. We believed that we were in the process of dismantling racism and destroying capitalism in the US—in "the belly of the beast." Laura Whitehorn's wonderful introduction describes what it was like to experience the urgency of revolution. Safiya, and others like her, performed the kind of work that made it possible for us to sustain those beliefs.

I appreciate the straightforward way in which Safiya recounts the subjugated histories of that era, punctuated by the ironic and critical tone she occasionally adopts. In the chapter "We Too Are Veterans" she points out that many activists, who saw themselves as literally engaged in war, suffered—and continue to suffer—from post-traumatic stress disorder:

> We theorized about what we were up against. We marched, sang, and rhetoricized about the implications of being in "the belly of the beast." We dissociated ourselves from anything or anyone who had been close to us and regurgitated the bravado about the struggle being primary—that in order to win we must be willing to sacrifice mother, father, sister, or brother. We embraced all this in much the same manner that the drill sergeant in the Marine Corps psyched up the recruits to fight in Vietnam. (80–81)

Laura Whitehorn points out that Safiya's opinions around issues of homophobia changed over time, although this is not necessarily reflected in her writings. In the passage above, I read a critique of the masculinist and militarist romanticism, which was so seductive to many of us. I thus find myself wishing that she had left us with writings that describe the transformation of her ideas.

But Safiya was not concerned with producing a comprehensive history of her activism. That is why this collection is so powerful. Although she did not intend to focus on herself, except insofar as she could illuminate the importance of mass struggle, Safiya left us with a powerful legacy. Laura points out that all the people who worked with her said the same thing when they were asked to describe her contributions: "no one worked harder than she did" (34). She was not only the moving force behind huge operations—the Jericho Movement and the campaign to free Mumia, for example—she combined her ability to build mass movements with close contacts with all those, regardless of their relative prominence, who remained in prison on charges related to their political beliefs and activities. She corresponded and visited with them, and urged others to communicate with them.

I remember how inspired I felt after my own last visits with Mongo we Langa and Ed Poindexter. Marilyn Buck has never curtailed her participation in our movement to abolish the prison-industrial complex. Leonard Peltier's vigor continues to inspire us. Each message from Mumia is a powerful reminder of why we need to redouble our efforts to free him. Safiya was in close contact with every one of the approximately one hundred political prisoners who were on the list she compiled. When we give thanks that the list is somewhat smaller today—it can be found on page 110—we recognize what an important contribution she made to the release of Geronimo ji Jaga Pratt, the Puerto Rican independistas, Linda Evans, Laura Whitehorn, Susan Rosenberg, and others. But there are still seventy-five political prisoners behind bars. I hope the readers of *The War Before* will commit themselves to the campaign to bring Assata Shakur home, and to freeing Mumia, Leonard Peltier, and every one of the human beings for whom Safiya Bukhari so passionately gave her life.

Angela Davis
Oakland
2009

Introduction

For many, the iconic image of the 1960s is not a picture of hippies with daisy-wreathed hair dancing in the rain during the days of peace, love, and music at Woodstock. It is a photograph splashed across the front pages of Chicago newspapers in December 1969. Four grinning Chicago police officers, all of them white, carry a trophy: the bullet-ridden body of a young Black man.

Fred Hampton, leader of the Illinois chapter of the Black Panther Party, was twenty-one years old when the cops murdered him. Other photos show his body lying face down on the floor of the apartment where he and fellow Panther member Mark Clark had been shot to death in their sleep. Still another depicts Fred's blood-soaked mattress.

At first, the photos appeared accompanied by accounts from Illinois State Attorney Edward Hanrahan saying that the police had been defending themselves from bullets fired by Panthers within the apartment. But it quickly emerged that this "shootout" had been something quite different. As the Panthers and their lawyers unveiled physical evidence showing that all but one of the more than ninety shots had come from the police, it became clear that this had been a deliberate police assassination, targeting the powerful Black Panther Party leader. This was, in fact, a premeditated act of war conducted by police—assisted, we were later to learn, by the FBI.

Other images of Fred Hampton and the Black Panther Party describe another side of that war—and help explain why the

Panthers, and Fred in particular, were targeted. These photos, taken at rallies, marches, community-organizing projects and meetings, are flooded with a riot of emotions: anger, joy, humor, and most profoundly, the tremendous creative energy unleashed by a struggle for liberation. The Panthers sparked that energy. Their programs and their organizing led Black people around the country to take control of their communities. In those programs, many of the people in these communities saw themselves—not white institutions or politicians—as the source of change, achieved by working collectively.

Another emotion visible in those images—and palpable to anyone who attended a Panther rally in a park or church or on a street corner at that time—was hope. In the context of a struggle for justice and freedom, hope was such a powerful emotion that the FBI and police found it necessary to use the tools of warfare to obliterate it.

■ ■ ■

When we learned that night that Fred had been killed, those of us in a collective of Weatherman (soon to become the Weather Underground Organization) felt fury and grief, but not surprise. We had been prepared for this. My own preparation had been short and dramatic. It had only been fourteen months since, one hot August afternoon in 1968, I had been sitting at my desk in Hyde Park, Chicago. I was then a disaffected, twenty-three-year-old graduate student preparing for PhD exams in English literature. In my second-floor apartment, I looked up from Milton's *Paradise Lost* to gaze out the open window onto a quiet street scene: a sidewalk, some trees, a fire hydrant, and a young Black man walking down the block.

Suddenly a police car pulled up. Two officers jumped out and grabbed the man, throwing him up against a building, frisking him, and demanding that he tell them who he was and what he was doing on that street. Impulsively, I ran outside, where I tried to convince the cops to let him go. They threatened to arrest me as well. The young man struggled a little, then was arrested— not for anything he'd done, but for answering police questions too slowly. He was later released with a warning.

I did not go back to my desk that day. I did not return to my studies at all.

That past April, a few months before I'd moved to the city, the mayor of Chicago had called to the West Side not just the police but also the National Guard. They were given orders to "shoot to kill" anyone caught destroying property in the outburst of grief and rage following the murder of Martin Luther King Jr. After years of standing up to the fire hoses, bullwhips, and billy clubs of southern police forces during the civil rights movement, Black people now watched their northern communities turn into occupied territories. Instead of accepting and meeting Black people's demands for equal rights, the government had responded by initiating a domestic war in the streets of our country.

The domestic war was easier to comprehend in the context of international events. I had already developed a vague sense of this context from teach-ins and rallies during those years when protests against the threat of nuclear war expanded into something broader and more radical. In stuffy, darkened high school and college classrooms, I had watched grainy newsreel films and documentaries showing how the US government habitually intervened both clandestinely and openly in suppressing democracies around the world. The United States was not only waging a war against the people of Vietnam. The government had also been complicit in the overthrow of the democratically elected government of Jacobo Arbenz in Guatemala in 1954 and the murder of Patrice Lumumba in the Congo in 1961. But another global phenomenon had emerged at the same time: third world people were fighting back, refusing to accede to oppression and, in many cases, seemed to be winning their battles—China in 1949, Cuba in 1959, Algeria in 1962. In 1955, progressive Asian and African nations had met in Bandung, Indonesia, uniting to condemn Western colonialism and challenge the European choke hold on world history. Bandung and its outgrowth, the Non-Aligned Movement, changed the balance of world power. Eleven years later, a similar meeting—the Tricontinental Conference in Havana—brought African, Asian, and Latin American nations closer together in an anticolonial movement.

In January 1968, the Vietnamese Liberation Army had surprised most of the world by launching a general offensive and popular uprising, a massive attack on US forces known as the Tet Offensive.[1] Suddenly it seemed possible that the liberation forces could succeed in defeating the US military—as, of course, they would go on to do.

Clearly, this war had two sides. The oppressed nations were refusing to be victims.

A week after I'd witnessed the cops beating that young man on my block—as if we were in apartheid South Africa—the Chicago police launched another attack, this time with tear gas and clubs, against thousands of young people who had gathered in Grant Park to protest the Vietnam War during the Democratic National Convention. The next day, I was there among the thousands shouting, "The whole world is watching," as TV cameras filmed us being gassed and chased by police and soldiers with fixed bayonets. Soon after, I began attending rallies held by the Black Panther Party, and I joined Weatherman—a group that would flourish, then disintegrate, in less than ten years. I also became part of a larger movement that will last well beyond my own lifetime.

■ ■ ■

Safiya Bukhari was and remains a catalytic part of that movement. According to her own accounts, Safiya was radicalized into the Black Panther Party at the business end of a billy club. Born Bernice Jones in the Bronx in 1950, she grew up among nine sisters and brothers in a devoutly Christian, middle-class family (the family moved south soon after Safiya's birth, then back to the Bronx). The children were relatively sheltered and were raised to believe they would succeed in the world through higher education. Safiya planned on becoming a doctor. In 1968 she was attending Brooklyn's New York City Community College as a premed student.

Her life to that point had been fairly conventional; she'd even joined a sorority. Along with two close friends, Yvonne and Wonda, Safiya pledged at Eta Alpha Mu, the college's only integrated sorority. Part of their assigned pledge duties was to show up in costumes at the Port Authority bus station, where they were instructed to entertain the crowd. "I was dressed as a ballerina," remembers Yvonne, "and Bernice came as Charlie Chaplin."

Even then, Bernice Jones was on her way to becoming Safiya.[2] Yvonne wrote, in a letter to Wonda Jones in 2005, "With our sorority there were parties and socials, of course. But Bernice, Wonda, and I were more interested in helping change the future for our youth. We petitioned our sisterhood about sponsoring a child in Africa. But it was Bernice who asked why we needed to invest in an African child when there were needy children in the United States."[3]

The sorority assigned the young women a field trip: they were to visit Harlem. "Bernice, Wonda, and I took the A train to 125th Street," Yvonne remembers. "Upon departing the train station, we encountered a member of the Black Panther Party selling newspapers. I recall that he talked about the Free Breakfast for Children Program offered to the children of the community and asked if we were interested in volunteering or contributing to the cause."

The women went to the church where the breakfasts were offered, to see for themselves. Safiya liked what she saw and kept coming back. It was at that time that she began to notice how badly the community was treated by the police.

"It wasn't the Panthers that made me join the Black Panther Party," Safiya often said; as she told an audience in Chicago in 1991, "It was the police."[4]

One time, Safiya tried to stop an officer from harassing another Panther selling a Party newspaper. "Stupid me," she said of herself, remembering the incident. "I said to the cop, 'He has a constitutional right to disseminate political literature.' He took my ID, told me get up against the car, and said I was inciting to riot. He arrested me, my friend, and the Panther [who'd been selling newspapers]. On the way to the Fourteenth Precinct, I learned that there was no such thing as a constitutional right when it comes to Black people."

■ ■ ■

History is made by thousands and thousands of individuals whose names you may never know. It's one thing to read the speeches of Martin Luther King Jr.—there's no way the civil rights movement or US history would have been the same without him. But if you want to understand those times—and how change is made—you need to know of the people who shared Dr. King's dream—those who heard his speeches and worked to carry out that vision, whose passion led them to build an entire movement.

Safiya Bukhari did the work and became, over the years, a leader among many people. Her name doesn't come up on the list of prominent women in the Panthers; she wasn't in front of the media. But from 1969, she was in the Harlem office of the Black Panther Party, working on all its projects—the Free Breakfast for Children Program, political education and outreach, and a health clinic to screen for sickle-cell anemia and other medical problems—and, of course, selling the Panther newspaper.

During those years, I worked with the Panthers in Chicago and saw them as the catalyst of liberation, not only for Black people but for all progressive activists. What I didn't fully realize until some years later is that, although they were probably the most successful in mass organizing on a countrywide scale, the Black Panthers were one of many Black groups of the 1960s and 1970s who defined their goal as trying to make a revolution. Many Black liberation groups flowered in those years—Safiya herself also joined the Republic of New Afrika, though she never left the Panthers. Using the politics of national liberation and independence, the Panthers probably reached further into more sectors of the Black community than other groups, building serve-the-people programs based on a class analysis.

■ ■ ■

The Black Panther Party's Ten-Point Program—their platform of goals—was modeled on Vietnamese, Chinese, and other liberatory struggles.[5] Like many progressive groups of that era, the Panthers saw other oppressed peoples rising up all over the world. In those years, all of us found ourselves witnessing a global revolution—one that was, amazingly, not dominated by white leftists. Malcolm X was saying to millions, "We are non-violent with people who are nonviolent with us." Why, asked Malcolm, are you applauded for picking up a gun and killing Germans and Koreans and Vietnamese, but you're not allowed to fight back against the Ku Klux Klan or the police who are trying to kill you?[6]

This was a profound argument. The point was not to attack nonviolence, but to show that it was only one tactic in an arsenal of struggle, and that armed self-defense was another. Self-defense was, in fact, taken up by some parts of the civil rights movement, as well as by many Black nationalists in and beyond the Black Panther Party. Robert Williams, leader of the Monroe, North Carolina, branch of the NAACP, was, for example, among the early advocates of armed self-defense—which he called "armed self-reliance"—to respond to racist violence. An integrationist, Williams was never suspected of hurting or killing anyone. He sheltered a white woman and her husband in his home for a few hours when they were threatened by a mob—for which the FBI accused him of kidnapping the couple. Williams fled to Cuba, a refugee from United States law enforcement.[7]

Back in New York, Safiya Bukhari had become a young mother. She formed a political and a romantic relationship with another member of the Panthers, Robert Webb, and gave birth to Wonda (named for Safiya's sorority sister, Wonda Johnson) in 1969.[8] In those years, revolutionaries usually saw ourselves as too busy making the revolution to engage in standard family life. The revolution, we felt, would make life better for our families and children. So Safiya devoted herself less to personal love and motherhood than to the Black Panther Party.

This meant embracing the Panther principle of self-defense. The Panthers patrolled their neighborhoods, keeping watch over the police and helping, when they could, victims of police brutality. At a time when police killings of unarmed Black and Puerto Rican youth in New York were frequent—and consistently went unpunished—there was much to do. It is hard to describe the impact that the concept of self-defense had on the Black community and progressive supporters. For the first time in many years, defending a community against police terror was widely promoted as a legitimate tactic. This gave teeth to the community's demand that Black lives be afforded equal value to white.

But the year 1969 was also the beginning of the Panther 21 case—a prosecution by the Manhattan district attorney, cooked up by the New York Police Department, to portray the Panthers as thugs and hoodlums. Charged with attempted arson, attempted murder, and conspiracy to blow up police stations, school buildings, a railroad yard, and the Bronx Botanical Gardens, the defendants were to spend more than two years in jail before all twenty-one were acquitted by a jury after deliberating for just forty-five-minutes.[9] As Safiya helped organize support for the defendants, the case not only disrupted her life and work—and that of the entire organization—it also confirmed her worst fears: the police were out to get the Panthers.

Other Panther arrests followed. Many of them were questionable; several were later proved in court to be frame-ups similar to that of the 21. Although many activists sensed that covert police surveillance was helping to provoke internal dissention in the Party, it wasn't until after 1975—when the US Senate's Church Committee confirmed the existence of J. Edgar Hoover's counterintelligence program (COINTELPRO)—that the broader community fully grasped the source of the damage:

since 1967 they had been targeted and infiltrated by the FBI, whose explicit purpose was to "expose, disrupt, misdirect, discredit, or otherwise neutralize" the Party.[10] Out of necessity, the Panthers began shifting their emphasis from community organizing to legal defense work. Exposing frame-ups—when it was possible to do so, when all the evidence had not been destroyed by the police—took years of work, not to mention years of the lives of those falsely accused.[11]

Way before we knew what it was, COINTELPRO exerted a tremendous influence on the consciousness and politics of all of us who belonged to or worked with the Panthers and other radical groups. We didn't know that it was a specific government program, but we did know that we were under surveillance and attack. Many of us were subjected to random bullets and rocks that broke our office windows; strange break-ins where only our notes and address books were taken; and odd, provocative phone calls to our homes, offices, and families. Any ambiguity about the source of these attacks ended for many of us on the night of December 4, 1969, with the assassination of Fred Hampton and fellow Panther Mark Clark in Chicago.

Not only did the police lie, claiming that Fred and Mark had been killed during a shoot-out initiated by the Panthers; it was also revealed that Fred and other Panthers had been drugged by William O'Neil, an FBI informant within the organization. The police had unleashed a firestorm against the Panthers that was both unprovoked and carefully premeditated. Here's what else we were sure of: Fred Hampton had been targeted for nothing other than his ability to articulate the problems, dreams, and goals of masses of Black people. Another Black leader had been killed. This was counterinsurgency—a tactic of warfare.

In this context, and with more and more energy going toward supporting the Panthers and other radicals in court cases, many saw the need for underground organizations to carry on community defense work. At the same time, the step many US radicals took in those years to go underground was a leap of hope: the world was in flames, and movements around the world were winning national independence by means of armed as well as political struggle. Many of us felt we were joining a global revolution, taking a chance on a strategy that held the prospect of bringing down the empire. That is why, in her writings and speeches, Safiya will sometimes refer to her years underground as a defense against repression, and sometimes as an attempt to build a national liberation struggle to contend for power.

In 1971, COINTELPRO succeeded in driving a wedge into the Black Panther Party, provoking a split that created separate organizations as well as enmities that resulted in killings. Safiya became communications director of the East Coast organization and edited its newspaper, *Right On!*[12] She also issued statements received from the clandestine Black Liberation Army (BLA), which was aligned with the East Coast Panthers. The split was deeply troubling, revealing how severely conflicts and divisions can corrode attempts to develop new values and better human relationships. In many of her later writings, Safiya explored the question of how the FBI had been able to create the split—what were the weaknesses, the failures, that allowed such fratricide to be instigated. She also entertained ideas for how to build a more cohesive organization, one that could withstand such assaults from within.[13]

By now, Safiya had devoted her life to the movement, setting aside the ordinary adventures of youth and responsibilities of family. The decision took a toll on her daughter, one both she and her mother later worked hard to repair.

■ ■ ■

Throughout these years, Safiya played a critical role in developing support for the increasing number of Black prisoners who had been arrested and charged with serious offenses, many tagged by police and media as actions of the BLA.[14] In December 1973, she was arrested and charged with plotting to break prisoners out of New York City jails. A few days after her arrest, out on bail, Safiya told a radio audience that her charges were bogus, an attempt by cops to stop her work on political cases. The charges against her were, in fact, soon dismissed.

Then she was hit with a subpoena to testify before a New York City grand jury that was preparing charges against other Black radicals. She couldn't bring herself to testify against her political associates. Safiya left her family and friends to continue her work underground.

She stayed under for almost two years, until 1975, when she was arrested at the scene of a grocery store shooting in Norfolk, Virginia. Convicted of robbery and felony murder, and sentenced to forty years, Safiya began serving her time in the prison for women at Goochland, Virginia.[15]

Long before her arrest, Safiya had developed massive fibroid tumors. In prison, her condition worsening, she received frighteningly little medical care. In late 1976, Safiya escaped.

Captured within a year, she was tried for escape and used her defense to garner attention to the appalling neglect of her medical condition. The result was that she finally got the operation she needed. But she was also placed in detention and spent nearly all of the following four years in solitary confinement.

True to form, Safiya organized, even when she was in the hole. She provided support to other women prisoners; once released into the general population, she created a group called Mothers Inside Loving Kids (MILK) to help long-term prisoners regain custody of their children. She edited a book of BLA poetry, *The Soul of the Black Liberation Army*. In fact, many of her early writings were produced in prison. Above all, calling on an enormous reserve of psychological strength, she fought to maintain her political identity.

In August 1983, after eight years and eight months in prison, she was, to her surprise, granted parole and released. She rejoined her daughter and her mother (who had been raising Wonda) in New York City and began the process of rebuilding a relationship with her daughter. She got a job as a social worker in the Bronx office of the Legal Aid Society, an organization providing legal services to indigent people. After years of stress and trauma, she found that she had more political work to do than ever.

■ ■ ■

Radical movements had grown and, by the time of Safiya's release, there were more than forty leftist political prisoners in the United States. They represented movements in the Black, Puerto Rican, Mexican, Native American, and white progressive communities. Within the following three years, some forty others would join them.[16] Between 1984 and 1998, numerous national and international conferences, publications, organizations, and events focused attention on these cases. Safiya was intimately involved in the efforts, becoming more central to them as time went on.

Safiya continually visited prisoners, wrote to them, and always accepted their collect phone calls. She communicated their needs and ideas to the outside world, and she wrote and spoke on their behalf, while the government, refusing to call them "political" prisoners, kept trying to bury them.

When you're inside, it means everything to know that there's someone who will care when you get thrown in the hole or when you don't have money in your commissary account—someone who will call people to help. Safiya was one of the people prisoners counted on. Sometimes, when fewer people were doing the work, Safiya—like Yuri Kochiyama for years before her—was *the* one.[17] In years when radical movements are in disarray or when activism is absent, work in support of political prisoners can be a way to keep some political issues alive. For prisoners, though, it is more than a tactic—it is a lifeline. That is why every current and former US-held leftist political prisoner knows and reveres the names of Yuri and Safiya in particular. Their work made it possible for political prisoners to have a voice, which meant we were still politically active human beings.

I say "we" because I was one of those prisoners.

In 1985, I was arrested with five other white activists for conspiracy to bomb several government buildings that were symbols of domestic racism, such as the office of the New York City Police Benevolent Association (known for supporting cops who had killed innocent civilians) following the murder of Black grandmother Eleanor Bumpurs. We were also charged with bombing buildings emblematic of US foreign policy—most famously the Capitol Building, after the US invasion of Grenada and shelling of Lebanon in 1983. We stuck to specific targets and planned with care: No one was hurt in any of the bombings.

Without adopting a consistent name for our group, we chose that moment to carry out these acts partly because the government and the police were hot on the trail of Puerto Rican and Black movement undergrounds, and we wanted to throw a distraction in their path. As white radicals, we refused to leave these liberation struggles to fight alone. We didn't want to say,

"Go, defeat the enemy! We'll be sitting here on the sidelines, clapping for you!" Supporting the struggles of people for freedom means that you take some risks yourself. It means stepping beyond your political comfort zone.

The six of us were charged with "conspiracy to influence, change, and protest policies and practices of the United States government by violent and illegal means." I received a sentence of twenty years. And it was in the visiting room of the federal women's prison in Dublin, California, that I met Safiya Bukhari.

She was there doing her work, visiting prisoners across the country, getting to know me and the six other women political prisoners in Dublin at that time.[18] She found out what we thought and what we needed, then met with activists outside, encouraging them to support us and all the political prisoners she encountered.

Out of this work she, along with political prisoner Jalil Muntaqim and former political prisoner Herman Ferguson, decided that a national mobilization to demand the release of political prisoners was needed. They created the Jericho Movement and called for a November 1998 rally in front of the White House to make the demand. The name Jericho was used to conjure up the image of massive resistance that would succeed in bringing down the walls of the prisons, freeing the more than one hundred political prisoners behind those walls at the time.

Safiya traveled around the country and abroad, speaking to anyone who might be interested, talking herself hoarse and exhausting herself in the process. She produced buttons, posters, fliers, mouse pads, T-shirts—anything that might generate awareness of political prisoners and make the Jericho rally a success. At the same time, she worked with Sally O'Brien on the weekly radio show *Where We Live*, on Pacifica station WBAI, delivering news and information about political prisoners. She was often seen at various conferences and events, behind a card table piled with leaflets, fliers, buttons, and books about the comrades in prison, handing out information, talking to anyone who stopped to look, asking people to sign a petition or attend an event. Along with her work in the Jericho Movement, she continued to work on the campaign to free Mumia Abu-Jamal. She had founded the New York Free Mumia Abu-Jamal Coalition a few years earlier and was still co-chairing the group. She never stopped. The people who worked most closely with Safiya during these years—including Mumia Abu-Jamal, Jalil Muntaqim, Yuri Kochiyama, Herman and Iyaluua Ferguson, Herman Bell, Pam Africa, Cleo Silvers, Suzanne Ross, Paulette d'Auteuil and Anne Lamb, Sally O'Brien, and Sundiata Sadiq— all now say the same thing when asked to remember Safiya: no one worked harder than she did.

Above all, Safiya was a passionate and effective organizer. In the summer of 2009 I discussed Safiya with Lumumba Bandele, who was raised in a politically aware and active family and community and is now a leading member of the Malcolm X Grassroots Movement (MXGM). He said, "Safiya was the reason I do work supporting political prisoners." With other young activists, Lumumba remembers that "in 1994 or 95" he arranged an organizer training session, The Azabache Youth Leadership Conference, for young people. Seasoned organizers were asked to speak, offering guidance to the several hundred younger activists who attended the session. A prearranged plan was to be presented at the end of the session, outlining the next steps everyone would take together, "but Safiya diverted those plans," Lumumba said. "She gave a fiery speech, 'Which Way Forward?' in which she convinced everyone to join together in work for Mumia. She swept us all up, and we spent the following months plastering the streets of New York with posters, talking to everyone who would listen—organizing support for Mumia. Someone asked her why people should support Mumia and other political prisoners. Safiya said, 'anyone who is truly passionate about social justice has the capacity to become a political prisoner.' Listening, I recognized in her words all the people from my childhood who were like that—the elders of our struggle, the people who'd worked so hard and given so much of themselves. As she spoke, I felt she represented me and my history and identity."[19]

■ ■ ■

By the end of the twentieth century, some of us began to get out, having completed our sentences or been released on parole. In 1999, I "maxed out," having served the bulk of my sentence (the two-thirds mandated under then-current federal law). In 2000, as he left office, President Bill Clinton commuted the sentences of eleven Puerto Rican *independentista* prisoners in federal custody, along with those of Linda Evans and Susan Rosenberg, two of my codefendants. To Safiya, this was a miracle—and a blow: Clinton did not release any of the Black prisoners, nor did he release Native American leader and internationally recognized political prisoner Leonard Peltier (whose conviction arose from a historic event of the 1970s, the Native American takeover of Wounded Knee).[20]

Today, I look at the videotape of the "coming out" party that friends threw for me a week after my release. Safiya, of course, was there. Getting up to speak, she tells us that she is talking from the point of view of someone who had been in prison. Then she says: "Every time a freedom fighter comes home, it's like a part of us is out there again, it's like a ray of hope for everybody else. But when you leave, and you leave those others behind, it's like you leave part of you inside the institution. So you have to continue to do the work, because as long as there's a political prisoner—any prisoner—inside this country, that means that you're not truly free."

Watching the tape now, I see Safiya's pain and grief, mixed with joy, fueling her buoyant delivery. And I notice that she's organizing me. I could show it to you. She stands up there, revealing her own pain because she knows that helps other people deal with their pain—and because she wants them to join, to do the work with her.

In the early years of this century, Safiya's health deteriorated. Not many of us knew how badly she suffered from a variety of ailments connected with hypertension. A week after the death of her mother in 2003, Safiya died of a pulmonary embolism to the lungs. Her death at the age of fifty-three was mourned by leftists and progressives across the globe.

Safiya's life is a story that stands for all of us who have not been defeated but have yet to win. In the speeches and writings you'll find here, two emotional strands compete. There's the excitement and energy she brought to her life's work, motivated by her desire for social change and her awareness that imprisonment is one consequence of any serious struggle for liberation. But there is also the sorrow of losing people and leaving others behind—what Safiya once called the hole in her heart caused by the deaths and imprisonment of so many comrades.[21] As she spoke over the years, that sorrow crept in more frequently. The years pass, and she sounds angrier, talking about a lack of organizing, the absence of what she calls a "serious" movement for change.

I understand those feelings. Even though I'm out of prison, a part of me remains there. Political prisoners are, in fact, a part of all of us who were part of the 1960s. I hold them the way I hold myself. And I forgive the mistakes we made along the way and their human toll, or how we might have been too extremist at times. I forgive us the simplistic "us/them" binary (reflected in our use of "them" to mean anyone associated with the ruling class or the state), our failure to specify who was being held responsible for crimes of oppression and greed. I forgive us the stances that look silly in hindsight—the posturing, the drama, the self-seriousness. I forgive us the arrogance that allowed us to think we could create revolution by sheer force of will and example—a tendency we sometimes called "voluntarism." Those were parts of our attempt to find our own place in the whirlwind of change swirling across the globe. We stepped forward, saying, "Okay, I'll risk. And if we fail, I won't abandon our principles or those who fall." It's what it means to live in this world, what underlies solidarity, that wonderful quality of being human.

That, in Safiya's words, is worth fighting for.

■ ■ ■

When Wonda Jones first asked me to help edit her mother's papers for publication, we both thought it would be a small task. Safiya, after all, was an organizer, an activist, not an author or scholar. Safiya was all about the work; she rarely seemed to have time for writing.

But our project quickly grew. As soon as we began looking, we realized that recordings of Safiya's many interviews and speeches must exist somewhere. In addition to the packet of essays Safiya left, all written in prison or late at night, additional articles and interviews began turning up. Ashanti Alston, Safiya's longtime comrade and fellow activist (and former political prisoner), found his and Safiya's marriage contract along with Safiya's articles from old, yellowing issues of Panther newspapers. Wayne Lum, who had worked with Safiya on behalf of leftist US-held political prisoners, furnished the unique tape of a TV interview. Claude Marks and Billy X Jennings in the San Francisco Bay Area; Jalil Muntaqim and Herman Bell, then held in the San Francisco County Jail; Nancy Kurshan and Hondo T'Chikwa in Chicago; Herb Boyd, Michael Tarif Warren, Barbara Zeller, Sundiata Sadiq, Robert Boyle, Sally O'Brien, Lumumba Bandele, and Matt Meyer in New York; and Roz Payne in Vermont all contributed recordings and documents from their own archives. The themes here are disparate; they were determined not by a plan for a book, but rather by Safiya's need to argue for various positions at various times and, more than anything else, to urge people to join her in supporting political prisoners.

What you see in this book is not a verbatim version of everything Safiya wrote or spoke, nor are the pieces ordered as they were in her papers. Her goal was not so much to leave a print record, but rather to organize. Each essay or speech was directed at a particular audience at a particular moment, producing a lot of repetition in the compendium of texts and speeches she left behind. I have tried to cut, combine, and edit these in a way that reflects her ideas and her goals. I have tried to make this Safiya's book—the one she might have wanted to see published. Many of the original texts can now be found in their entirety at safiyabukhari.com and freedomarchives.org. The videos of several speeches can be viewed at thejerichomovement.com.

I am certain that there are other materials, more of Safiya's words, out there. There are also oceans of memories held by her family, her friends, and all the people whose lives she touched—those who worked with her and benefited from her activism. This book doesn't include those. It lacks the full, vivid portrait of Safiya that would emerge from such remembrances—by prisoners as well as family members and political associates on the outside. That book, the one *about* Safiya, remains to be written.

As I typed and edited, I often talked aloud to Safiya, telling her how badly I miss her and how badly the movement misses her, and sometimes arguing with her about things she'd written. Transcribing her essay on Islam and revolution, for example, I came across her comment about resisting the "temptation" of homosexuality in prison and chastised her for failing to update the essay to reflect her own changing attitude about this issue. "I know you don't think that way anymore," I argued, wondering how I would make it clear to readers that this negative connotation doesn't represent what Safiya believed in the years before her death. I knew this from my own comradeship and talks with Safiya, but also because so many of us have evolved in our thinking from some earlier rigid and limited viewpoints.

But of course Safiya didn't take the time to go back and rewrite old articles and essays, for the same reason she wrote many of them in the first place. She wasn't thinking about leaving her papers to posterity; she was thinking about writing in the moment as part of her organizing work. She wrote these pieces and gave these speeches and interviews out of her enormous passion for change and her rock-solid loyalty to political prisoners. Over and over, when Safiya told her own story, she made it serve the purpose of organizing. Her account of her early years doesn't include many personal details that would depict her particular life experiences. Rather, she consistently recounts the parts of her own history that elucidate general political points, such as how events pushed her to realize the necessity to fight for justice. She's not particularly interested in telling her story; she's interested in how her narrative might help others see that a struggle for justice is necessary—and worth joining. A clear portrait of Safiya the woman does, however, emerge from these writings. If you read the chapters from first to last, you will meet a woman who was not afraid to grapple with hard questions stemming from the heady days when we saw revolution on the horizon. In particular, Safiya wrestles over and over with the problem of how our own weaknesses allowed government repression to confound our work and divide our organizations.

In some speeches and writings, when Safiya discusses events she's talked about elsewhere, she provides what at first seems to be a conflicting account. But what these discrepancies represent, I think, is a search for the whole story: we don't always take action for just one reason, and we sometimes see our own life stories from differing angles at different times. Taken together, Safiya's accounts provide a multifaceted view of her life and politics.

In her later writings, you can feel an undertow of frustration that the prisoners—particularly the Black prisoners—were not being released, that all the hard work to generate support for them was not opening up the prison gates. Her heart continually expanded to embrace all the political prisoners, as well as her friends, family, and clients at Legal Aid who needed her help. It expanded until it broke, and we all lost a champion.

Safiya found it frustrating and ironic, as I do, that there is so much interest in the 1960s and the years of revolutionary movement, but so little interest in the plight of the political prisoners who were among the revolutionaries of those years. So much enthusiasm for the radicalism of the 1960s, but so little progress in winning the release on parole of Black political prisoners who have served more than forty years in prison and counting. I hope that this collection of her writings helps provide some context for all of us to address this contradiction and to build successful campaigns in support of political prisoners. I hope that the collection would make Safiya happy, as I hope it makes Wonda even more proud of her mother.

Abiding thanks go to Wonda Jones and her family for offering me the wonderful opportunity to work on this project; to Mumia Abu-Jamal and Frances Goldin for reading the original manuscript and offering helpful advice; to Amy Scholder for her vision and her faith in this book, her insights, and her editing skills; and to the wonderful staff at the Feminist Press for their clarity, generosity, and hard work. Jalil Muntaqim, Michael Tarif Warren, Ashanti Alston, Herman and Iyaluua Ferguson, Masai Ehehosi, Herman Bell, Pam Africa, Mumia Abu-Jamal, Claude Marks, Lumumba Bandele, Sally O'Brien, Billy X Jennings, Cleo Silvers, Diana Block, Sundiata Sadiq, Suzanne Ross, and Eve Rosahn deserve my gratitude for generously sharing their memories of working with Safiya, and for discussing this project. Appreciation is also due Barbara Zeller and my late comrade Alan Berkman for their consistent, soulful assistance and support as I talked out ideas about the book—even as they faced, with grace and courage, Alan's final illness and death, and as Barbara has mourned.

Thanks don't seem quite enough to offer my partner Susie Day for her extensive, expert aid in editing (and helping to write), her work in preparing the manuscript, her always open ear and mind, and her infinite patience over the four years this project has required.

Laura Whitehorn
New York City
2009

Notes

1. Tet is the Vietnamese lunar New Year; the offensive was begun on January 31, 1968.
2. In 1971 Safiya became a Muslim and took the name Safiya Asya Bukhari. See chapter 7, "'Islam and Revolution' Is Not a Contradiction," p. 64.
3. In a 1996 interview with Kim Wade, a student at Hunter College in New York, printed in the Black Student Union newspaper, *The Shield*, Safiya said: "I would have to say my first involvement with the movement was with the Brothers and Sisters for Afrikan-American Unity on the campus at [New York City Community College], now [New York City] Technical College in Brooklyn. That was more cultural than anything." So her political consciousness was in process even as she joined Eta Alpha Mu.
4. See chapter 12, "Talks on the Black Panther Party and the Black Liberation Struggle," p. 119.
5. The Ten-Point Program was the founding document of the Black Panther Party. The demands ranged from, "*We want freedom. We want power to determine the destiny of our Black and oppressed communities*," to, "*We want an immediate end to all wars of aggression*," and, "*We want land, bread, education, housing, clothing, justice, peace, and people's community control of modern technology*." For the complete text, see blackpanther.org/TenPoint.htm. See also chapter 10, "On the Question of Political Prisoners," note 4, p. 102-3.
6. The first quotation is a frequently cited statement that Malcolm made in various ways in several speeches and interviews. The argument referring to Germany, Korea, and Vietnam is found in his "Message to the Grassroots," a speech delivered to the Northern Negro Grass Roots Leadership Conference in Detroit, November 1963.
7. There are many sources for these facts, including BlackPast.org, University of Washington, Seattle. See also Timothy B. Tyson, "Robert F. Williams, NAACP: Warrior and Rebel," *New Crisis*, December 1997.
8. In one 1996 interview, Safiya mentions that she was previously married to one of the Panther 21, Abayama Katara (Alex McKiever).
9. For more on this case, see Kuwasi Balagoon et al., *Look for Me in the Whirlwind: The Collective Autobiography of the New York 21* (New York: Random House, 1971); Murray Kempton, *The Briar Patch: The Trial of the Panther 21* (New York: E. P. Dutton, 1973).
10. COINTELPRO was computer shorthand for the FBI's secret counter-intelligence program against the Black Panthers and other progres-

sive groups in the United States. The existence of the program was first discovered in 1971 by activists who broke into an FBI office in Media, Pennsylvania. For more on the Church Committee, see chapter 11, "Building Support for Political Prisoners of War Incarcerated in North America," note 10, p. 117. See also Ward Churchill and Jim Vander Wall, *Agents of Repression: The FBI's Secret Wars Against the Black Panther Party and the American Indian Movement* (Boston: South End Press, 1988). Various former informants and FBI agents have confirmed the existence of COINTELPRO and their roles in it. For example, Earl Anthony, who joined the Party and then became an FBI informant, wrote *Spitting in the Whirlwind: The True Story Behind the Violent Legacy of The Black Panther Party* (Malibu, CA: Roundtable, 1990).

11. Geronimo Pratt spent twenty-seven years in prison while law enforcement and government lawyers withheld evidence that he was innocent of a murder (see also chapter 11, "Building Support for Political Prisoners of War Incarcerated in North America," note 3, p. 116.); Dhoruba Bin-Wahad was in prison for nineteen years. Both men were released by courts that recognized that the two had been falsely imprisoned; both received large sums in recognition of the injustices. In other cases, the truth is only now being documented, after many years of imprisonment for the defendants. For one example, see the case of the Omaha Two, detailed in articles by Michael Richardson at opednews.com. These and other former Panthers remain, however, behind bars.

12. "The newspaper *Right On!* was published beginning in March 1971 by the East Coast Black Panther Party" (New York Public Library, Schomberg Center for Research in Black Culture, New York, NY).

13. See, for example, chapter 4, "What is Security? And the Ballot or the Bullet . . . Revisited," p. 36, chapter 5, "Enemies and Friends: Resolving Contradictions," p. 43, and chapter 6, "On the Question of Sexism in the Black Panther Party," p. 52.

14. Between 1970 and 1975, literally hundreds of articles in New York newspapers suggested that various acts had been committed by BLA members. See also chapter 1, "Coming of Age," notes 2 and 3, p. 15.

15. For details of these events, see chapter 1, "Coming of Age," p. 1.

16. See Dan Berger, "The Real Dragons," in Matt Meyer, ed., *Let Freedom Ring: A Collection of Documents from the Movements to Free US Political Prisoners* (Oakland, CA: PM Press, 2008). Some of those prisoners (for example, Grand Jury resisters) were released before 1998, when

Safiya noted that there were "more than sixty" political prisoners. See Chapter 20, "Q&A on Jericho," p. 206.

17. Yuri Kochiyama is perhaps best known as an associate of Malcolm X and the person who held him as he died at the Audubon Ballroom in 1965. She has for many decades been a tireless and inspiring advocate for political prisoners and freedom struggles. For many years she was also the person you would call if you were arrested or there was trouble. See Diane Fujino, "Richard Aoki and Yuri Kochiyama," in Fred Wei-han Ho and Bill Mullen, eds., *Afro Asia: Revolutionary Political and Cultural Connections Between African Americans and Asian Americans*" (Durham, NC: Duke, 2008).

18. These were the Puerto Rican *independentista* prisoners Lucy and Alicia Rodriguez, Carmen Valentin, and Dylcia Pagan, and two of my codefendants, Marilyn Buck and Linda Evans.

19. Conversation with Lumumba Bandele, New York City, August 24, 2009.

20. Clinton did not have jurisdiction to grant release to any of the political prisoners in state jurisdiction.

21. Kim Wade, a student at Hunter College in the late 1990s, had a similar impression of Safiya: "For Safiya Bukhari, to give of herself, her time and her essence is about all she can do to heal the scars and wounds she's attained from the war of liberation" (Kim Wade, introduction, "Interview with Safiya Bukhari," *The Shield*, December 1996).

1. Coming of Age: A Black Revolutionary[1]

Greek mythology tells the story of Minos, ruler of the city of Knossos. Minos had a great labyrinth (maze) in which he kept the Minotaur, a monster that was half man and half bull, whose victims were boys and girls who would make it to the center of the maze only to be killed when they came face to face with the Minotaur. If an intended victim chanced to survive the encounter with the Minotaur, the person perished trying to find a way out of the many intricate passages. Finally, Theseus of Athens, with the help of Ariadne, Minos's daughter, entered the labyrinth, slayed the beast, and found his way out by following the thread he had unwound as he entered.

The maturation process is full of obstacles and entanglements for anyone, but for a Black woman in America it has all the markings of the Minotaur's maze. I had to say that, even though nothing as spectacular takes place in the maturation process of the average Black woman. But the day-to-day struggle for survival and growth reaps the same reward in the end in ten thousand different ways. The trick is to learn from each defeat and become stronger and more determined, to think and begin to develop the necessary strategies to ensure the annihilation of the beast. . . .

I am one of a family of ten children. My parents were strict and religious, but proud and independent. One of the strongest influences of my childhood was my mother constantly telling us to hold our heads up and be proud because we were just as good or better than anyone else, and to stand up and fight for what we believe to be right.

There was a lot of competition in my family. You had to be competitive with ten children (all two years apart) growing up, each trying to live up to the other or be better. We were determined not to be caught up in the rut of the ghetto. We were going to get out, so each of us worked on our separate goals, ten individuals, one family, in our separate world.

We believed that with the right education we could "make it," so that is the route we took searching for the "American Dream." I was going to be a doctor. In my second year of college, I pledged a sorority; it was here that the rose-colored glasses were cracked and rays of reality were allowed to filter in.

The sorority had decided to help "disadvantaged" children as one of our projects for the year and we were trying to decide what country to work with when one of the sisters suggested that we work in the ghettos of New York. Personally, I had never even thought of people in the United States being disadvantaged, but only too lazy to work and "make it." I was in for one of the biggest rude awakenings of my life.

A few of us were sent to Harlem to investigate the situation. We talked to people on the street, in the welfare centers, from door to door, and watched them work and play, loiter on the corners and in the bars. What we came away with was a story of humiliation, degradation, deprivation, and waste that started in infancy and lasted until death—in too many cases, at an early age.

Even at this point, I did not see this as affecting me personally, but only as a sorority project. I was sort of a tourist who takes pity on the less fortunate.

The sorority decided to do what we could to help the children. The Black Panther Party was already running a free breakfast program to feed the children. I had a daughter of my own at this point and decided that I would put my energies into this.

I could not get into the politics of the Black Panther Party, but I could volunteer to feed some hungry children; you see, children deserve a good start and you have to feed them for them to live to learn. It is difficult to think of reading and arithmetic when your stomach is growling. I am not trying to explain the logic of the Free Breakfast for Children Program, only showing how I had to be slowly awakened to the reality of life and shown the interconnection of things.

At five a.m. every morning, my daughter and I would get ready and go to the center where I was working on the breakfast program. It entailed cooking and serving breakfast, sometimes talking to the children about problems they were encountering, or helping them with their homework. Everything was going along smoothly until the number of children coming began to fall off. Finally, I began to question the children and found that the police had been telling the parents in the neighborhood not to send their children to the program because we were "feeding them poisoned food."

It is one thing to hear about the underhanded things the police do—you can choose to ignore it—but it is totally different to experience it for yourself. You must either lie to yourself or face it. I chose to face it and find out why the police felt it was so important to keep Black children from being fed that they told lies. I went back to the Black Panther Party and started attending some of their community political education classes.

First Encounter with the Police

Not long after that, I was forced to make a decision about the direction I was going in politically. I was on Forty-second Street with a friend when we noticed a crowd gathered on the corner. In the center of the crowd was a Panther with some newspapers under his arm. Two police officers were also there. I listened in. The police were telling the Panther he could not sell newspapers on the corner and he was insisting that he could. Without a thought, I told the police that the brother had a constitutional right to disseminate political literature anywhere, at which point the police asked for my identification and arrested the sister and myself, along with the brother who was selling the papers.

I had never been arrested before and I was naive enough to believe that all you had to do was be honest and everything would work out all right. I was wrong again. As soon as the police got us into the backseat of their car and pulled away from the crowd, the bestiality began to show. My friend went to say something and one of the police officers threatened to ram his nightstick up her if she opened her mouth again, and then ran on in a monologue about Black people. I listened and got angry.

At the Fourteenth Precinct, they separated us to search us. They made us strip. After the policewoman searched me, one of the male officers told her to make sure she washed her hand so she would not catch anything.

That night, I went to see my mother and explained to her about the bust and about a decision I had made. Momma and Daddy were in the kitchen when I got there. Daddy was sitting at the table and Momma was cooking. After I told them about the bust, they said nothing. Then I told them about how the police had acted, and they still said nothing. I said I could not sit still and allow the police to get away with that. I had to stand up for my rights as a human being. I remember my mother saying, "If you think it's right, then do it." I went back to Harlem and joined the Black Panther Party.

I spent the next year working with welfare mothers, in liberation schools, talking to students, learning the reality of life in the ghettos of America, and reevaluating many of the things I had been taught about the "land of the free and the home of the brave." About this time, I quit school and looked for a full-time job. I had education and skills, but there was always something wrong. What it was only became clear after I went to International Telephone and Telegraph to apply for a job as a receptionist-clerk. They told me I was overqualified. I ended up working in my friend's mother's beauty parlor and spent all my spare time with the Party.

By the summer of 1970, I was a full-time Party member and my daughter was staying with my mother. I was teaching some of the political education classes at the Party office and had established a liberation school in my section of the community. By listening to the elderly, I learned how they could not survive off their miserly social security checks—not pay the rent and eat, too—so they would pay their rent and eat from the dog food section of the supermarket or the garbage cans. I had listened to the middle-aged mother as she told of being evicted from her home and how she was sleeping on a subway with her children. She did so because welfare refused to help her unless she signed over all her property; out of desperation, she fraudulently received welfare. I watched a mother prostitute her body to put food in the mouth of her child, while another mother, mentally broken under the pressure, prostituted her eight-year-old child. I had seen enough of the ravages of dope, alcohol, and despair to know that a change was needed to make the world a better place in which my child could live. My mother had successfully kept me ignorant of the plight of Black people in America. Now I had learned it for myself, but I was still to learn a harsher lesson: the plight of the slave who dares to rebel.

The year 1971 saw many turbulent times in the Black Panther Party and changes in my life. I met and worked with many people who were to teach and guide me: Michael Cetewayo Tabor of the Panther 21; Albert Nuh Washington; and "Lost One" Robert Webb, who was responsible for my initial political education. Cet taught me to deal in a principled fashion, Nuh taught me compassion, and Robert taught me to be firm in my convictions.

When the split took place in the Black Panther Party, I was left in the position of communications and information officer of the East Coast Black Panther Party. Much later, I was to discover the vulnerability of that position. Many Party members went underground to work with the Black Liberation Army (BLA).[2] I was among those elected to remain aboveground and supply necessary support. The police murders of youths such as Clifford Glover, Tyrone Guyton, etc., and the BLA's retaliation with the assassinations of police officers Piagentini and Jones and Laurie [and Foster] made the powers-that-be frantic.[3] They pulled out all the stops in their campaign to rid the streets of rebellious slaves. By spring 1973, Comrades Assata Shakur and Sundiata Acoli were captured, along with Nuh and Jalil (Anthony Bottom); Twymon Myers[4] was on the FBI's Ten Most Wanted List, and I was still traveling back and forth across the country trying to build necessary support mechanisms.

In 1972, I had recognized the need to depend on something other than myself. In less than two years, I had come to realize that nothing is permanent or secure in a world in which it is who you know and what you have that counts. I had seen friends and loved ones killed or thrown into prison; associates who I believed would never go back turned state's evidence or melted into the woodwork. Nuh introduced me to Islam, which gave me a new security, sense of purpose, and dignity.

By 1973, I was receiving a great deal of flak from the police because of what they "suspected" I might be doing. Mostly, it was because I did not have a record, they could not catch me doing anything, and I had gained the community's support. All the while, I actively and vocally supported BLA members.

Capture

On January 25, 1975, some other members of the Amistad Collective of the BLA[5] and I went into the country in Virginia to practice night firing. We were to leave Virginia that night on our way to Jackson, Mississippi, because I wanted to be there on Sunday to see someone. Before returning to the crib where we were staying, we decided to stop at a store to pick up cold cuts for sandwiches to avoid stopping at roadside restaurants on the way down. We drove around looking for an open store. When we came to one, I told the brothers to wait in the car and I would go in and be right back.

I entered the store, went past the registers, down an aisle to the meat counter and started checking for all-beef products. I heard the door open, saw two of the brothers coming in, and did not give it a thought. I went back to what I was doing, but out of the corner of my left eye, I saw the manager's hand with a rifle pointed toward the door. I quickly got into an aisle just as the firing started. Up to this point, no words had been spoken. With the first lull in shooting, Kombozi [Amistad] (one of my bodyguards and a member of the Amistad Collective) came down the aisle toward me. He was wearing a full-length army coat. It was completely buttoned. As he approached, he told me he had been shot. I did not believe him at first, because I saw no blood and his weapon was not drawn. He insisted, so I told him to lie down on the floor and I would take care of it.

Masai [Ehehosi] (my codefendant) apparently had made it out the door when the firing started because he reappeared at the door, trying to draw the fire so we could get out. I saw him get shot in the face and stumble backward out the door. I looked for a way out and realized there was none. I elected to play it low key to try to get help for Kombozi as soon as possible. That effort was wasted. The manager of the store and his son, Paul Green Sr. and Jr., stomped Kombozi to death in front of my eyes. Later, when I attempted to press countercharges of murder against them, the Commonwealth attorney called it "justifiable" homicide. Five minutes after the shoot-out, the FBI was on the scene. The next morning, they held a press conference in which they said I was notorious, dangerous, etc., and known to law enforcement agencies nationwide. My bail was set at one million dollars for each of the five counts against me.

Trial and Imprisonment

On April 16, 1975, after a trial that lasted one day, I was sentenced to forty years for armed robbery; that night, I arrived here at the Virginia Correctional Center for Women in Goochland. Directly following my arrival, I was placed in the maximum-security building. There I stayed until the threat of court action led them to release me into the general population. The day after my release to general population, I was told that the first iota of trouble I caused would land me back in the maximum-security building and there I would stay.

My emphasis then and for the next two years was on getting medical care as well as educational programs and activities for myself and the other women, with the priority being on medical care for myself. Inside the prison, I was denied care. The general feeling was that they could not chance hospitalization for fear

I would escape; as such, they preferred to take a chance on my life. The courts said they saw no evidence of inadequate medical care, but rather a difference of opinion on treatment between the prison doctor and me.

The quality of "medical treatment" for women prisoners in Virginia must be at an all-time low. Their lives are in the hands of a "doctor" who examines a woman whose right ovary has been removed and tells her there is tenderness in the missing ovary. This "doctor" examines a woman who has been in prison for six months and tells her that she is six weeks pregnant and there is nothing wrong with her. She later finds her baby has died and mortified inside of her. Alternatively, he tells you that you are not pregnant and three months later, you give birth to a seven-pound baby boy. The list includes prescribing Maalox for a sore throat and diagnosing a sore throat that turns out to be cancer.

In December 1976, I started hemorrhaging and went to the clinic for help. No help of any consequence was given, so I escaped. Two months later, I was recaptured. While on escape a doctor had told me that I could endure the situation, take painkillers, or have surgery. I decided to use the lack of medical care as my defense for the escape to accomplish two things: (1) expose the level of medical care at the prison and (2) put pressure on them to give me the care I needed.

I finally got to the hospital in June 1978. By then, it was too late. I was so messed up inside that everything but one ovary had to go. Because of the negligence of the "doctor" and the lack of feeling on the part of the prison officials, I was forced to have a hysterectomy. When they brought me back to this prison in March 1977, because of the escape, they placed me in cell 5 on the segregation end of the maximum-security building—the same room they had placed me in on April 16, 1975. Today I remain in that cell, allegedly because of my escape, but in actuality because of my politics.

How do I know? Since I was returned to this institution on March 24, 1977, other women have escaped, been brought back, and been released to general population. Yesterday, after twenty-two months, my codefendant on the escape charge was okayed for release to general population. I was denied.

Despite my emotional and physical setbacks, I have learned a great deal. I have watched the oppressor play a centuries-old game on Black people—divide and conquer. Black women break under pressure and sell their men down the river. Then the oppressor separates the women from their children. In two strokes, the state does more damage than thirty years in prison could have done if the women had supported the men.

Now, more than ever before, Black women (New Afrikan women[6]) have developed a mercenary outlook on life. No longer are they about family, community, and us as a people. They are about looking good, having fun, and "making it." Women's liberation is what they are talking about. Genuine women's liberation for Black women, however, will only come about with the liberation of Black people as a whole; that is, when for the first time since our forefathers were snatched from the African continent and brought to America as slave labor, we can be a family, and from that family build a community and a nation.

The powers-that-be were disconcerted when Black mothers, wives, and daughters and Black women in general stood by and, in many cases, fought beside their men when they were captured, shot, or victimized by the police and other agents of the government. They were frightened of the potential of Black women to wreak havoc when these women began to enter the prisons and jails in efforts to liberate their men. They were spurred into action when they were confronted with the fact that Black women were educating their children from the cradle up about the real enemies of Black people and about what must be done to eliminate this ever-present threat to the lives of Black people.

During the last four years of my incarceration, I watched and refrained from speaking because I did not want to alienate the "Left." Black men and women have fooled themselves into believing we were "making progress" because Patricia Harris, a Black woman, joined the president's cabinet and Andrew Young became ambassador to the United Nations. They failed to realize that it is simply politics, American style. There is no real progress being made. Indeed, one of Jimmy Carter's best friends, Vernon Jordan, head of the Urban League, had to concede in his annual economic review, *The State of Black America*, 1979, that the "income gap between Blacks and whites is actually widening."[7]

The sacrifices made by Black women in search of Black womanhood, like those made by the people of Knossos in attempting to slay the Minotaur, have been many, harsh, and cruel. We, too, can slay the beast (in our case American racism, capitalism, and sexism) and out of the ashes build a true and independent Black Nation in which we can take our rightful place as women, wives, and mothers, knowing that our children will live to be men and women, and our men will be allowed to recognize their manhood—to support and defend their families with dignity.

Together building a future for ourselves! Build to win!

Afterword One: Coming of Age; An Update [January, 1981]

It has been two years since I wrote the original article. Many things have happened: Assata Shakur was liberated, Imari Obadele (former president of the Republic of New Afrika) was released, the Ku Klux Klan regrouped and was revamped, sixteen Black children are missing and presumed to be dead in Atlanta, eight Black men were murdered in Buffalo, pregnant Black women were shot in Chattanooga, and Ronald Reagan takes office in two days.[8]

It has been two months since I was released from the maximum-security building (after spending a total of three years and seven months). I had to go to court to do it . . . it too was an eye-opening experience. The reason they were keeping me housed in that building was that I was a "threat to the security of the free world."

What can I say? It seems that the political scene in America has come full circle and Black people are once again the scapegoats for everything that goes wrong in white America. They no longer feel the need to pacify us with poverty programs and token jobs.

Sitting in a maximum-security cell for three years and seven months afforded me an opportunity to reflect upon my life and the lessons I was forced to learn. Now the learning process is over . . . it is time to put what I have learned into practice; freedom will only be won by the sweat of our brows.

Afterword Two: [Thirteen] Years Later

Yesterday, October 21, 1994, we buried a close comrade, friend, and brother—Breeze Barrow. Less than two weeks ago, we buried another close comrade, friend, mentor, and father figure—Nathaniel Shanks.[9] Both of these brothers were strong Panthers and had been on the streets holding the line, maintaining the stand while we had been locked down in the dungeons of this country.

Reverberating through my mind for years has been the incantation of Che Guevara: "Wherever death may surprise us, it will be welcome as long as this our battle cry reaches some receptive ear and new hands reach out to intone our funeral dirge with the staccato of machinegun fire and new cries of battle and victory." Today, this minute, this hour (as Malcolm would say), I have come to realize that picking up the gun was/is the easy part. The difficult part is the day-to-day organizing, educating, and showing the people by example what needs to be done to create a new society. The hard, painstaking work of changing ourselves into new beings, of loving ourselves and our people, and working with them daily to create a new reality—this is the first revolution, that internal revolution.

I am coming to understand what they meant when they sang the words, "The race is not given to the swift, nor is it given to the strong, but to him that endures to the end," and what was meant by the fable of the hare and the tortoise. Some people declare themselves to be revolutionaries, members of one organization or another, i.e., "I was one of the first Panthers," or "I used to be a Panther." They only come out when there is a major celebration where Panthers are on display and live off their former glory, not understanding that it is not about what you used to be, but what are you doing now. They ran a quick race, using all for the moment, grew tired, and gave up. It may take a little longer to do it the hard way, slowly and methodically, building a movement step by step and block by block, but doing it this way is designed to build a strong foundation that will withstand the test of time and the attack of the enemy.

If we truly are to create a new society, we must build a strong foundation. If we truly are to have a new society, we must develop a mechanism to struggle from one generation to the next. If we truly are to maintain our new society after we have won the battle and claimed the victory, we must instill into the hearts and minds of our children, our people, ourselves this ability to struggle on all fronts, internally and externally, laying a foundation built upon a love for ourselves and a knowledge of the sacrifices that went before and all we have endured.

There is much to be done to achieve this. There is a long road ahead of us. Let's do it.

Afterword Three: 2002

> Safiya originally wrote this third afterword as an introduction to "Coming of Age" in the journal *Social Justice*.[10] In early 2002, Joy James, then professor in the department of Afrikana Studies at Brown, and others organized a conference at Brown University titled "Imprisoned Intellectuals: A Dialogue with Scholars, Activists, and (Former) US Political Prisoners on War, Dissent, and Social Justice." The invited speakers were asked to submit a version of their remarks for inclusion in a journal. Safiya spoke at the conference and submitted the essay, "Coming of Age: A Black Revolutionary," with this new introduction.
>
> Many sixties radicals distrusted an overemphasis on theory, which we saw as an excuse for inaction by radical generations before our own. In this short piece, Safiya sums up her ambivalence about the project of writing, which she began while in prison. Her conclusion—that we must write our own history—provides the impetus for the collection of her writings and speeches.

At the beginning of this conference, I had problems with accepting the label of being a "prison intellectual." "Intellectual" had always carried the connotation of being a theorist, an armchair revolutionary, if you will. Therefore the idea of being seen as an intellectual was anathema to me. I had always thought of myself as an activist, an on-the-ground worker who practiced rather than preached.

This conference forced me to face a reality. I was there because I had spent some time in prison writing and thinking. Thinking and writing. Trying to put on paper some cogent ideas that might enable others to understand why I did some of the things that I had done and the process that had brought me/us to the point we were at. I had also come to the conclusion that if we didn't write the truth of what we had done and believed, someone else would write his or her version of the truth.

If we can't write/draw a blueprint of what we are doing while we are doing it, or before we do it, then we must at least write our history and point out the truth of what we did—the good, the bad, and the ugly.

Notes

1. Safiya wrote "Coming of Age" in 1979. It was first published in New Afrikan Prisoners Organization, *Notes from a New Afrikan P.O.W. Journal*, book 7 (Chicago: Spear and Shield, 1979). It was reprinted in Joy James, ed., *Imprisoned Intellectuals: America's Political Prisoners Write on Life, Liberation, and Rebellion*, Transformative Politics Series (Baltimore: Rowman and Littlefield, 2003). Some footnotes have been added or expanded here.

2. For information on the Black Liberation Army and its relationship to the Black Panther Party, see Akinyele Omowale Umoja, "Repression Breeds Resistance: The Black Liberation Army and the Radical Legacy of the Black Panther Party," in Kathleen Cleaver and George Katsiaficas, eds., *Liberation, Imagination, and the Black Panther Party* (New York: Routledge, 2001).

3. On April 28, 1973, police officer Thomas Shea, searching for "two black males in their early twenties," shot and killed ten-year-old Clifford Glover in a South Jamaica, New York, lot after pursuing Glover and his fifty-year-old stepfather Add Armstead. Shea was later acquitted. See Murray Schumach, "Police-Call Tape Played at Trial," *New York Times*, May 24, 1974, 37; Laurie Johnston, "Jury Clears Shea in Killing of Boy," *New York Times*, June 13, 1974, 1. New York police officers Joseph A. Piagentini and Waverly M. Jones were murdered in Harlem on May

21, 1971. While the legitimacy of the evidence in the case was questionable, Jalil Abdul Muntaqim (Anthony Bottom), Herman Bell, and Albert Nuh Washington—all of whom had been members of the Black Panther Party—were convicted of the murders. NYPD officers Rocco Laurie and Gregory Foster were killed in January, 1972 on New York City's Lower East Side. Witnesses were unable to identify any suspects, but police announced that the killings were carried out by the BLA. (Gerald Fraser, "4 at Murder Site Testify at Trial," the *New York Times*, 30 January 1974, 21.)

According to Akinyle Umoja, "Between 1971 and 1973, nearly 1,000 Black people were killed by American police. . . . American police were seen as the occupation army of the colonized Black nation and the primary agents of Black genocide. So the BLA believed it had to defend Black people and the Black liberation movement in an offensive manner by using retaliatory violence against the agents of genocide in the Black community." ("Repression Breeds Resistance: The Black Liberation Army and the Radical Legacy of the Black Panther Party," Akinyele Omowale Umoja, in Kathleen Cleaver and George Katsiaficas, eds., *Liberation, Imagination, and the Black Panther Party*, New York: Routledge, 2001, 12.)

4. Twymon Ford Myers, a twenty-three-year-old BLA member, was killed in a shoot-out with the FBI and New York Police Department officers on November 14, 1973. See John T. McQuiston, "Fugitive Black Militant Is Killed in Bronx Shootout with Police," the *New York Times*, November 15, 1973, 93. Police had named Twymon as a suspect in the shooting of Foster and Laurie.

5. Amistad was the name of a slave ship involved in a famous mutiny. In 1839, a group of African people who were sold into slavery and were being shipped from Cuba to the United States rebelled and commandeered the ship. The participants, led by a man named Cinqué, were recaptured and prosecuted for murder and piracy. The rebellion and trial fueled the growth of the abolitionist movement.

6. New Afrikan is a term used to denote the membership of Black people in a nation. See chapter 4, "What is Security? And the Ballot and the Bullet . . . Revisited," note 2, page 42.

7. Vernon Jordan, *The State of Black America* (New York: National Urban League, 1979).

8. From September 22 to 24, 1980, four Black men were shot in the head in Buffalo. On October 8 and 9 the same year, two Black Buffalo taxi

drivers were murdered and found with their hearts cut out. On December 29 and 30, two Black men were fatally stabbed, one in Buffalo and the other in Rochester. In addition, four men of color, three Black and one Latino, were stabbed to death in New York City, an incident that police suspected was linked to at least some of the Buffalo-area murders. Joseph Christopher, a white private in the US Army, was convicted of three of the Buffalo shootings, but the decision was overturned by the New York State Court of Appeals in 1985 ("Murder Convictions Against '22-Caliber Killer' Overturned," *Los Angeles Times*, July 6, 1985, 11; "Inquiry on Killings Shifted to Georgia," the *New York Times*, April 26, 1981, 43). Dorothy Brown, a pregnant Black woman, was shot to death by police in Jackson, Mississippi, in August 1980. A week later, Black and some white community members marched in front of the City Hall in protest of Brown's death and several other incidents of police violence against Black people. The murder of Brown may be the incident to which Safiya refers.

9. Edwin "Breeze" Barrow died on October 16, 1994, and Nathaniel A. Shanks died on October 9, 1994. Both were former members of the Panthers memorialized in articles in *The Black Panther, Black Community News Service* 4, no. 1, Winter, 1995 (Kai Lumumba Barrow, "Edwin 'Breeze' Barrow, the Stand-Up Warrior, 1951–1994" and Mumia Abu-Jamal, "Nathaniel A. Shanks, The Passing of a Panther, 1926–1994").

10. *Social Justice* 30, no. 2 (2002).

2. Testimony: Experiences in the Black Panther Party

In 1988 and 1989, Safiya testified at a deposition for Dhoruba Bin-Wahad in his federal suit against the FBI and the New York City Police Department. Dhoruba sued these agencies for illegal acts they had carried out against him, resulting in his imprisonment. The actions of the law enforcement agencies were part of the government counterintelligence program COINTELPRO.[1] In 1990, as a result of the suit, Dhoruba was released from prison, his conviction reversed.

For Dhoruba's case, Safiya agreed to be questioned by government attorneys about police and FBI attacks on the Black Panther Party. From a court transcript of her hours of testimony, stretching over several days, arises an unusually intimate portrait of the Party's daily operations and culture. The following are excerpts from Safiya's testimony. These provide a sense of what went on in those days of resistance in the late 1960s and early 1970s—and of how it felt to be carrying out community organizing while surrounded by hostile and dangerous law enforcement agencies. It is a view of daily life during the heyday of COINTELPRO.

The Black Panther Party Program

The Free Breakfast for Children Program remains one of the better-known community programs run by the BPP. The program was designed to provide free breakfast for school children so that they could concentrate better in school.

The Black Panther Party had a Ten-Point Program. We wanted land, bread, justice, housing, and peace. As our major political objective, we wanted a United Nations–supervised plebiscite to be held throughout the Black colony, where only Black colonial subjects would be allowed to participate, for the purpose of determining the will of the Black people concerning our national destiny. Different organizations were advocating establishing a Black nation on the land base of five separate states in the United States or going back to Africa. We needed a plebiscite to see what the people wanted, and the Party would go along with that. Just like the Declaration of Independence— of the people, by the people. The government wasn't dealing with the needs of the people, and the people had the right to throw off that government and create a new government for the needs of the people. The media said we were advocating the overthrow of the government. But we were just doing the same thing the United States did when it declared its independence from England. It was an either/or situation: either we become viable citizens with the same rights and recognition as everyone else or we needed to look realistically at bringing about the changes necessary to govern ourselves. But before you could do anything else, you had to educate the Black community about what was going on.

The purpose of the Black Panther Party was to establish revolutionary, politically powerful Black people. In order to carry out our purpose, we had to work. If you were going to bring about social change, you had to institute programs. Community service was part of the programs.

I started working with the Panthers by working with the Free Breakfast for Children Program, even before I was actually a member of the Panthers. I began in the spring of 1969. I got up early in the morning and went over to Chambers Street Memorial Church in Manhattan and made breakfast for the children. I cooked breakfast for them and helped them with their homework and got them off to school.

Before I joined the Party, I didn't believe the things being said about police brutality or about justice not being done. When the police acted against the community, I thought it was because there was something wrong being done by someone in the community. But once I became victimized myself, I began to look at what the Panthers were doing and saying differently. Once I joined the Party, it became even more clear.

For example, while I was working with the breakfast program, the number of children attending started dropping off. We went around and talked with the parents to try to find out why this was happening. What we found out was that the police were telling the parents we were poisoning the children, feeding the kids poisoned foods. That made me angry, and it was one of the things that encouraged me to take the next step and join the Party. The police weren't feeding the children. But to keep us from feeding them, they were saying we were giving them poisoned food. So the children were doing without because of the police's own bigotry. That was a lesson for me in how the police lie, how the system lies and hurts people.

I also learned that the cops were trying to discourage the merchants from donating food or providing other assistance to the program. A few times, I was responsible for picking up the donations from various merchants. I remember two times on 135th Street, at a food co-op, the people told me that they'd been told by the cops that the food wasn't going for the breakfast program, that instead it was being resold. The police had told them the food wasn't being used for what it was supposed to be used for. Later, after COINTELPRO was revealed, we saw, in the FBI files, the actual letters that were sent to contributors talking about how the food and funds were not being used for what they were supposed to be used for. The letters said that the breakfast program was being used as a means to subvert the minds of the children and how dangerous it was. And we learned that this was done as part of that program to disrupt and destroy the Panther Party. And the same was done to the liberation schools the Party ran.[2]

While I worked in the breakfast program I met members of the BPP who rotated responsibility for working in the program. They worked side by side with members of the community who volunteered in the breakfast program. Those members of the Party were responsible for educating the rest of us, for political education.

On Joining the Party

I remember I came into the Panther office and told the OD (officer of the day) that I wanted to join.[3] He gave me a handful of papers and rules and regulations and told me to study. I had to be at PE (political education) classes. Political education included all the Panther politics and rules—the Ten-Point Program and Platform, the Eight Points of Attention, Twenty-six Rules and Regulations of the Black Panther Party, the "Red Book" by Chairman Mao Tse-tung, and the basics—things like do not swear at the masses, do not steal from the comrades or the masses, speak politely, etc. These classes were held for about an hour every night for all Party members. But Wonda and I had intense class sessions at home, because we were still going to school at the time—though I dropped out of college soon after.[4] We also had skills from our education, so we could do more and had greater abilities—and therefore had to meet greater requirements. I used to edit things such as Bobby Seale's book, helping with grammar and typing. And we were being groomed to become teachers for the PE classes, so that the responsibility for teaching didn't always fall on the same Panther members. I didn't know that at the time, but it later became clear.

Technical education included breaking down weapons, learning how to put them together blindfolded, and learning how the weapon works. We also learned never to aim a weapon at a person, a comrade, and not to play with loaded weapons. We learned weapon safety. Those of us with no criminal record applied for firearms licenses and used regular training facilities. I got a permit for long arms. We had legally registered firearms. The training involved firearms, never explosives.

The physical education classes were more about how you handled yourself physically, hand-to-hand combat, and your health—being physically fit. We learned basic martial arts, how to defend ourselves.

These classes took the form of drills, sometimes held in front of the office, other times held in Mount Morris Park in Harlem, and sometimes in Central Park, depending on the extent of the drills.[5] If it was an endurance training, where you had to run three miles instead of one, or if we were going to do extensive calisthenics and then run, or if we were going to do the kind of training that involved jumping out of a tree or hiding behind a tree, we would go to Central Park.

I remember going through the calisthenics, the whole thing from jumping jacks to deep knee bends, then running from the office to wherever we were going to do the exercises, spending forty-five minutes doing the exercises, then running back to the office. Some of the exercises involved climbing trees and survival techniques like learning the foliage. We also had pep rallies and pep talks.

In addition, I was given a form for reporting my daily activities, including the time, what happened from the time you came into the office to the time you went off duty at the end of the day. I had to be at the office at about eight a.m.—if you were late, you were disciplined: you had to run around the block five times.

That discipline was used for other things, too. I was disciplined once for not changing my baby's diaper. I was brought up on charges for that. The child wore the diaper for so long that it constituted neglect. My daughter stayed in the office a lot and if they felt she was not getting cared for properly, I was brought up on charges. I had to fulfill my parental responsibilities in addition to Party ones.

But another time I was brought up on charges for stupid stuff. The Party had a policy of free love. Well, they called it free love. I called it political pimping. One of the Panthers decided he wanted to sleep with me. I was brought up on charges of refusing to sleep with him.

Charges had to be written. You had to be able to bring something up in a principled way. Then I could address the issues and defend myself. It was a procedure held right in the office.

On the charge of child neglect, I was found guilty and suspended. I had to clean somebody's apartment building.

Another time Wonda and I were brought up on charges for fighting. I had a huge fear of snakes, and Wonda had thrown a rubber snake on me. Our punishment was to read Fanon's *The Wretched of the Earth* and each write a paper on what the book said about mental disorders. That time, our punishment included having to do security on weekends at a Panther facility.

The section leader would go through the drills—calisthenics, etc.—and then assign you a task for the day. And once I became a full-time Party member, the work was 24-7. But you didn't work unless you were detailed to work. Everyone had a section. Mine was from 110th Street to 116th Street, between Eighth Avenue and Pleasant Avenue. I had the barrio.

The Party earned money through newspaper sales, speaking engagements, and donations. Sales of the newspaper, pamphlets, and buttons brought in a lot.

On Party Structure and Programs

The other programs of the Party at the time, in addition to the breakfast program, were the health clinic, housing, and tenant-landlord relations; we organized welfare parents, we organized against police brutality, and a lot of effort went into defending political prisoners. In New York, we were specifically organizing in support of the people arrested in the Panther 21 case. I worked on political prisoner support. I also belonged to the medical cadre of the Party. We were responsible for the medical health of the people in the office and for setting up the health clinic, working with the community, taking care of the health needs of the Party and the community.

From about January 1971 to March that year, I was the officer of the day for the Harlem office, at 202 Seventh Avenue—it was a storefront. The officer of the day opened the office; accounted for everything, including the security of the office; made assignments, and basically made any decisions necessary. Those who came through the office included Party members, members of the National Committee to Combat Fascism (NCCF), and community workers or members of the community.[6] Following the split in the Party, later in 1971, I became communications and information officer of the East Coast faction, the [Eldridge] Cleaver faction of the Party.[7] I was part of the central leadership. I was also in charge of the national committees for the defense of political prisoners within the Party. At first we just dealt with the Black Panthers who were incarcerated. Later, we began to deal with other political prisoners as well.

After the arrest of the Panther 21 in April of 1969, there was a freeze on Party recruitment. With the bust of the twenty-one came the uncovering of a number of undercover agents. A freeze was placed on membership so that anybody couldn't just come up and say, "Because I'm down and everything, I want to be a Panther," and just come on into the Party. A procedure was put in place and you had to go through it to become a member. You had to prove you were trustworthy. People would join the NCCF in order to go through that process. Before the freeze on membership, the NCCF was also used to provide an organization to people who weren't Black but wanted to work with the Party. After the freeze it became predominantly Black. It was like a military academy in relation to the army. A training ground. But from the outside, you couldn't tell who was NCCF and who was a Party member.

There was a ministry of information in the Bronx. That ministry was for the regional staff. The regional staff had the responsibility to determine who did what. They had regional meetings on Sunday mornings in the Bronx and decisions would come down from there for the region. They decided what each member would do.

In the Harlem office we had a branch captain, then the officer of the day, the secretary, the section leader, and the subsection leader.

I never stopped being a member of the Party, but I did become a member of the Black Liberation Army once I went underground.

On the Heightening of Repression Against the Party

When I first joined the Party, the morale was spirited. Later, that gave way to apprehension and guardedness.

J. Edgar Hoover, the head of the FBI in those days, declared the Black Panther Party the most dangerous threat to national security. Because of that, there was the Bureau of Special Services (BOSS) and the Red Squad, both in New York.[8] They were in collusion to destroy us, along with the police department and the court system. This was how COINTELPRO played out on the local level. Later on, when I was in prison, I received my FBI files. Those files talked about informants inside the New York office of the Black Panther Party, informants who were in the office with me. During and after my arrest, I became aware of two undercover police officers, members of the New York City Police Department, who were assigned to be informants in the office.

The media was working hand in glove with the police on this, too. You didn't pick up a newspaper without seeing something about a crime being committed by the Black Panther Party. The Mafia hadn't gone out of existence; there were still drugs downtown; there were those shadows in Chinatown. But they were not getting the press coverage that we were getting at this point. The connections between the police agencies have been documented in COINTELPRO files. But even before we saw those documents, we knew it had to be a national campaign. Logic dictated that all these things were connected.

Through these programs, a split was created between the East Coast and West Coast sections of the Party. From about February 1971, when this occurred, the community programs stopped, because all we could do was focus on self-defense work. When things settled down, we started the community programs again. But then there were more arrests and trials, and we had to cut back again to focus on those. And the fact that we were able to keep doing work as long as we did, in the face of all the trials, the deaths, the constant counterintelligence program activities that were happening—under all those pressures, we were able to survive. That was a success. We were there when the community needed us. We dealt with their problems. We kept the free health clinic going in Brooklyn. We worked with welfare mothers. We worked on housing issues. We protected the community, keeping the older people from being attacked in the streets. And we expected that the police would tap our phones—even my mother assumed that. We expected that they would follow us and watch us. But some of the things they did, we did not envision. We did not envision that they would send undercover agents to come up with ideas that were badder than bad. We did not envision that they would be able to kill people and create huge divisions between people. We were not able to analyze what was happening when we were hit by COINTELPRO. That was a failure. We had to cut back and allow the attacks to stop us from doing community work. We reacted with more intensified rhetoric, instead of continuing our programs.

In the early days after I joined the Party, the police consistently confiscated the newspapers Panthers were selling. I was never arrested, but I was told to get off the corner when I was selling papers. I would sell papers mostly in the community, where I could do community work. But once, I was down on Forty-second Street selling papers, and I was told to move on by the police. They told me I couldn't sell papers there; I had to move. A uniformed officer got out his gun and a nightstick, and I moved. But the police arresting people was a daily thing. Panthers would be selling papers on the corner, and they'd end up getting arrested and going back and forth to court, and it got to a point where people were told to cop a plea, to get it over with. Sometimes, sisters were physically assaulted while being arrested. It was just a constant thing. We had to go in pairs, so that if one person got arrested, the other one could call the office to tell people.

In those early days, we had pep rallies and pep talks at the office and in the street out in front. But this changed at the point when the Party went on the defense, in late 1970, because conditions had changed—then the drills became more about self-defense. At that time, the atmosphere became much more tense, more defensive. It was as if something was about to happen and we had to be prepared. In December 1969, two members of the Illinois Panther Party—chairman Fred Hampton and Mark Clark—were gunned down in a preplanned raid by the Chicago police. We later learned that the FBI had played a role in the attack, planting an informant among Fred's inner circle and drugging the Kool-Aid the Panthers had had with dinner. But even at the time, we knew the police had set the whole thing up—they claimed there were shots from inside the apartment, but it was proved quickly that all the shots were fired by the police, not by the Panthers. A few days later there was an assault by police on the Los Angeles office of the Panther Party.

Members were not required to carry a firearm, until the fear of being attacked became so predominant that several of us were obligated to carry weapons for defense. And as officer of the day in the Harlem office, I was one of those required to carry a weapon. This took place during the course of the split in the Party.

You never went anywhere by yourself; you never went anywhere without somebody in security knowing where you were. You couldn't be out of contact for any length of time without cause. This was around the time of the split in the Party. We felt that we had two major enemies: we had the other side of the Party and we had the state apparatus. It was like being in a war situation and you didn't know where your enemy was lurking. You were constantly looking over your shoulder.

The media was saying that the Panthers were racists, anarchists, and thugs. But when I joined, I saw that the Panthers did not use violence against its members. They were not violent. But once the FBI began instigating through COINTELPRO, things changed. After the split, it was a time of paranoia. The resulting violence was totally opposed to what the Party was about. COIN-TELPRO brought about a war inside the Party. Through COIN-TELPRO, people worked under the guise of being Panthers and instigated incidents. Threats were made over the telephone, and we feared for our lives. They created a war atmosphere.

One example of what happened was that one member, Robert Webb, was told in a phone call with the West Coast that people were coming to take care of him. Then in March 1971, he was shot and killed on 125th Street and Seventh Avenue. To show further how the police were involved, this is now 1988 and no one has yet been tried or even arrested for Robert's death. It was as if it were sanctioned. We knew who killed Robert, and we made that very well-known. It was even published in the paper, yet no one ever did anything. The person was a paid killer, receiving thousands of dollars. Robert was killed right out on a Monday afternoon in front of Chock Full o'Nuts on 125th and Seventh Avenue. His bodyguard had been pistol-whipped, and he was killed, and the police did nothing. It was clear that they were working in conjunction with the killers. So our paranoia wasn't really paranoia at all—we actually had a basis in fact to be on the defensive.

We sandbagged the office and our living quarters, and security was beefed up. We weren't allowed to be around family members, and the children were put in safe locations. We were trying to protect our families and to continue as best we could doing our work. But finally it was decided that the Party could no longer function aboveground because of the conditions.

It was clear that differences that emerged between the West and East Coast Panthers provided a prime opportunity for the government to destroy the Party. At that time, there were also a number of burglaries and break-ins at our houses. One time, files were destroyed at the office; machinery was stolen. Another time, when I was living on St. Nicholas Avenue, a neighbor told me to look out my window because my car was being burglarized; someone was in it. (When I'd moved into the building, I did what was standard BPP procedure—letting all the neighbors know they are in the building with a Panther so that we'll look out for one another.) After my neighbor called, I looked out the window and saw police going through my car, with two squad cars parked nearby. One police officer was standing outside the car and one was inside, going through the glove compartment. They actually stole some parking tickets out of the glove compartment. I hope they paid them. I called the police station and reported a burglary in process, but nobody ever came to investigate.

Even after the Party disbanded in the late seventies, people were watched and checked on, had their fingerprints checked, their phones tapped, their phone records subpoenaed.

The Use of Torture by Police Against the BPP

In May 1971, Ruben Scott, a California member of the Panthers, was tortured to try to force him to testify against Herman Bell, Anthony (Jalil) Bottom and Albert Nuh Washington (the New York Three).[9] He was arrested in New Orleans and tortured. He was beaten and had cattle prods applied to his genitals; pins were stuck into him. He was beaten so badly that he made statements in New Orleans that were later thrown out by a judge—they could not be admitted because they were the result of extensive torture. And a New York City district attorney and New York City detectives were on the scene. They also threatened him with other cases—murders—if he didn't testify. He subsequently testified against the New York Three and then recanted his testimony. Since that time, he has appeared on television, on Gil Noble's show, *Like It Is*, and told what happened to him. He made his position known and signed an affidavit to that effect. But when he attempted to tell the judge at the New York Three trial in New York City about what happened, the judge consulted with the district attorney, and Scott was not permitted to recant.[10] Other ex-Panthers were also tortured in New Orleans at the same time, but not to the same degree as what happened to Ruben.

Most of the time when someone testified against other Panthers, it was not members of the Party who did the testifying. It was wives or friends or someone who was arrested at the time. For the most part, members of the Party weren't the people who were forced to give testimony.

All this made it very hard to continue carrying on the work of the breakfast program and other programs of the Party.

Notes

1. For a definition of COINTELPRO, please see the introduction, note 10, p. xxxvi.
2. The Black Panther Liberation schools were projects to bring political education to Black communities.
3. For a fuller story and the background on how Safiya came to join the Party, see chapter 1, "Coming of Age," p. 1.
4. Wonda was Safiya's sorority sister and joined the Party shortly before Safiya did.
5. Mount Morris Park is now Marcus Garvey Park.
6. The National Committee to Combat Fascism (NCCF) was a broad organization created by the Panthers to incorporate supporters and activists who were not Black or were not ready to join the more disciplined ranks of the Party. The NCCF was formed during a three-

day conference in Oakland, California, in 1969. "Led by Panthers, there were some twenty-five hundred participants, including Students for a Democratic Society, the Young Patriots, Brown Berets, Young Lords, and the Communist Party. The principal proposal of the conference was community control of the police." *The Black Panther Party [reconsidered]*, Charles E. Jones, ed., (Baltimore: Black Classic Press, 1998).

7. In 1971, with FBI provocation but also reflecting political disagreements over the role of armed struggle, the national leadership of the Party led by Huey P. Newton expelled the Panther chapters in Los Angeles and New York, the International Section of the Party, and other members. See "Repression Breeds Resistance: The Black Liberation Army and the Radical Legacy of the Black Panther Party," Akinyele Omowale Umoja, in Kathleen Cleaver and George Katsiaficas, eds., *Liberation, Imagination, and the Black Panther Party*, (New York: Routlege, 2001), 4. Also see Muhammad Ahmad, *We Will Return in the Whirlwind: Black Radical Organizations, 1969–1975*, (Chicago: Charles H. Kerr Publishing Company, 2007), 196–211. The expelled Panthers, who were seen as supporting not only the politics that the Party had always represented, but also the position that Black people were involved in a war of national liberation like those occurring in Latin America, Asia and Africa, were sometimes referred to as the East Coast faction or Cleaver faction. Eldridge Cleaver headed the International Section, based in Algeria. Before joining the Panthers, Eldridge had served time in prison for assault. In prison he had written essays for *Ramparts* magazine and a book, *Soul on Ice* (New York: McGraw-Hill, 1968), which delineated some of the thinking that characterized the resurgence of Black radicalism in the 1960s. After leaving prison in 1966 Eldrige became the Black Panther Party Minister of Information. Among other things, Eldridge was famous for saying, "You're either part of the problem or you're part of the solution." Eldridge died in 1998. (See John Kifner, "Eldridge Cleaver, Black Panther Who Became G.O.P. Conservative, Is Dead at 62," the *New York Times*, May 2, 1998, B-8.)

8. The statement by Hoover was the basis for COINTELPRO. That program involved FBI and local police working together. BOSS is an acronym for Bureau of Special Services, an intelligence division of the NYPD. It was often referred to as "the Red Squad" because its task was to spy on and gather information about radical groups and individuals.

The best known cop functioning under BOSS was Gene Roberts, who infiltrated Malcom X's organization as well as the Black Panthers.

9. The New York Three were convicted of the May 1971 fatal shooting of two NYPD officers. Originally, five men were arrested; two were acquitted. The case went through several trials before convictions were obtained. For details on this case and on the role of Ruben Scott, see chapter 14, "CBS Tries the New York Three," p. 156.

10. Detectives from New York and San Francisco were present at various points during the torture. These facts have been presented in numerous court papers in both the New York Three case and the subsequent case of the San Francisco 8, a case also based on tortured confessions by Scott (see FreetheSF8.org). The judge who ignored Scott's assertions that he had been tortured and that his confession and testimony were false was Edward Greenfield, who presided over the original trial.

3. Marriage Contract: Safiya A. Bukhari and Michael M. [Ashanti] Alston

> Safiya and Ashanti were legally married in 1984 by the Muslim chaplain at the prison where Ashanti was incarcerated. After Ashanti's release in 1985, he and Safiya drew up this marriage contract. It was never intended to be a legal document, Ashanti says, but was created "because we wanted something in writing, something that we were consciously agreeing to, to show what this marriage would mean and what we'd do if we had difficulties. We wanted to act consciously instead of just getting married and saying, 'Everything is going to be lovely.' We knew that kind of thinking isn't realistic—we already knew that from what had happened during the split in the Panthers." The marriage itself lasted only a few years, though the two did not divorce and remained partners in order to care for Safiya's daughter Wonda and granddaughter Shylis.

The party of the first part, hereinafter known as Safiya A. Bukhari, and the party of the second part, hereinafter known as Michael Maurice Alston, do consent and agree to abide by the following contractual agreement; to wit:

1. The basis for the continuation of this relationship, commonly known as a marriage, is and will continue to be a common desire and commitment to the struggle for the liberation of oppressed people wherever they may be found. It is understood that if at any time either of the parties reneges upon this commitment, the relationship is subject to dissolution.

2. That the relationship is a partnership based on equality, autonomy, mutual trust, respect, love, companionship, friendship, and freedom.
3. That we work to promote the health and welfare of our family unit so that we develop our social skills to be successful in reaching personal and collective goals.
4. That we will dare to be honest and courageous in giving of ourselves so that our relationship becomes and remains a safe haven, a source of joy and a place to unfold grander human qualities.
5. That whenever contradictions arise that threaten to become antagonistic in nature, we will use the principles of constructive conflict resolution to remedy the situation. If at such time the contradictions have reached the stage where they cannot be resolved without outside mediation or intervention, then we agree to give each other space and seek the guidance of friends, comrades, or professional counseling to alleviate and diffuse the situation, with the understanding that all of us are human and subject to human frailties.
6. If it ever reaches the point where we decide to end or sever our relationship, we will remain/redevelop friendship and comradeship.

The foregoing is agreed to willingly and without compulsion or duress.

SIGNED: M. Ashanti Alston
SIGNED: Safiya A. Bukhari
November 18, 1985

4. What is Security? And the Ballot or the Bullet . . . Revisited

This essay is undated; it was probably written in the mid-1990s. The Sun Tzu quote is in the original. The essay seems to have been written by Safiya in her capacity as a member of the Republic of New Afrika (RNA).[1]

In this essay and others, Safiya grappled with the significance of COINTELPRO: What did it mean for organizers? How could the damage to relationships and organizations be repaired, and how could similar rifts be avoided in the future? While some survivors of the COINTELPRO years drew grim lessons that encouraged them to drop out of political activism, Safiya drew different conclusions. Her realization of the lengths to which the government and law enforcement would go to extinguish the challenge of Black liberation only fueled her determination to continue organizing.

*Know yourself and know your enemies
and in a thousand battles you'll never be defeated.*
—*Sun Tzu*

The word "security" most often brings to mind a uniformed person presenting an image of authority and sending out "I'm in control" and "Don't mess with me! I'm bad!" and "Don't even think about it!" signals. The next thing people usually think about—and do—is to go into the basic-training (calisthenics) and technical-training (weapons) mode. While this has passed for security, it's on a very superficial level.

Once you dig a little past the obvious, it usually proves to be no real security at all.

By definition, security means the freedom from danger, fear, and anxiety. Individual and organizational safety and well-being begin with the knowledge of what you're about, what the organization is about, your limitations, the organization's limitations, your strengths, and the organization's strengths. Knowledge is the key to security. History has shown that the best security depends upon the internal strength of the organization and the internal principles of the people who make up the organization.

Inherent in the Creed of the Republic of New Afrika (RNA) is a line that says, "I will steal nothing from a brother or sister, cheat no brother or sister, misuse no brother or sister, inform on no brother or sister and spread no gossip." This is an extremely important component of individual and organizational security. The knowledge that the person next to you—the person working beside you—will not cheat you or lie and spread gossip about you is the basis for your feeling secure in your environment or within your organization. The ability to trust your comrades implicitly and to know with certainty what they will do in any circumstance is the best security.

The question, then, is how do we get to this point? It begins with knowing what you're about—what you want and what you believe in and how far you will go to obtain it. The reciprocal reality is knowing what the organization is about. If the purpose and mission of the organization is clear, not subject to interpretation, then people joining will not be able to say that they thought the organization was about one thing when they joined, only to find out later that it was about something totally different.

This means that both the individual and the organization need to be open and honest. My rule of thumb is, "If the police know, the people should know." The history of COINTELPRO shows that the enemy will use anything and everything they know about you to their advantage. If there are no "dirty little secrets" that the enemy can drop in the media or tell your next-door neighbor or your comrades, then we have managed to take one weapon from them. As we shed the ego and survive all the knocks of revealing these little truths about ourselves to one another, we become stronger, our organization becomes stronger and more secure, and our goal becomes realizable because we have begun to sublimate the big "I" to the collective "us" or "we."

An example of "what the police know, the people should know" is the social security number. We give this number to anybody who asks for it—the credit card agency when we apply for a card, the employer, the school . . . anybody, that is, except the organization that we believe will lead us to liberation. Then there's our telephone number. The government can obtain it at will; they bug it, they get copies of our telephone bills, they own it—but we don't want to give it to each other. In application after application we tell them our mother's maiden name, how many siblings we have, our children's names and social security numbers, where we work and how long we've worked there, where we live and how long we've lived there, and where we lived before that. We voluntarily give up this information because there's something we want in return.

Then there's the information they get through investigating or surveilling us. They find out who our friends and associates are, what organizations we belong to and which ones we used to belong to. They find out whether we have a criminal record and where we went to school. They find out our sexual liaisons and even some of our proclivities. They know our religious background. They know whom we owe what to and how much we're in debt. The enemy knows all this, and what they don't know already they investigate and make every effort to find out. We're left at the gate.

What's wrong with this picture? The root word of "security" is "secure." Inherent in this is feeling protected, safe, and guarded. This is all based on the trust we have in the entity or organization with which we are working or the people we have around us. If we trust them, we feel secure. Is the fact that we readily reveal information about ourselves to the US government and its agencies a statement of our trust in the US government—or the credit card bureaus, landlords, and places where we apply to work? Is the fact that we do not feel secure giving the same information to the organizations or people we work with a sign of our lack of trust in them?

The basic element of security is trust. Without trust there is no security. Trust comes through knowing and believing that you're safe within a specific area, whether it's a company of people or the confines of a building. When the Creed of the Republic of New Afrika says, "I will steal nothing from a brother or sister, cheat no brother or sister, misuse no brother or sister, inform on no brother or sister and spread no gossip," the citizens of the RNA know that they can trust that this will in fact be the policy of the Provisional Government (PG-RNA). This security in the knowledge that the PG-RNA will protect its citizens will go a long way toward providing for the security of the Provisional Government.

What About Self-Defense?

Now that we've established what security really is and put this level of security into practice, the rest becomes much easier. Our Provisional Government takes on the character of a liberated zone—a place where we feel secure and where we can carry out the task of freeing the land. Within the framework of this liberated zone the organizations that make up the New Afrikan Independence Movement (NAIM)[2] can begin to develop security units to protect our communities from outside elements harmful to our people. The first element of this is self-defense training. Every element of defense begins with self. We must be able to defend ourselves.

The first step is being in shape. For years following my incarceration, I had gained a lot of weight and felt incapable of losing it. I was very unhealthy and unable to defend myself. I felt vulnerable and worried about being able to defend anyone else. Finally I decided I had to get myself in shape and under control. I had to lose the weight and get myself into a position where I could defend my community and myself again. Once the weight began to come off, I started to exercise and practice martial arts again. I'm still not where I should be, but my confidence in my abilities is rising again and I am feeling more secure.

That's where it has to start. I recommend that we all begin to take stock of ourselves and take care of ourselves. Our internal security depends on how much we're capable of defending ourselves.

Personal self-defense training, such as martial arts training, can be obtained in a number of ways. We can use the expertise of people from within to set up training for our groups, or we can take classes at outside dojos.[3] Either way is okay. We just have to develop and maintain the discipline to carry through on our objectives. This kind of training boosts our confidence in ourselves as well.

What About Community Defense?

Defending our communities from outside forces is a natural outgrowth of self-defense. Building trust within ourselves and our organization and the Provisional Government makes it easier to build our defense effort. Let's lay the foundation by making that security real so that we can move forward, developing our community, building our national defense effort, and advancing to free the land!

The Ballot or the Bullet . . . Revisited[4]

Debating whether to work within the system, using the electoral process to achieve equality, or to work outside the system, using armed struggle to achieve liberation, is tantamount to comparing apples and onions.

The initial premise—that the question of whether electoral politics or armed struggle within the context of the liberation of people of Afrikan descent is debatable—is erroneous. A debate poses two sides of the same question against one another. Equality (uniformity, conformity, likeness) and liberation (deliverance, emancipation, freedom) are not the same. In order to understand the issues we must understand the language.

The bottom line is that we can no longer assume that we're all striving for the same thing. Equality simply means that you want the same thing, same privileges, same access to things that the next person—the person with whom you seek to be equal—has. Freedom means you want the ability to determine for yourself, without social and political pressures, tainted as they are by racism, how you want to live your life and what you want to achieve for your family and community. How do you know if you've achieved equality? Can you ever achieve equality? Now, freedom is different. When you have the power to determine your destiny, you have achieved freedom. It's as simple as that.

When El Hajj Malik el Shabazz posed the question of the ballot or the bullet,[5] he raised it in the context of the struggle for our freedom. The concept was that we would either win our freedom using the ballot or we would take it with the bullet. The choice was up to the system—what would be possible, and how. What do we visualize? What is our goal?

Notes

1. The Republic of New Afrika was founded in the right of self-determination for Black people in the United States. Its name refers to the five states in the South (Mississippi, Alabama, Louisiana, Georgia, and South Carolina) that Black people developed and enriched with their labor and where they have lived for more than four hundred years. Because of this history, these states form the land base of an independent nation for whose liberation Black people fight. The Provisional Government of the Republic of New Afrika (PG-RNA) was formed in 1968 at a conference in Detroit. "The Creed" refers to a set of personal principles to which citizens of the Republic of New Afrika adhere.

2. "New Afrikan Independence Movement" refers to the breadth of groups and organizations working for the self-determination of Black people in the United States. In general, these groups are united by the concept that Black people never freely chose US citizenship (nor have they been accorded full rights of citizens, free of racism) and that they are united by African ancestry. The term "New Afrikan" denotes a political identity based in a common history, geographical origin, psychology, political life, and culture. These categories of commonality also give rise to nationhood: the concept that New Afrikans in the United States are a nation of people, colonized and oppressed by the government of the United States and entitled to self-determination. The PG-RNA is one part of the NAIM.

3. Dojos are martial arts studios. In the 1970s and 1980s, many progressives and revolutionaries joined dojos for training in karate, judo, and other martial arts.

4. This is a fragment of an unfinished essay.

5. Malcolm X delivered a speech titled "The Ballot or the Bullet" in Cleveland, Ohio, in April 1964. The text of the speech appears in Malcolm X and George Breitman, *Malcolm X Speaks: Selected Speeches and Statements* (New York: Grove Press, 1965).

5. Enemies and Friends: Resolving Contradictions

It is not clear exactly when this essay was written—probably sometime in the late 1980s or early 1990s. During those years, people who had been in any of the radical organizations targeted by COINTELPRO tried to reconstruct relationships and create a basis for continuing to do political work together. This essay is one of Safiya's many attempts to contribute to that process, to examine what she sees as her own weaknesses in working with others, and to establish some firm foundation for encouraging people to unite to support the comrades left in prison. Since one of those people, Geronimo Pratt (Geronimo ji Jaga), had been unable to prove his innocence partly because of the rancor among some former Panthers, these questions had particular significance for Safiya's work.

Over the past several years, the movement—or what is left of it—has been bogged down in a quagmire of infighting, backstabbing, manipulation, and one-upmanship. Those of us in the movement don't see it this way. But to the people outside looking in—those we are attempting to organize—this is what appears to be happening. We see ourselves as being involved in concrete political work. Depending on what political formation we belong to, we consider ourselves the sole standard bearers of revolutionary principles, the ones with the correct path—and everyone else who is not down with us is incorrect, fools, or napes.[1] If we were able to take a step back to look at the situation objectively, we would get a different view.

The first thing that you recognize from that perspective is that there's a big world out there and the "movement" is very small. Not only is the movement small, but it's an extremely incestuous bunch of people. I don't mean that blood relatives are actually indulging in sexual relations. I mean that the movement is so small that it is hard to find someone who has not been party to a relationship—political or sexual—with someone else in the movement. In effect, we're all connected to one another in some convoluted way. In a very concrete sense, the movement has become like *Peyton Place* or any other soap opera you see on television. Contradictions between people and organizations usually develop out of personal problems that escalate into political differences.

Because the movement is rife with disorganization and lacks cohesion, people make decisions about whom to work with based on personal relationships. As a result, one might wonder whether we can be taken seriously when we talk about making a revolution in this country. I cannot exclude myself from this criticism, because I've found myself deciding on occasion to take the easy way out rather than stay and wage struggle to combat these tendencies and build a stronger movement.

My own inability to confront the problems and struggle to eradicate counterproductive tendencies within our formations stems from a fear of having my motives misconstrued or of being subject to personal attack. Sometimes it's extremely hard to deal with situations in a principled manner when people call one another "comrade" but treat each other in a manner that belies the use of that term. Social practice is the criterion for truth. If you talk about people behind their backs, have hidden agendas, or manipulate situations so that certain people are not privy to what's going on—and I'm not talking about a "need-to-know" situation—it makes it hard for people to criticize such activity without fearing retaliation.[2]

The real problem begins with what Mao Tse-tung called liberalism.

In "Combat Liberalism," Mao Tse-tung said, "Liberalism is extremely harmful in a revolutionary collective. It is a corrosive that eats away unity, undermines cohesion, causes apathy and creates dissension. It robs the revolutionary ranks of compact organization and strict discipline, prevents policies from being carried through and alienates the Party organizations from the masses which the Party leads. It is an extremely bad tendency."[3]

I have read and studied "Combat Liberalism" more times than you can shake a stick at. But reading doesn't necessarily mean understanding—and understanding doesn't necessarily mean internalizing. Within the past few months, I have been taking stock of myself and trying to understand what is making it hard for me to make real progress, to engage in constructive criticism and open myself up to criticism and self-criticism. It wasn't until the past few weeks, when I was trying to determine whether it made sense to continue to try and work with certain people, that I had to look into myself and recognize that I was again refusing to engage in constructive criticism. I was walking away and allowing a situation to continue without struggling to resolve contradictions. I asked myself, "How can you talk about taking on the United States government when you are afraid to struggle with a few people?" That is the biggest contradiction of them all.

Now, for the first time, I understand what Mao Tse-tung meant when, in a speech before the Chinese Communist Party's National Conference on Propaganda Work on March 12, 1957, he said, "He who is not afraid of death by a thousand cuts dares to unhorse the emperor." Whatever is unprincipled, incorrect, and counterproductive about you and your style of work, you have to be willing to subject to the rapier knife of revolutionary criticism if you are serious about creating a revolution. Everything—action or inaction, the way you relate to people you work with, how you deal with the masses, how you deal with your family, how you deal with personal relationships, how you deal with people with whom you disagree—has to be open to criticism and self-criticism. None of us is perfect, but we all claim to want to create a revolution. In order to create this revolution we must be willing to sublimate our egos for the good of the movement and suffer death of these egos by a thousand cuts. It is only when we are able to do this that we will truly be able to move forward and create a revolution—and win.

If we continue to practice liberalism and do not engage in struggle against incorrect views for the sake of unity or progress or "getting the work done properly," then we will continue to walk away from organizations and groups, creating new groups of two or thirty. This practice has permeated the movement and helped to create the sectarian problem we're experiencing today. We cannot organize our communities for revolution if we cannot resolve the contradictions among ourselves. It's not good enough to say, "We agree to disagree." That usually means that you've decided to go your separate ways and not interfere with each other. If a contradiction is of such magnitude that you cannot work together, even with the knowledge that you're involved in building a revolution—something that requires a coordinated effort between revolutionaries and the masses, something that is highly life threatening—then you cannot just go your separate ways. There is no separate way in a revolutionary struggle. We're all either in this together or we're working at odds with each other. The sooner we recognize this and begin seriously working to resolve the contradictions among us, the sooner we can seriously begin to build a foundation for revolution.

To simply say that we're going to work together is not enough, either. We're all human beings. We all have our own idiosyncrasies. What is necessary is that we stop the liberalism, place all our cards on the table, and hash out our differences. We can no longer afford the luxury of rumormongering, making unsubstantiated allegations, or harboring ill feelings without airing them.

The original split within the Black Panther Party in 1971 went down because we practiced liberalism, harbored ill will, believed rumors without investigation, and allowed this to go on until it grew so large that we believed the only way out was fratricide. If we had nipped it in the bud, COINTELPRO would not have been able to do its job. A lot of comrades would not have been killed, many more would not have ended up in prison for all these years, and countless others would not be members of the class of the walking dead.

Only when we lay all our cards on the table, reveal all our heretofore hidden agendas, and determine that we are working on the same agenda will we be capable of waging struggle over disagreements to build a strong, solid organization that will lead us to freedom and liberation.

In understanding this, I have come to recognize that everybody does not take this view. For those who do, I would like to offer this view of how to resolve contradictions among the people so we can begin to move forward in the struggle. The first step is to discuss our goals and see whether they are the same, or at least whether they fit with one another.

We often assume that because we all say, "We're involved in a struggle," we mean we're involved in the same struggle, with the same objectives and goals. Here's what I mean by that phrase: I believe that nothing short of a revolution will eradicate the racism, capitalism, and imperialism that oppress me and my people as well as other exploited and oppressed people everywhere. I believe that the capitalist system of this country has to be destroyed and replaced with an economic system built on the premise "From each according to his ability, to each according to his needs." That is, every man, woman, and child contributes to the whole what he or she is capable of contributing, and, whether that contribution is highly skilled labor or unskilled labor, each receives from the whole the basic necessities of life—what is necessary for maintaining a humane and dignified existence.

Once we have established a commonality of goals, the method we use in resolving contradictions should be determined by a number of factors, chiefly, (1) whether the contradiction is with our enemy or between friends and, (2) what is the desired outcome of the contradiction.

Once it has been established that the contradiction is between friends (for the purpose of this paper, "friends" is not being used to mean cut buddy, homey, or pal. Here it is merely a way of saying that the person is not an agent, pig, provocateur, or someone working against the interest of the people), then the next step is to determine what the desired outcome is.

If the contradiction is between friends, then the desired outcome must be to resolve the contradiction in order to move forward. If the allegation is that the person is an agent or enemy of the people, the desired outcome is to resolve the contradiction in order to verify the charge or exonerate the individual. The method used to resolve the contradiction starts from the premise "No investigation, no right to speak."

The first order of business is to investigate the allegation. Not to spread rumors or vilify the person, but to conduct a thorough, objective investigation of the circumstances that led to the charge. Too often in our movement, as in our everyday lives, we hear rumors about individuals and, without thought for consequences or making any effort to determine the validity of the rumor, we simply pass them on to someone else. On the streets, outside political formations, we're very clear that when we do this we're indulging in gossip. Within the movement, we talk about COINTELPRO all the time but don't realize that what we're doing is continuing the pattern of behavior that allowed COINTELPRO to succeed.

The object of investigation is to get to the truth. This requires that we enter into the investigation from the point of neutrality. This can best be done by empowering a minimum of three people to conduct the investigation and arrive at an objective conclusion. We must be objective and give no greater validity to one side than to the other. The axiom is that there are three sides to a situation: side one, side two, and the truth. In getting to the truth we must hear all sides of the question first. Once all sides are heard, if the truth is not easily discerned, then it becomes necessary to continue the investigation by questioning witnesses to the situation. During the course of the investigation, depending upon the nature of the charge, we conduct business as usual.

The movement has long talked about people being "tried before the people in a people's court." But the theory has far outweighed the practice. The Provisional Government of the Republic of New Afrika (PG-RNA)[4] has gone so far as to elect judges to its People's Court. But trying issues of dispute before a People's Court is not a working practice. In order for it to be a working practice, we

Enemies and Friends: Resolving Contradictions

have to begin implementing it. If we are to educate our people on the correct method of resolving contradictions by example, then we can ill afford to continue making allegations, spreading and embellishing them without moving to resolve them.

A Model for a People's Court

I recently engaged in such a dispute. The model that was used to resolve the dispute was a people's tribunal. The person bringing the charges put them on paper. The person the charges were brought against prepared a written response. These were disseminated to all parties involved. A date, time, and place were set for a hearing. Both sides were able to have witnesses present. Three independent hearing officers (having no involvement in the dispute and trusted by both sides) were chosen, and an odd number of (not less than five) jurists were chosen, also with no involvement in the charges.

The hearing officers set the tone and laid out guidelines for the proceeding. The charges were read into the record and tape-recorded. Then the person bringing the charges presented her point of view, followed by the reading of the written response to the charges. Next, the person bringing the charges called and questioned her witnesses. The person charged then questioned the witnesses, followed by questions from the hearing officers and jury panel. The witnesses were not allowed to ask any questions; their part in the proceeding was simply to be witnesses. The proceedings were handled the same way for the person being charged when she presented her witnesses.

All the parties involved had agreed to abide by the decision of the court, and they did. This is only a model. It was not perfect, and it is possible that the resolution was accepted and the episode laid to rest for reasons other than the fact that the proceedings were handled in a principled manner.

Maybe We Really Haven't Identified the True Contradiction?

I suggest that the real contradiction may be that we really are not about the same thing, the same goals, and some of us are not willing to admit it. Not yet, anyway . . .

Notes

1. "Napes" is a variant of "jackanapes"; both words mean conceited, and using them is similar to calling someone a jackass. "Nape" was often used by members of the Black Panther Party.

2. A "need-to-know" situation: in an attempt to minimize gossip and spreading of information within revolutionary organizations, a standard was employed, whereby information was only given to those who needed to know it in order to carry out their work. This was also a practice within clandestine organizations, to prevent sensitive information from being exposed.

3. Mao Tse-tung, "Combat Liberalism" (September 7, 1937), in *Selected Works of Mao Tse-tung* (Peking [Beijing]: Foreign Language Press, 1967), vol. 2, 32.

4. Republic of New Afrika: see chapter 4, "What is Security," note 1, p. 42.

6. On the Question of Sexism Within the Black Panther Party

Safiya's original introductory paragraph is included here. This essay was published, in unedited form, in the fall/winter 1993 issue of the *Black Panther, Black Community News Service*.[1] It has also been posted on various websites and is quoted in several books about the Black Panther Party.[2] The Black Panther Party had a reputation for sexist politics and mistreatment of women members. Certainly the media encouraged that view. The tendency of white observers to pounce on examples of sexism in Black groups and culture also created the atmosphere in which Safiya was moved to write the essay, to put such criticisms in context and to point out that sexism is no more endemic in oppressed communities than in privileged ones.[3]

This piece was initially written as a response to the May 5, 1993, *New York Times* op-ed page exchange between former Black Panther member Elaine Brown and Alice Walker, author of *The Color Purple*. This exchange was the culmination of a running discussion about former Party member David Hilliard's book, *This Side of Glory*.[4] Walker had criticized the Party's male leadership as sexist. In what was hyped to be an attack on sexism within the Party, Walker seemed to spend more time attacking what she presumed to be the sexuality of the male leadership: she made many allusions to homoeroticism. She had a clear problem with using the terms "sexuality" and "sexism" interchangeably. Exchanges like this make it glaringly obvious that it's necessary to put the issue of sexism in the

Black Panther Party in its correct perspective. While Alice confuses sexuality and sexism, I will attempt to address the issue of sexism within the Black Panther Party.

The error everyone—Black Panther Party supporters and detractors alike—seems to make is to look at the Party in a vacuum, separating it from its time and roots. The Party came out of the Black community and its experiences. In order to understand the issue of sexism in the Party, it is necessary to review the historical experience of Black people in this country as well as the climate in which the Party came into being. This is not to say that there was nothing wrong with the way Black women were treated in the Party. But we should not simply decry the role of women in the Party. Instead, we should analyze the development of the situation and make the necessary moves to correct it.

What, then, was—is—the Black experience in this country?

We were all brought over in the same condition, packed like sardines in the bowels of slave ships. We were herded like cattle to the slave auctions and sold to the highest bidder to be used as workhorses, studs, breeders, and household help. We were defined by our capacities as breeders, studs, and slave laborers. The women were further categorized by how pleasing they were to the eyes of the slave masters. The destruction of our culture, which started with the stealing of our language, religion, and children, was completed when we began to measure our own worth by how many women the Black man could "pleasure" at a time and how many children we could have.

The Black woman worked right alongside the Black man in the field, and she worked in the master's house. The Black man could not defend or protect his family. In most cases the Black woman was the one who defended or protected the family from the slave master's wrath—by any means necessary. Since Black men had been stripped of their manhood in every way but the ability to "pleasure" women and make babies, the sexual act soon became the standard by which the Black man measured his manhood.

Having been deprived of our culture, we began to take on the persona of our slave masters, filling the void of our lost culture with the slave culture that was foisted upon us. This is the root of the sexism that is plaguing our communities today. Unlike the sexism characteristic of the white community, the sexism of the Black community has its basis in racism and self-hate.

The division in the Black community between the Black male and Black female did not just come about on its own. It was carefully thought out and cultivated. After the end of chattel slavery, Black men, for the most part, couldn't get jobs. The Black woman had to be the breadwinner as well as homemaker. This—in conjunction with the already festering sore of having to stand by and watch while the woman was raped, made to bear the master's children, and then made to wet-nurse the children of the white woman—was too much for the Black man to handle psychologically. This resulted in the Black man casting the blame for his situation at the feet of the Black woman. As time went on, the love-hate-anger triangle began to manifest itself in the sexism present today in the Black community.

Which brings us to 1966 and the founding of the Black Panther Party.

Nothing had changed in terms of the quality of life in the Black community; nothing had changed in terms of racism in this country. We were still slaves in every way, except we were no longer bound and shackled. We still didn't have a culture. Our Africanism and sense of identity were gone and had been replaced by Western civilization. We were busy trying to be like the rest of the people in America. We had taken on the persona of sexist America, but with a Black hue. It was into this context that the Black Panther Party was born, declaring that we were revolutionaries and a revolutionary had no gender.

Bobby Seale and Huey Newton envisioned the Black Panther Party for Self-Defense as just that: a community-based organization that sought to defend the community against police brutality and to set an example of revolutionary activism. The membership of the Party was recruited from the ghettoes of the inner cities. The Party itself was founded in Oakland, California, in the spring of 1966, by two Black men who came straight out of the ghetto and met on the campus of Merritt College. The Party was founded as a response to the rampant episodes of police brutality committed by the notorious Oakland Police Department against the Black community.

On October 28, 1967, only one year after the founding of the Party, Huey Newton was incarcerated after an incident in which a police officer was killed and Huey wounded. This, along with the march on the California state capitol at Sacramento with guns,[5] catapulted the Party into national prominence.

Whatever was going on in the community and society as a whole was reflected in the interaction of the members of the Party. The ideology of the Party developed out of the struggle of people of Afrikan descent in the United States for freedom. This struggle began on the slave ships and continues today. Seen through the prism of Marxism-Leninism and scientific socialism, the Party's ideology was an attempt to overcome the romanticism and idealism that were characteristic of Black organizations at the time and replace them with a pragmatic analysis that allowed for social practice as the criterion for truth. Nonetheless, the Party had its own unique analysis about which social and economic class was the vanguard of the struggle for Black liberation.

The Party believed that the only group capable of moving the struggle forward was the lumpenproletariat (or lumpen)[6]—the brother and sister "off the block," the unemployed (last hired and first fired), the hustler, the welfare mother, etc. The Party felt that this group was at the bottom rung of the totem pole and had nothing to lose. It was this element that the Party recruited from the ghetto and tried to politicize. In its view of what they represented, the Party romanticized the lumpen.

In defining the work of the Party, the leadership looked to other struggles around the world and to Mao Tse-tung's "Red Book"—*The Quotations of Chairman Mao Tse-tung*—for direction.[7] The Party's Eight Points of Attention and Three Main Rules of Discipline were lifted directly from this book. One of the eight points was "Do not take liberties with women." The recognition of this point and its addition to the catechism of the Party was a monumental step forward in addressing the treatment of women. The simple fact that the issue was placed in—or on—the books was a step forward. Now we had to make it a part of our everyday lives, the everyday lives of the so-called lumpen who were the majority element of the Party.

The simple fact that the Black Panther Party had the courage to address the question of women's liberation in the first place was a monumental step forward. In a time when the other nationalist organizations were defining women as barefoot, pregnant, and in the kitchen, women in the Black Panther Party were working right alongside men, being assigned sections to organize just like the men, and receiving the same training as the men. Further, the decisions about what a person did within the ranks of the Party were determined not by gender but by ability.

In its brief seven-year history women had been involved on every level in the Party.[8] There were women like Audrea Jones, who founded the Boston chapter of the Black Panther Party; women like Brenda Hyson, who was the OD (officer of the day) in the Brooklyn office of the Party. There were women like Peaches, who fought side by side with Geronimo Pratt in the Southern California chapter of the Party; and Kathleen Cleaver, who was on the Central Committee. There was Sister Rivera, who was one of the motivators behind the office in Mount Vernon, New York. On the other hand, there were problems: men who brought their sexist attitudes into the organization. Some of the men refused to take direction from women. We had a framework established to deal with that. But many times the framework was not used because of liberalism, cowardice, and fear.

The other side of the coin was women who sought to circumvent the principled method of work by using their femininity as a way to achieve rank and stature within the Party. They also used their sexuality to get out of work and avoid certain responsibilities. This unprincipled behavior within the Party (just as on the streets) undermined the work of other sisters who struggled to deal in a principled manner.

Thus, there were three basic evils that had to be confronted: male chauvinism, female passivity, and ultrafemininity (the "I'm only a woman" syndrome).

The advent of the women's liberation movement during the late 1960s sought to equate what was happening with white women in this society with the plight of Black women. The white women were seeking to change their role in society vis-à-vis the home and workplace. They sought to be seen as more than just mothers and homemakers; they wanted to be afforded the right to be fully active members of the workplace and to take on whatever role they wanted in society. But our situation was different. We had been working outside the home and supporting our families. We had been shouldering the awesome responsibilities of waging a struggle against racist oppression and economic exploitation since we had been brought to these shores in the slave ships. Our struggle was not a struggle to be liberated so that we could move into the workplace, but a struggle to be recognized as human beings.

Sexism, or the degeneration of the relationship between the Black man and woman into antagonism and brutality, is a byproduct of our history. While I am clearly opposed to the way this history plays out in our community, I am not a feminist. I am a revolutionary. I am a scientific socialist. I believe that we have to struggle on all fronts against those attitudes that threaten to destroy us as a people.

It is extremely important that we remember that even though the Black Panther Party had established a built-in process to deal with male chauvinism in its ranks, the members of the Party were products of the society in which they lived. We struggled against those tendencies whenever possible, but they were reinforced by the larger society.

In order to create a new society we have to create a new being. We are all products of the society we come from and live within. We have internalized the negativisms of this society. Our every thought and manifestation (or way of acting on that thought) has been ingrained within us by the circumstances that make up the environment from which we emerge. In changing this society we have to change how we deal with each other. We have to acknowledge that there is something wrong with how we view each other, how we deal with each other, and how we think of each other. After acknowledging what is wrong, we have to understand how it developed and why it is wrong. Only after we do this will we be in a position to change the thinking and the behavior.

If we simply change the color of the oppressor, we have not moved forward. We must change the mindset of the people so that the oppression does not continue. We must cast out the oppressor's culture, including sexism. It is easy to decry from afar the sexism of the leadership of the Black Panther Party, without having struggled along with that leadership. If we are truly about the task of revolution, then we must jump into the trenches and struggle together.

While the Party was dealing with the issue of politically educating its ranks, it was also feeding hungry children, establishing liberation schools, organizing tenants and welfare mothers, and establishing free health clinics. Simultaneously, the Black Panther Party was under attack from the local, state, and federal government. Offices of the Party from California to Louisiana, from Texas to Michigan—all across the country—were under physical attack. Panthers were being killed and imprisoned. We were not theorizing about struggle; we were in constant struggle on every level.

Finally, I would like to remind you of two things. First: everybody who is Black is not involved in the Black liberation struggle. Therefore, their critiques of that struggle are not carried out with the motivation of curing the sickness to save the patient. They seize opportunities like the publication of Elaine Brown's and David Hilliard's books to vent their personal beliefs and agendas. Alice Walker has suggested that the male leadership of the Party feared being perceived as having homosexual love for each other—whether or not they had actually been lovers—and that this fear accounted for their macho sexist attitudes toward women. This raises a tantalizing question: is her assertion an example of people coloring the facts to fit their own leanings?

The second point is this: while the primary struggle the Black community faces is against racist oppression and economic exploitation, we must still deal with the problem of male chauvinism and sexism—along with domestic violence—in our communities. These problems are not just problems that exist in the Black community, but in the whole of society. The problem for us is that we are having to deal with these issues simultaneously with the primary struggle.

The Black Panther Party put into place a mechanism for dealing with this—starting with political education and ending with bringing the responsible parties up on disciplinary charges. We must not be afraid of allowing the old self, rife with the negativisms of this society, to die so that a new, more revolutionary and progressive self can be born. Then and only then do we stand a chance of destroying this oppressive society. It is with this thought in mind that we use the weapon of criticism and self-criticism to correct the way we deal with each other. It is through study and practice that we strengthen our own self-esteem and gain the courage to challenge chauvinist and sexist attitudes we encounter as we struggle. Finally, it is through our social practice that we set the example to our community and advance the overall struggle.

The Black Panther Party may not have completed the task of eradicating sexist attitudes within the Party and in the community. But we did bring the problem out in the open and put the question on the floor. As we struggle against our primary enemy, it is extremely crucial that we remember that ours is a collective struggle, a struggle for human rights for all our people, men and women. As long as one of us is oppressed, none of us is free. We cannot, as women, struggle side by side with our male comrades for freedom for our people and then be oppressed by our brothers. Our struggle for freedom as a people must mean freedom for all of us. Freedom for men, freedom for women.

But the enemy of our people will not wait for us to resolve the questions of gender and sexism. We have to find a way to put all our cards on the table, to struggle together to cure the sickness and save the patient. Those of us who are truly about the work of making revolution and creating a revolutionary culture must be willing to die the death of a thousand cuts. We must exorcise those characteristics of ourselves and traits of the oppressor nation in order to carry out that most important revolution—the internal revolution. This is the revolution that creates a new being capable of taking us to freedom and liberation. As we are creating this new being, we must simultaneously be struggling to defeat racism, capitalism, and imperialism—and liberate the Black Nation.

Notes

1. The *Black Panther, Black Community News Service* was a newspaper founded in the spring of 1991 by a collective of people who "all were members of the Black Panther Party" before the Party was destroyed by COINTELPRO. The group "came together because of a compelling need to address the critical issues facing the Afrikan-Amerikkan community" ("Editorial Statement," *Black Panther Newspaper Committee* 1, no. 1, Spring 1991, p.1). The newspaper had a home office in Berkeley and addresses in cities around the country, including New York City. The original newspaper of the Party, *The Black Panther Intercommunal News Service*, which published for about thirteen years beginning in 1969, was sometimes called the *Black Panther Black Community News Service* or the *Black Panther Community News Service*. And in chapter 9, "This is Worth Fighting For," Safiya describes the genesis of another newspaper, *Right On! Black Community News Service*, which she says was begun "directly following the split" in the Party.

2. For example, Jama Lazerow and Yohuru Williams, eds., *In Search of the Black Panther Party: New Perspectives on a Revolutionary Movement* (Durham, NC: Duke University Press, 2006) and Mumia Abu-Jamal, *We Want Freedom: A Life in the Black Panther Party* (Cambridge, MA: South End Press, 2004).

3. A similar point is sometimes raised about hip-hop culture. See, for example, Thien-bao Thuc Phi, "Yellow Lines," in Fred Ho and Bill Mullen, eds., *Afro Asia: Revolutionary Political and Cultural Connections Between African Americans and Asian Americans* (Durham, NC: Duke University Press, 2008). Bao writes, "Let's make something clear: sexism and patriarchy are not unique to hip hop or men of color," (p. 307). He footnotes this sentence with the following: "Let me say that one more time: sexism and patriarchy are not unique to hip hop or men of color," (p. 317 n. 23).

4. David Hilliard and Lewis Cole, *This Side of Glory: the Autobiography of David Hilliard and the Story of the Black Panther Party* (Boston: Little, Brown, 1993).

5. On May 2, 1967, the Panthers staged a march of some thirty armed Party members to the state assembly in the capitol to protest the Mulford Bill, a gun control bill then under consideration. The march captured wide media attention as well as the imagination of many in the Black community.

6. "Lumpenproletariat" is a German word used by Marx to describe a sector of the working class composed of thieves, swindlers, beggars, and others—the "raggedy-proletariat." But in the context of the United States, where racism barred many Black people from membership in the working class, the term came to mean those permanently without jobs and without hope of regular employment. In a "study guide" attributed to the Black Liberation Army and dated 1977–78, "lumpen proletariat" is defined as "the under class, unemployed, marginally employed and those who live outside of the law, i.e., criminal element. The aged, infirm, and disabled are also part of this class because they are marginally employed, therefore, not a secure part of the productive process. Those on welfare, social security are also members of this class" ("Study Guide 1977-78," signed Coordinating Committee, NYURBA, out-of-print pamphlet).

7. Many organizations during this period were strongly influenced by Mao Tse-tung and the Chinese Revolution, especially the "little Red Book" to which Safiya refers. The "Red Book," *Quotations from Chairman Mao Tse-tung*, is a collection of excerpts from longer writings by the leader of the Chinese Revolution. For a fuller discussion of this influence, especially as it emerged among Black organizations, see Fred Ho and Bill Mullen, eds., *Afro Asia: Revolutionary Political and Cultural*

Connections Between African Americans and Asian Americans (Durham, NC: Duke University Press, 2008).

8. Note by Safiya: "1966–73: The Black Panther Party split in 1971. From that time until 1976 there existed an East Coast and a West Coast Black Panther Party. For purposes of this writing, the Black Panther Party was destroyed in 1971."

7. "Islam and Revolution" Is Not a Contradiction

The notes for this chapter are Safiya's original notes; in some places updated information has been added. The essay is undated; it was probably written in the late 1980s.

I became a Muslim (one who submits to the will of Allah) while in the Black Panther Party, and as a result of defending the rights of members of the New York Three.[1] As someone who had been reared in the Christian Church and a family full of ministers and deacons, I knew the Bible well and had participated in the choir, usher board, and Sunday school in church. I had also been privy to a lot of things being done by people who were supposed to be "saved" and "going to heaven" that made me doubt the existence of God. I had decided that there could not be a God if these people were going to heaven and others weren't.

It was Nuh Quyyam [Albert Nuh Washington] who inadvertently made me see things differently. When they were captured and returned to New York, the New York Three were housed in the Tombs.[2] People within and close to the Black Panther Party were criticizing and questioning how Nuh and Jalil could be Muslims and revolutionaries—questioning their commitment to the struggle. I looked upon Nuh as a mentor; as a matter of fact, I called him my teacher. So instead of joining in the criticisms of him, I defended his right to self-determination. I reminded those who objected to his being Muslim that we were fighting for the right to freedom and self-determination. I said, "How can we talk about self-determination if we would deny someone their freedom to determine whether or not they want to believe in the existence of God?" The debate became hotter and hotter, and to shore up my position, I decided to study the religion for myself.

Nuh turned me on to a book by Muhammad Qutb called *Islam: The Misunderstood Religion*. That book answered a lot of my questions about religion. It especially answered my questioning how there could be a God while people who said they worship Him were doing the things they were doing. But it was reading the Qur'an for myself that made me decide that I wanted to seriously study the Islamic way of life. As I studied, I learned that Allah makes Muslims, man does not. Which to me meant that simply declaring, "There's none worthy of worship but Allah," does not make you Muslim. It is the intentions of your heart and your determination to struggle in the way of Allah that makes you Muslim. I read sura 2, ayats 190–93, where Muslims are admonished to "fight in the cause of God those who fight you . . . and fight them on until there is no more tumult or oppression . . . for tumult and oppression is worse than slaughter." So, in 1971 in Sankore Masjid in Greenhaven Correctional Facility at Stormville, New York, I declared Shahadah (testified faith) and determined that I would strive to stay and struggle in the "straight way."

Prior to becoming Muslim I ate whatever I felt like eating, had the foulest mouth in town, and had no qualms about exercising my authority over others. Even after becoming Muslim I still had something of a "God complex." I had a tendency to demand that people live up to my standards for their life, and if they didn't, I relegated them to the backseat of life. There was no gray in anything, only black or white. There were no excuses for not living up to my expectations. I was the judge, jury, and executioner. I had learned that there indeed was a God and Allah *subhanahu wa ta'ala* (glorious and exalted) was He, but I had not learned temperance, compassion, or forgiveness.

Then, on January 25, 1975, while a member of the Amistad Collective of the Black Liberation Army, I was involved in a shoot-out in Norfolk, Virginia. One of my comrades was killed, another was shot, and I was captured. My bail was set at one million dollars on each of five counts, and on one of the counts I was facing the electric chair. While the shoot-out was occurring and the capture was going down, I was on autopilot. I didn't have time to think, only to react. But when I finally had time to reflect, what kept going through my mind were all the things I had read in the Qur'an about the intentions of the heart and how, if those were correct, Allah would allow you to be victorious.

I began to question Allah, "Why? Why did you allow this to happen to me?" Over the next two months, while awaiting trial in the Norfolk City Jail, while making *salat* (prayer) five times a day, while being kept in solitary confinement in the "bama" cells,[3] I repeatedly posed this question. Finally, the answer began to come to me: "Think ye because you say, 'I believe,' that you will not be tested in your belief?" Even though I was having these conversations with God about why He was allowing this to happen to me (notice, I was still wondering why *me*), I was not afraid—I still recognized that Allah was God and as long as He was with me, I was not alone.

My political convictions vis-à-vis the Black Panther Party and Black Liberation Army, my citizenship in the Republic of New Afrika, and the struggle for freedom and self-determination were as strong as ever—maybe even stronger, because I had just seen firsthand what the state would do to a slave who dared to rebel. My belief in Islam as a way of life was becoming more solidified also. On the one hand, I was faced with revolutionaries who had problems with my being Muslim. On the other hand, I was being told by Muslims that in order to receive support from them I had to denounce the Black liberation movement and my codefendant who was not Muslim.[4] All this was happening while I was in jail awaiting trial on a capital case.

I didn't denounce anything or anyone. We went to trial on April 17, 1975, and by the end of that day we had been sentenced to forty years each and I was on my way to the Virginia Correctional Center for Women in Goochland, Virginia—known to everyone simply as Goochland.

Being a practicing Sunni Muslim in prison was not easy. Being an orthodox Muslim, a political prisoner, and a woman was unheard of. When I arrived at Goochland I was placed in maximum-security confinement, on the pretext that there was no space available for me on the quarantine hall, where new prisoners were normally placed. The discipline of making *salat* five times a day and having Allah constantly in your remembrance is a wonderful thing, because it enables you to deal with the madness around you. It worked for me in the Norfolk City Jail, and it continued to work for me in Goochland. I could take time out from the insanity of prison life to communicate with the things that centered me.

I was still asking the question, "Why me? Why did you allow this to happen to me?" Internally, I was trying to get the answer to that question; externally, I was preparing myself for the struggle to maintain my political integrity while incarcerated in Goochland. I knew that the stated reason for housing me in the maximum-security segregation unit was a lie, because I had been in an empty cell on quarantine hall before I was brought to segregation. I asked for the rules of the institution and found that the only reason someone could be placed in this unit was for a violation of the rules of the Department of Corrections or the institution. I had violated neither. I told them that if at the end of the twenty-one-day quarantine period I was not out of segregation, I would begin a suit against them for discrimination based on political beliefs and affiliations. I then settled back to wait out the twenty-one days.

It was during the twenty-one days that my spiritual understanding began to kick in. One day the message came to me, "Stand still and know that I am God." It kept reverberating through my head. "I am omnipotent and omnipresent." I didn't have books—or anything else—in my cell, so I had to wrestle with this on my own. This was strictly between me and Allah. I was reminded of the story of Saul on the road to Damascus when Allah knocked him to his knees and reminded him that He was God. I was reminded that I couldn't just declare, "There is no God but God" and go on my merry way—that more is required of me.

Over the next two years, both my political and my spiritual beliefs were to be tried by fire. In addition to being in prison with a forty-year sentence, I was also in constant pain from fibroid tumors. During my sojourn in the city jail awaiting trial, I had repeatedly been denied medical care. I'd been told that I would be taken care of when I arrived in the state system. During my initial examination upon arrival, a doctor told me the tumors were the size of oranges and asked me how long my sentence was. I told him forty years; he told me to come back to see him in ten. I had learned to incorporate Allah into every facet of my life, so I turned to Allah for guidance on this. My answer was, "You go as far as you can in fighting this battle for medical treatment and I will handle the rest."[5] So I followed the prison's rules. I filed a grievance. In response, I was told that the lack of medical treatment constituted a difference of opinion between myself and the doctor on whether treatment was needed at this point.

On the spiritual front, I was struggling to get a halal (permitted foods) diet, to observe *Jummah* (Friday prayer), and to fast for the month of Ramadan. There were women in the institution who considered themselves Muslims but had never observed Ramadan because they were followers of the Nation of Islam. They also did not observe *Jummah* or a halal diet. They also, for the most part, practiced homosexuality. What was I to do in this situation? Maintain the *deen* (Islamic way of life)! Judge not the workings of others, but pull their coattail to what Allah says in *al'Kitab* (scripture), and maintain the deen. Allah alone makes Muslims. I informed the institution of the requirements in practicing Islam, and I continued to do what was required of me.

The first year, I observed Ramadan in my cell. I was not allowed to have any meals after sundown or prior to sunrise. I purchased necessities from the commissary and as the women in the institution observed my practice, they began to make things available to me. The next year, the institution made arrangements for me to observe Ramadan.

It's extremely hard to maintain your principles, politics, and beliefs when all around you others are compromising and giving in to temptations. I watched as women who came into the institution at the same time I did, who had never been involved in relationships with women before, began to get involved. I, too, might have succumbed if it had not been for the mercy of Allah.

One of the things that hit me strongest when I submitted myself to the will of Allah was the knowledge that Allah is all-knowing, omnipotent, and omnipresent. Those were not just words for me, not just ritualistic sayings. It was and is a belief that is part of my core. I'm saying this because, knowing that Allah is already aware of what transpired inside Goochland while I was incarcerated there, there is no need for me to lie to you. I forged friendships while I was there; I was tempted to form a homosexual relationship. But Allah is merciful and the temptation was only a brief one. I had never been in prison before. I had never been alone so far from home. I was alone without a support mechanism. In my darkest hour of despair, Allah quickly let me know that I was not alone. I was never tempted again in that manner. I can truly say, "There but for the grace of Allah go I."

Two years after entering Goochland, I escaped. Everything came to a head at one time. I had decided that I would wait for word on my appeal before doing what I had been trained to do. At the same time, I had begun to hemorrhage from lack of medical care for my ovarian tumors. I was in constant pain, hemorrhaging, and not receiving any medical care. Even though I had followed the prison rules, I still hadn't obtained any medical care. I had even offered to pay for the medical care myself, but the prison said no. I knew then that the only way I would get the medical care I needed was to go out and get it for myself.

I made up my mind to leave the institution. But I prayed over it first. I needed to make my peace with Allah. I had gotten to the point where I truly believed that Allah *subhanahu wa ta'ala* (glorious and exalted) must be consulted in all things. While I was talking to Allah about my decision to leave, He showed me that I would, indeed, get away from Goochland. But He also showed me that I would return. On the evening of December 31, 1976, I escaped.

I was on escape from that date until February 21, 1977. While on escape, I was seen by two doctors and told that I would have to make a decision: to have an operation, or to be in pain for the rest of my life. When I was recaptured and returned to Goochland, I realized that one of the reasons I was incarcerated was that Allah had a plan for my life. You see, nothing happens without out Allah allowing it to happen.

Three things were happening simultaneously in my life. I was being reminded of *a khutbah* (sermon) that Imam Rasul Sulaiman had given at Sankore Masjid in Greenhaven when I declared Shahadah. In this *khutbah*, Imam Sulaiman stated that there were three forms of jihad (duty). The first was the internal jihad, wherein you struggle to change those things within that are incorrect. The second jihad is with your immediate family; the third is with the community. I was, and still am, engaged in the first jihad. I was learning that there was only one God, and that He is all-knowing, all-wise, and all-powerful. I was learning that Islam is not a religion that you observe only on Friday or when you are in the company of other Muslims. Islam is a way of life. You live within its tenets 24-7. Allah is constantly in your remembrance.

At the same time that I was dealing with that jihad, I was reminded of the admonishment to "wage struggle against tyranny and oppression wherever it may be found." The lack of quality or even adequate medical care at Virginia Correctional Center for Women was an issue over which to wage struggle. I determined that when I went to trial, I was going to plead not guilty to the escape charge by reason of duress and necessity, citing the lack of medical care and the fear for my life as the reasons for my escape. I also decided that I would represent myself.

I received support from many people in preparing my case. Some of the legal research was done by brothers who were locked down in various prisons across the country. The law library at Goochland was virtually nonexistent, since it was a women's prison and the prevailing belief was that women didn't need a law library. I also received assistance from the People's Law Office in Chicago. I even received some support from some of the correctional officers in the prison. But the support that was most unforeseen and extremely appreciated came from the people of the town of Goochland who sat on the jury.

During the course of the trial, I made the court aware of the lack of medical care at the prison. I subpoenaed witnesses who told of misdiagnoses such as ovarian cysts in an ovary that had already been removed, sore throats that turned out to be cancer, and fibroid tumors that were really pregnancies. At the end of the trial, the judge instructed the jury that they had to deliver a guilty verdict because escape was like murder: either the victim was dead or not. Either I was at the prison during that time period or I wasn't. Since I hadn't been at the prison during the time period in question, the judge told the jury, they had to find me guilty of escape.

The jury stayed out for a couple of hours. Then the judge called them back and told them that if they didn't find me guilty he would hold them in contempt of court. They found me guilty, but sentenced me to only a year, not the five years they could have given me. Then they waited outside the court until I was brought through on my way back to jail. There, they apologized for giving me the year.

I was also given the right to have an outside doctor handle my medical case. The institution later gave me a list of three doctors and said I could choose one from among them. The doctor I chose was a woman named Wanda (I don't remember her last name). She was on staff at the Medical College of Virginia in Richmond. I'd had a male physician who related to the women in prison as little more than animals—or as a means of obtaining a paycheck without having to be competent at what he did. I felt that I stood a better chance at receiving understanding and compassion with a female doctor at this point, largely because of the nature of my medical problem. As I said earlier, Allah was constantly with me throughout this process. I know this because when I finally had to undergo surgery to remove the tumors, I almost died. Allah stepped in and stayed death's hand.

Here is what happened. I had just been sedated in preparation for surgery. I was strapped to a gurney and the anesthesia was taking effect. I started choking on my saliva, but no one was paying attention. I tried to call out, but no one heard. I tried to signal, and could not get anyone's attention. Then, from somewhere in the depth of my being, Allah gave me the strength to rise up against the straps that were holding me down. When the attendants saw what was going on, they rushed over and assisted me.

I spent more than nine hours in surgery. Later, when I came to, Wanda was still there waiting to talk with me. I had asked her, before I went into surgery, to do what she could to save as much as possible. I wanted to have more children. When I awoke, she told me that the internal situation was so damaged that the only thing she could save was one ovary. I couldn't help but believe that if I had been given the medical treatment I needed in a timely fashion, this could have been avoided. But I was thankful for Wanda's ability to save the one ovary.

There was one more thing I had to learn as a Muslim—and as a revolutionary. From the day I became Muslim, I had been told about *shirk*, the assigning of partners to Allah (polytheism). There is no greater sin than *shirk*—believing that there is someone or something more worthy of worship or fear than Allah. I thought I had that one down pat. I knew that there was no other God but the one God. Inshallah illallah illallah. I bear witness that there is nobody worthy of worship or of fear but Allah. The problem was that I also had an overwhelming fear, an uncontrollable and irrational fear. This fear superseded and overshadowed even my faith in Allah. "What could that be?" you ask. I was scared beyond reason of snakes.

I keep going back to my capture in Norfolk and the things that went through my mind then. I knew I was facing the death penalty. For thirty days, this hung over my head. That didn't worry me. I was alone in a hostile environment. That didn't worry me. What worried me was how I would handle it if they attempted to use my fear of snakes to obtain information about my comrades and activities in the Black Panther Party or Black Liberation Army. I didn't know how I would stand up to that kind of interrogation. I knew how real my fear was.

I never thought about that kind of fear being *shirk*. I had never actually come face to face with a live snake before. I had seen pictures of snakes in books and had nightmares. I had seen pictures of snakes on television and had nightmares. I had even heard my mother and grandparents talk about snakes and had nightmares. My fear was all-consuming.

Prior to my arrest I had seen the movie *Tomasina and Bushrod*. One scene in that picture showed one of the co-conspirators being dangled over a hole full of snakes to induce him to give information to help capture two Black bank robbers. After he gave the information, he was still dropped into the hole with the snakes. I can still hear his screams. This movie made my fear even more real.

After I was brought back from escape, I was again taken to the maximum-security unit at the prison and placed in isolation. I was kept in this building in isolation and segregation for three years and seven months. During this time, I went from my cell to the showers; my cell to the recreation area (either downstairs or in a room on the same floor); and in the last months, from my cell to another room on the same floor to work. One day, when they had taken me out of my cell for an hour of exercise, they took me downstairs. A metal door was locked behind you as you went through each section of the building. As we approached the area leading to the downstairs recreation area, I looked into the rec room. Under the television stand I saw something coiled and black, with its tongue flicking in and out. I had no conscious thought and performed no conscious act. I reacted totally on instinct. I began screaming and running for the door. When I reached the door, it was locked. There was no way to get out, so I slid down the wall, curled myself into a fetal position, and kept screaming.

It was as though I was outside my body, watching myself go through these machinations. I could not stop myself from screaming, nor could I get control of myself. There was no thought process going on, just screaming and the regression to the fetal position. I had sunk into the darkest recesses of my mind in an attempt to protect myself from my worst fears. My fear of snakes was clearly greater than my belief in and love of Allah.

Somehow, the guards managed to return me to my cell. I don't know how they dealt with the snake. When I had finally managed to calm down and was myself again, I knew that I had to confront my fear. The institution was not going to do it for me. No one was going to guarantee that I wouldn't have to confront a snake again in life. The only positive thing about this experience was that I learned that they could not use the threat of exposure to snakes to gain information from me. This confrontation had made me know that my reaction would be so elemental that there was no way anyone could use it to extract information.

The other problem, for me, was much greater. My reaction to this fear made a lie of my statement of belief, that there is nothing more worthy of worship or fear than Allah. Was not this fear, at its very essence, saying that snakes had a greater power over my life than Allah? How could I rationalize this fear of snakes without ascribing a partnership to God in this snake, or without deifying this snake itself? The resolution of this spiritual and intellectual conflict would do two things for me. It would deal with my fear of snakes, and it would resolve my problem of *shirkism*.

Over the next month, I went back and forth between reading the Qur'an and making *salat* over this issue. I studied hadith (written traditions of the prophet Muhammad) on *shirk*. I read the Qur'an on faith and the oneness of God. I wrestled with my belief. Finally, on a basic level, I concluded that nothing happens to us without the permission of Allah. This may sound simple and matter of fact, but it's not. There was an entire analysis and process I went through before this became real to me. For me as a revolutionary, death was something I lived with daily and constantly. I enunciated clearly the concept that "wherever death may surprise us it will be welcome, as long as this our battle cry reach some receptive ear and another hand reach out to intone our funeral dirge with the staccato of machinegun fire and new cries of battle and victory." In dealing with the government of the United States of America, I was very clear that they were just men and women, while Allah was God. Him alone should I fear.

Then I thought about my reaction to the snake. If Allah is God—all-powerful, all-knowing, and all-wise, the arbitrator of the universe and creator of all things—then He created the snake. All things occur by the permission of Allah. If the snake should bite me, what could be the end result? Death. If in fact I had already conquered the fear of death and in fact welcomed it on the battlefield, then why did I fear the snake? After death, there is the judgment, the day of requital. The day when we all have to give an accounting of our lives and be weighed in the balance. That is to be feared. The day when Allah will look into your heart and determine whether your good outweighs your bad. *Shirk*—ascribing a partner to Allah, believing that anything or anyone other than Allah is worthy of worship or fear—is a sin. The first pillar of Islam is to believe in the oneness of God. You can't be one and also have a partner. One and one equals two. This undermines the fundamental pillar of Islam.

As I worked this out in my mind and in my heart, I grew stronger and my fear abated until finally it was gone. I could truly say with conviction, with a rock-solid belief system in place, "There's no God but God and Muhammad, *pbuh* (peace be upon him), is His messenger!"

After I came home from prison in August 1983, the first opportunity I got, I went to the Bronx Zoo. They have a reptile house there. I had never been in one before, but I was determined to test myself and my belief. I walked into the reptile house and looked at all the snakes, walking throughout the reptile house making sure that I took my time and observed everything. I emerged from that place with the courage of my convictions intact. *Allah subhanahu wa ta'ala is Allah, having no partners. There is nothing worthy of worship or fear but Allah.*

Now I can answer the question, Why me? The process of killing off those things within me that undermined my ability to submit myself to the will of Allah—as well as to learn what Che Guevara knew early on, that "a true revolutionary is motivated by great feelings of love"—was a time-consuming process. I had a lot of plans for how I was going to conduct my life as a revolutionary. Allah had other plans.

Now I conduct my life on the basis of two things. I follow the dictates of my conscience. I remember Allah in all things. If a thing is at war with my conscience, I don't do it. If it does not fall within the dictates of the sunnah (Islamic custom), I don't do it. Then I remember the admonishments of Allah: "It is incumbent upon Muslims to wage struggle against tyranny and oppression wherever it may be found . . . and fight in the way of Allah until tyranny and oppression is no more."

Notes

1. Albert Washington (Nuh Quyyam), Anthony Bottom (Jalil Muntaqim), and Herman Bell, the New York Three, are former members of the Black Panther Party, wrongfully convicted in the death of two New York City police officers (Waverly Jones and Joseph Piagentini), in 1971. [Nuh Washington died of cancer at Coxsackie prison on April 28, 2000. For recent information on the New York Three, see chapter 14, "CBS Tries the New York Three," p. 156.]

2. The official name for the Tombs was the Men's House of Detention. It was located at 125 White Street in Manhattan and was given that name because of its tomblike aura.

3. This was a row of cells separate from the rest of the population in the women's section of the jail where they kept women who were mentally ill, suffering from withdrawal, or drying out. They were individual cells and it was nothing for women to throw feces, have hallucinations, etc., all around you.

4. Masai Ehehosi, the one who had been shot, was later captured when he sought medical treatment. Masai is now a Muslim too.

5. I am not trying to say that Allah spoke to me. What I'm saying is that when I went to Him in faith and acquiescence, with the belief that He was all-wise, all-powerful, and all-knowing, He showed me the path I was to travel. By faith I believe He showed me the straight way that was to lead me in the way I should go.

8. We Too Are Veterans: Post-Traumatic Stress Disorders and the Black Panther Party

This is a slightly edited version of an article by Safiya in the *Black Panther, Black Community News Service*, February 1991. In talks she gave in Chicago that year, Safiya mentioned that she was working on a book on this topic. According to Ashanti Alston and a parenthetic line at the end of the original article ("The above is an excerpt from a book on the subject to be released in the spring"), this essay would have been a chapter in that book. But Safiya was too busy with organizing work to write the book. In several interviews and speeches, Safiya returned to this topic of the psychological and health damage suffered by people involved in the battles of the 1960s and 1970s. She also talked about the psychological effects she and others experienced as a result of incarceration and especially of solitary confinement. This article, including its title, reflects the general understanding that the movements of those years arose in the context of a state of domestic war between oppressed communities and the US government and law enforcement structures. It also hints at Safiya's ongoing battle with her own grief at the loss of too many of her comrades to death, prison, or exile.

I was nineteen when I joined the Black Panther Party and was introduced to the realities of life in inner-city Black America.

From the security of the college campus and the cocoon of the great American Dream Machine, I was suddenly stripped of my innocence by a foray into Harlem and indecent housing, police brutality, hungry children needing to be fed, elderly people eating out of garbage cans, and hopelessness and despair everywhere. If I hadn't seen it for myself, I would never have believed that this was America. It looked and sounded like one of those undeveloped third world countries.

Between 1966 and 1975, eager to be part of the fight for the freedom and liberation of Black people in America from their oppressive conditions, thousands of young Black men and women from all walks of life and backgrounds joined the ranks of the Black Panther Party. They were met with all the counter-force and might of the United States war machine.

Not unlike the young men who went off to fight in the Vietnam War believing they were going to save the Vietnamese from the ravages of "communism," the brothers and sisters who joined the ranks of the Black Panther Party, with all the romanticism of youth, believed that the rightness and justness of their cause guaranteed victory. We were learning the contradiction between what America said and what it did. We were shown examples of the government's duplicity and we became victims of its counterintelligence program (COINTELPRO), an all-out multiphasic war designed to stifle dissent in America in general and in the Black community in particular.

We came into the struggle believing that we would prevail. Because our struggle was right and just, we said, "We shall win without a doubt!" All we had to do was present an organized and disciplined united front and be determined to gain our freedom by any means necessary and our victory would be assured.

We theorized about what we were up against. We marched, sang, and rhetoricized about the implications of being in "the belly of the beast." We dissociated ourselves from anything or anyone who had been close to us and regurgitated the bravado about the struggle being primary—that in order to win we must be willing to sacrifice mother, father, sister, or brother.

We embraced all this in much the same manner that the drill sergeant in the Marine Corps psyched up the recruits to fight in Vietnam.

Veterans of the War in Vietnam

In 1967 my brother came home from Vietnam. He looked good. There were no scars or missing limbs. We were ecstatic. His bedroom was next to mine on the second floor of our duplex apartment in the Bronx. In the middle of the night I heard agonized screams coming from his room. Not knowing any better, I went to him and touched him to soothe him. He instantly went on the attack. He grabbed me with one hand, his other like a claw. I don't know what saved me, whether it was my screaming his name or throwing myself on him, but he came to himself before he harmed me.

That night he told me about watching his entire platoon get wiped out, about gouging eyes out with his bare hands, about not knowing who was the enemy and what direction it would come from the next time, and some of the other nightmares of Vietnam. After that we never talked about it again.

Before going to Vietnam, my brother had wanted to become a doctor. After returning from Vietnam, he could not stand the sight of blood. He drank straight gin continuously, like ice water, without getting drunk.

My brother made the horror of Vietnam real to me in 1967. I wasn't to experience anything remotely close to that again until I joined the Black Panther Party and came to realize that you didn't have to travel around the world to experience the ravages of war. The physical conditions of the Vietnam War were not present here. But for those of us who had been raised to believe that America was the land of the free and the home of the brave, and who were now involved in a struggle for liberation and human rights for Black people, the psychological conditions were just as intense.

We joined the Black Panther Party (and therefore the Black liberation struggle) with a lot of hope and faith. We believed that the struggle would end for us only with our death or the freedom of all oppressed people. With the destruction of the Black Panther Party while freedom was still not assured, we were left with no sense of direction or purpose—no one to tell us what to do next—and the knowledge that the job was not done. We hadn't just mouthed the words "revolution in our lifetime"; we had believed them. We sincerely believed that the Black Panther Party would lead us to victory. The only way we wouldn't live to see it would be if we died in battle. Alprentice "Bunchy" Carter, in his poem, "Black Mother," summed up how we felt:[1]

> Black Mother i must confess that i still breathe
> Though you are still not free
> What could justify my crying start
> Forgive my coward's heart
> . . . But blame me not the sheepish me
> For i have just awakened from a deep, deep sleep
> And i be hazed and dazed and scared
> And vipers fester in my hair
> BLACK MOTHER, i curse your drudging years
> The rapes and heartbreaks, sweat and tears
> . . . but this cannot redeem the fact
> You cried in pain, i turned my back
> And ran into the mire's fog
> And watched while you were dogged
> And died a thousand deaths
> But i swear i'll seize night's dark and gloom

A rose i'll wear to honor you
And when i fall
A rose in hand
You'll be free and i a man
For a slave of natural death who dies
Can't balance out two dead flies
i'd rather be without the shame
A bullet lodged within my brain
If i were not to reach our goal
Let bleeding cancer torment my soul.

We had experienced the death and/or imprisonment of countless of our brothers and sisters who had struggled right beside us, slept in the beds with us, eaten at the same table with us. (As I write this, the picture of Twymon Myers's bullet-riddled body flashes before my eyes. Shot so many times that his legs were almost shot off. Then the desecration of his funeral by the FBI's jumping from behind tombstones and out of trees at the cemetery, with sawed-off shotguns and machine guns pointed toward the mourners. "This is your FBI! Get out of the cars with your hands in the air and line up in a single file with enough distance between each of you so we can see you clearly.") Pictures pop in and out of our minds with no prompting.

Then there were the murders of Fred Hampton and Mark Clark, Alprentice "Bunchy" Carter and John Huggins, Sandra Pratt and Little Bobby Hutton, not to mention Fred Bennett, the countless shoot-outs, the infiltrations and setups that left you leery of strangers or of anyone getting too close or acting too friendly.[2] This left you constantly on guard and under the pressure of not knowing who your friends were and from which direction the next threat was coming.

Still, I think I'm one of the lucky ones. In 1983, after serving eight years and eight months of a forty-year sentence, I was released on parole. While in prison I maintained my commitment to the struggle for the liberation of Black and oppressed people. What kept me going was knowing that the reason they were killing and locking up Panthers was to break them and therefore to break the back of the struggle. I was determined that I would survive and, one way or the other, live to fight another day. We languished in the prisons and watched the growing lack of activity on the streets and promised ourselves that things would be different when we came home.

Our intense belief in the rightness and justness of our cause, and that things would be different when we returned to the streets, our awareness that we are still alive while our people's conditions have grown worse despite all our sacrifices—all this produces a traumatic shock to our system. This is the ultimate shock. We survived while others died. Despite all their intents and purposes, their deaths were in vain. The struggle hasn't been won. I contend that these elements have caused us to suffer post-traumatic stress disorder.

The *Diagnostic and Statistical Manual of Mental Disorders* defines post-traumatic stress disorder (PTSD) as "an anxiety disorder caused by the exposure to a psychologically distressing event that is outside the range of usual human experiences." Such events might include watching a friend die violently or unexpectedly; experiencing serious threats to home or family; or living under constant or prolonged fear or threat. PTSD symptoms include the following:

Recurring dreams (while asleep) or intrusive thoughts
(while awake) of the traumatic events
Flashbacks to the incidents triggered by sounds or pictures
or illusive smells

Inability to make or maintain relationships or friendships

Emotional isolation

Fantasies about living alone on a mountain or other isolated place

Feeling that no one is able to understand his/her situation or that no one would believe it if he/she tried to explain it

Constant fear of "losing control," and therefore refusing to allow oneself to show or feel emotions

Sense of helplessness, worthlessness, dejection

Feeling of guilt because comrades/friends who worked alongside you are in jail or prison and you survived

Suppressed rage that surfaces inappropriately at family or is controlled through the use of narcotics or alcohol

Inability to sleep

Being uncomfortable when in a crowded room or around a lot of people

Startle response

Inability to trust anyone

Substance or alcohol abuse, usually to numb the pain or drown out the memories, guilt, or both

Inability to maintain a job or deal with authority figures

Since coming home from prison I'd become more and more disillusioned with my comrades and the things I saw happening around me. I'd become dismayed by their seeming loss of principles and vacillation. I knew that I couldn't go back on my beliefs and principles, because the ghosts of Twymon Myers, Robert Webb, Anthony "Kimu" White, Timothy "Red" Adams, and all those other 'rades wouldn't let me. Nor could I turn my back on my comrades inside prison.

As I looked over the list of PTSD symptoms, I recognized

myself. And the first step to resolving the problem is recognizing that it exists.

And it wasn't just me. More and more there seemed to be some kind of pattern developing in the behavior of my other comrades who had survived the Black Panther Party and Black Liberation Army. I decided to do a psychological study of the problem because *We too are veterans and suffer from post-traumatic stress disorder.*

Notes

1. Alprentice "Bunchy" Carter was a Los Angeles Panther who was killed, along with John Huggins, on the campus of the University of California, Los Angeles by members of the US (United Slaves), an organization led by Maulanga Ron Karenga. The murder was later shown to be a classic example of machinations by the FBI under COINTELPRO.

   The cultural nationalist group US was founded in 1965. According to a message from Dr. Karenga on the organization's website, "From the beginning, the essential task of our organization US has been and remains to provide a philosophy, a set of principles and a program which inspire a personal and social practice that not only satisfies human need but transforms people in the process, making them self-conscious agents of their own life and liberation" (www.us-organization.org). Sowing divisions between radical organizations was an explicit tactic of COINTELPRO. See "Human Rights in the U.S.: The Unfinished Story of Political Prisoners and Victims of COINTELPRO," in Matt Meyer, ed., *Let Freedom Ring: A Collection of Documents from the Movements to Free U.S. Political Prisoners* (Oakland, CA, PM Press: 2008), 643.

2. The murders are chronicled in chapter 13, "Lest We Forget," p. 135.

9. This Is Worth Fighting For

Another piece that is hard to date. In Safiya's original manuscript, this essay was the final chapter, suggesting that it was written in the late 1990s.

Often, over the past ten years, I've gotten to the point where I've questioned what this was all about. I've wondered whether the sacrifices of the lives of comrades and friends were in vain and whether the continued incarceration of so many political prisoners and prisoners of war has been for nothing.

As my mind returns to the beginning of my politicization on the campus of New York City Community College all those many years ago, I wonder whether I made the right decision. Robert Frost wrote about two roads diverging from a single path in his poem, "The Road Not Taken." He wasn't talking about the choice between the path of revolution and the path of least resistance—of going with the flow and maintaining the status quo. But envisioning the choices in life, the poem clearly defines the moment of choice at some interval or moment in life.

The point when I was on the college campus at eighteen years of age, making the decision to work with the Free Breakfast Program of the Black Panther Party was one of those "fork in the road" situations. After learning about the hungry children in our communities who needed to be fed—the children who were going to school without a warm breakfast or any breakfast at all—I could have ignored the situation, as so many others do. But I chose to help to do something about it. No regrets.

That small crack in the window to another world, another side of life in these United States of America, led to other decisions. I was still in college. I was still not so disillusioned with and by the state of affairs in the United States that I was ready to commit myself to fighting for change. I still had a dream of what I could accomplish in America as it was.

My first encounter with the New York City Police Department posed another question for me about which road to take. That encounter forever ripped the rose-colored glasses from my eyes. Again, one choice was the path of least resistance, which would allow me to back up and not get further involved in the conflict between the people and the agents of repression. That choice would have meant allowing the police to carry out business-as-usual policies that place them above the law. The other choice was to join the Black Panther Party. I chose to join the Black Panther Party. I chose the path of resistance.

I was a reluctant revolutionary. I'm not even sure I could be considered a revolutionary at that time. The episode with the police department had just made me so angry that I decided I could not allow them to get away with what they'd done to me. No, I wasn't a revolutionary then. I was an angry Black woman.[1]

I owe my transformation from just another angry Black woman into a revolutionary to people like Robert "Coffeeman" Webb, Big Bashir Saunders, Afeni Shakur (who was my Winnie Mandela), Michael Cetewayo Tabor, Twymon Myers (whom I will talk about later), Albert Nuh Washington (my mentor), as well as many, many other people whom I worked alongside daily, or those like Ernesto "Che" Guevara whom I read about or observed.[2] I learned to look up to and emulate so many.

It was Robert Webb who spent countless hours turning an emotionally charged, undisciplined, apolitical, motivated-by-hatred girl into a disciplined, politically motivated woman.

Robert would spend hours sitting by my bedside at night going over the Black Panther Party's Ten-Point Program and Platform, along with the Eight Points of Attention; the Three Main Rules of Discipline, Criticism, and Self-Criticism; and the Twenty-six Rules and Regulations of the Black Panther Party. He spent time explaining how these sets of rules and principles made Panthers capable of carrying our struggle through to victory. He used examples of how this internal discipline was derived from the knowledge of who we were and why we were who we were.

Robert had fought in the US military and then come back to fight for the liberation of his own people. His weapon of choice was a .357 Magnum with a hair trigger. After he felt I had internalized the political dogma of the Party and understood that politics guide the gun, not the other way around, he gave me my first weapons training. He used his .357 to do it.

Robert Webb was shot on the corner of 125th Street and Seventh Avenue on March 6, 1971. He was the victim of the COINTELPRO-instigated fratricidal warfare between opposing factions of the Black Panther Party.

While Robert taught me the discipline and technicalities, Bashir Saunders taught me the basics. We called him Big Bashir because of his size. I'm five feet tall, so forgive me if I tend to exaggerate Bashir's size. Bashir seemed to be seven feet tall to me. He towered over me and he weighed about three hundred pounds.

He was OD (officer of the day) of the Harlem office of the Black Panther Party. He was a grizzly bear with the heart of a pooh bear. Where Robert taught me to be unemotional and pragmatic in my dealings with the world, Bashir taught me that we were working for the people. We were servants of the people. He had an undying love for the people that he tried to instill in all of us who worked under him.

Although Bashir died years after the Party did, I believe that the dissolution of the Party—the organization that many of us saw as the best chance for the liberation of our people—was a major factor contributing to his death. The death of a dream led to the death of the spirit and the death of the man.

But coming into the Black Panther Party and being exposed to heavy hitters like Bobby Seale, Geronimo Pratt, Kathleen Cleaver, Richard Dhoruba Moore (now Dhoruba Bin-Wahad), Robert Webb, and on and on and on did not have the effect on me that the exposure to an elfin, dark-skinned woman with a very short Afro did. Afeni Shakur walked tall and proud among these people. She emitted an inner strength and assuredness that made me say to myself, "This is a Black woman worthy of respect."

Other than my grandmother on my mother's side, up to that point I had not met a woman I could look up to. (It wasn't until much later in my life that I would add my mother to this list.) At a time when I needed it most, Afeni Shakur exemplified the strength and dignity amid chaos that I needed to see. Despite the setbacks, slip-backs, hard times, and tragedies that Afeni has undergone and endured over the years, I still hold the image of this fierce, small, strong, take-no-prisoners Black warrior woman before me. Afeni—in all her regality—surviving! Setting an example for me!

My mother always says, "Give me my flowers while I'm alive and can smell them." Well, here are your flowers, Afeni. Afeni never knew she was having this effect on me. I don't even think she was attempting to affect the lives of the people as she did. She was just being Afeni. Maybe if she had realized it, it would have helped her. The lesson I learned first from Afeni is that you can't define yourself by the person with whom you're in a relationship with. You have to define yourself by who you are and what you believe. You have to be a person in and of yourself. If you are a revolutionary, you have to be capable of carrying out the tasks assigned to you whether or not your mate supports you in that.

The second thing I learned from watching Afeni was that you have to have the inner strength to take responsibility for your actions. My mother and grandmother used to say all the time, "If you're woman enough to do it, be woman enough to tell the truth about it." But it's one thing for your parents to say something and another for a contemporary to show that thing by example. Here again was a Black woman who wasn't afraid to own up to her actions, be they good, bad, or indifferent.

What comes back to me most often when I think of Michael Cetewayo Tabor is a conversation I had on the phone with him during the height of the tensions surrounding the split in the Party. Cet was in exile. He was in Algeria, at the office of the International Section of the Black Panther Party. I was in the Harlem office, at 2026 Seventh Avenue in New York City.

Directly following the split, we had begun printing our own newspaper, called *Right On! Black Community News Service*. We'd begun it because Huey Newton et al. had maintained control of the Party newspaper, *The Black Panther*. A lot of the leadership of the Party had gone into seclusion for security reasons. There had been many threats on their lives, and now they were vulnerable not only to the forces of repression (such as the Joint Terrorist Task Force, the FBI, etc.), but also to the fratricidal elements within. *The Black Panther* was being used as a weapon.

Things were extremely destabilized in all the offices along the East Coast, but especially in New York, New Jersey, Connecticut, and Pennsylvania. We were on twenty-four-hour alert. We were never alone, always traveled in twos. Someone always knew where we were.

One particular night I and two other people were on security at the Harlem office when the phone rang. When I answered, an operator said, "Your overseas party is on the line. Go ahead, please." I said, "I didn't make an overseas call." I didn't make the call, but Eldridge Cleaver was on the line from Algeria. I asked him if he had placed the call and he said he had not. Neither one of us had placed the call, but we knew who had. It seems the government or somebody wanted us to talk about something.

We decided to talk despite not having initiated the call. Eldridge took the opportunity to tell me that it was time to escalate the struggle. He said it was time to take it to the streets and that's what I should tell people to do. I said, "No!" I was not going to tell people to do that. I told Eldridge that the conditions were not right, and I was not going to encourage our people to go out and take part in or become victims of a bloodbath. He told me that if I didn't do it there would be a second split in the Black Panther Party. I held firm because I truly believed I was right. Eldridge didn't know the objective conditions here. He was more than three thousand miles away, in Algeria.

When Eldridge saw he was getting nowhere with me, he put Cetewayo on the phone. Cet told me I should do as Eldridge requested. I asked Cet, "Do you remember what you taught me? To deal with the principle and not the personality?" Cet said, in that deep, melodious voice he possessed, "Yes." Then he was silent for a moment and after that made no further attempt to get me to do what Eldridge wished.

That was a very empowering moment for me, even though Eldridge was to go through with his threat of a second split, and would begin to publish *Babylon! Revolutionary People's Communications Network* (*RPCN*) shortly thereafter. In the months before Cet jumped bail in the Panther 21 case and left the country, he had played a significant role in my political development.

When he would come through the Panther pad on Eighth Avenue, where I lived collectively with other Panthers, he would stress adhering to principles. No matter what the situation, rely on the principle and not the personality.

It was one thing to be told to think for yourself, to gather all the facts and analyze them through the prism of scientific socialist analysis to come to an objective conclusion about what was to be done. It was another thing to do all that and then be able to act on it. All too often people will say, "This is the correct and principled way that we must act as revolutionaries." Then when it comes to issues they are involved in, it becomes a case of, "that applies to every other situation except for ones involving me." The fact that when it came down to the nitty-gritty Cet acquiesced to the principle was truly an empowering moment for me. It made me see that on the principle is a worthy place to stand. Cet reaffirmed this for me and made it possible for me to believe in myself. He made it possible for me to believe in the principles that he had told me were the foundation of a revolutionary ideology.

We were embarked on a campaign to change the world, one person at a time. That change begins with rebuilding the character into a revolutionary character, of which the central component is love. That means love of yourself and love of the people.

It took me forever to realize this. I believed that the motivating force was hatred of the oppressor and white people who were the oppressor, hatred of bootlicking Black folks who kowtowed to the oppressor, and hatred of other Black folks who preyed upon each other. This hatred was the driving force behind everything I did. I woke up with it in the morning and went to bed with it at night. It colored everything I did. I was in destruction mode.

The hatred of society was so extreme in me because I was a convert. I had been converted by the New York City Police

Department from someone who believed in this society and defended the police on every level to someone who believed nothing they said. I had long ago lost faith in the church and the family, and the last thing I had trust in had kicked me in the teeth. As you know, there's no fanatic like the new convert.

We did a lot of talking in those days about making revolution and creating a society where people didn't go without the basic necessities of life. But we had no game plan other than destroying the old society. We taught our children and our youth to hate the police, that they were pigs and that we didn't have to respect their authority. We taught them that religion was the opiate of the masses, that it was used to keep us down and make us obedient to the oppressor. We took away all the deterrents, the belief systems, and the limits, and we replaced them with nothing. We were able to do this because we did not understand the concept that freedom correlates with discipline. If the discipline is not externally imposed, then it must be an internal discipline. One or the other.

Ernesto "Che" Guevara's famous quote, "Let me say at the risk of seeming ridiculous that a true revolutionary is motivated by great feelings of love," along with Albert Nuh Washington's teachings of compassion were the forces that helped me understand this. Nuh turned me on to Islam, and then he helped me understand the true teachings of Islam. "A Muslim is a Muslim's brother (sister)." "(S)he wants for others what (s)he wants for herself." He went one step further and exposed me to Kahlil Gibran. He gave me *The Prophet* to read, and I kept on from there. The most important lesson that stayed with me from these teachings is that our children are not our property. Our children are little people who have been placed in our care, for us to nurture and guide. It is a most important charge, since they will one day be the ones who shape the direction of the world. It is not a responsibility that we can abdicate or pawn off on anyone. You cannot truly talk about being motivated by great feelings of love, or even about being a revolutionary, if you do not understand that it is indeed how we deal with the question of our youth that will determine the outcome of the revolution.

It begins with an anger at the forces with the immediate power to affect your life. For me, it began with an anger at the police force of New York City for abusing their authority and treating me as less than a human being. It grew into a determination to correct what is wrong with this, to make sure that it didn't continue solely because no one dared to stand up and speak out. It continued with the desire to make sure that my child would not have to endure the same kind of treatment. It was personal, but it became political. And it endures.

Notes

1. For a description of the encounter with the NYPD, see chapter 1, "Coming of Age," p. 1.
2. In her parenthetical comment about Twymon Myers, Safiya may be referring to "Remembering Twymon," a lost chapter of this book.

10. On the Question of Political Prisoners

Support for political prisoners became increasingly central to Safiya's work in the years following her own release from prison. After this essay, written sometime later than 1984, Safiya returned many times to the subject and integrated it into some of her other writings. Over time in these essays, Safiya grapples with the problem of how to generate popular support for the prisoners—people who ended up in prison for their participation in earlier phases of the Black liberation struggle, when militant, revolutionary politics and strategies were embraced more widely than at the time when she was writing the essays.

In 2001, Safiya repeated some parts of this essay in one she wrote for New York journalist and longtime activist Herb Boyd. He had requested that she submit a chapter for his book, *Race and Resistance: African Americans in the 21st Century* (Cambridge, MA: South End Press, 2002). Although he was unable to include the essay in the book, Boyd wrote, the piece showed "her profound insight and the passion she possessed for her comrades [in prison], a situation she knew first hand."[1]

There is no question that support for political prisoners and prisoners of war should and must be an integral part of any movement for liberation. There is no question, that is, for people who have dedicated their lives to the struggle for freedom in this country. Such people realize that it is not possible to talk about a movement for liberation if you fail to liberate people who are incarcerated as a result of that liberation struggle.

What is called into question, therefore, is whether or not we are serious about revolution and liberation.

I remember sitting in the back room of the Harlem office of the Black Panther Party on Seventh Avenue and listening to political education class where Mao Tse-tung's "Red Book" was being discussed.[2] This particular day the passage under discussion was "Tell no lies and claim no easy victories." I interpreted that to mean, Go to the people, organize the people, work among the people and tell no lies about what we want and what we've done and what we have accomplished. We have to build a strong bond of trust with the people and show them by example that we're different from the politicians and corporate businessmen and others who say anything and do anything to get the people to go along with their program.

This lesson has been the cornerstone of my understanding of what this struggle is supposed to be about. If we take the "tell no lies" approach to organizing, then we take the time to build the foundation for a movement that is destined to bring us the victory we say we're fighting for. Then there would be no need to organize separate programs to educate the community to the existence of political prisoners. No. Because while we were working to organize rent strikes and take control of abandoned buildings—to create decent housing in our community through our sweat equity—we would be talking about how Abdul Majid and others organized tenant associations such as the Ocean Hill-Brownsville Tenants Association in Brooklyn. While we're organizing around the issue of quality education that teaches our true history and role in this society, we would be talking about Herman Bell and Albert Nuh Washington and their work with the liberation schools. While we're organizing food co-ops and other survival programs, we'd be talking about Geronimo Pratt, Sundiata Acoli, Robert Seth Hayes, and all the other political prisoners and prisoners of war who worked in the free health clinics and day care centers—and who went to prison as a result of their active participation in organizing efforts around issues that directly affected the Black and oppressed communities.[3]

Because our "movement," for lack of a better word, has deteriorated to the point that the majority of our organizing is done through demonstrations, rallies, conferences, and press conferences, the only way we feel we can talk about the issue of political prisoners is when we drag them out for show-and-tell or when we need to legitimatize what we are doing. This raises the question, "Are we serious about struggle, or are we just profiling?" If we're not serious, then we need to let our political prisoners off the hook and tell them, "Do what you think is best for you." If we are serious then we need to stop ego-tripping, stop profiling, stop rabble-rousing, and get down to the serious work of organizing. Talk is cheap, action is supreme.

Political prisoners didn't become political prisoners out of a vacuum. They went to prison, for the most part, as members of political formations. There are more than 150 political prisoners in jail across this country. The majority of these brothers and sisters are serving upward of twenty-five years to life and at least one, Mumia Abu-Jamal, is facing death. At the time the majority of these people went to prison there was a thriving movement on the street. They are sitting there now and the movement is totally fragmented and in a state of disarray. They are being pulled in a lot of different directions by fragmented organizations that are more interested in posturing as the "vanguard" and jockeying for position than they are in doing the work of organizing people. I constantly wonder why it is necessary for them to be fighting among themselves to be the titular vanguard of a movement when there are millions of people that have to be organized. If they all got down today to the task of organizing New York City—or any of the other communities across the United States—there would still be room for more help. We wouldn't even step on each other's toes and would be glad to share the work because that's how much work there is to be done. That is, if we were serious about the job of organizing for liberation.

The term "political prisoner" means nothing to the average brother or sister on the block, because the terms "liberation" and "revolution" mean nothing. The words have no meaning for our people, no real meaning, because we have done no real organizing and educating for liberation. The lack of consciousness among our people, the lack of support for political prisoners, is a direct result of our lack of concrete work among our people. The day of people getting involved in struggle for great socialist ideas is long gone, if it ever existed. Our people require examples of the concrete changes in their conditions that will occur if we collectively fight for change. Once they are shown the example of what could be achieved, they are more likely to support struggle. When they are confronted by the way the state—the government, police, and other forces of repression—respond to people who dare to speak out and organize and educate against a system that has consistently exploited, brutalized, and oppressed them, they will be more likely to support political prisoners.

Some of us mistake the people's anger, frustration, and distrust of the system as meaning they are ready for revolution. It is true that they possess a deep-seated anger at the system. It's true that they distrust the system. But it's also true that they have not made the connection between the source of this anger and distrust and creating a revolution. Our people are more inclined to participate in a race riot than a revolution. They would support a drug dealer before they'd support a revolutionary. Why?

For a number of reasons, chief being that the drug dealer is in the community constantly. He is known by the community and has picked up on a lesson that the revolutionary used to know. The drug dealer understands that he has to give something back to the community. He employs the local people and therefore, even if it's pennies, makes a difference in the life of the community.

This is not an indictment of our people, but rather an indictment of the deterioration of the movement and our complete loss of direction. At some point we should have been able to stop and make an assessment of the state of the movement, especially following the major government offensives against the revolution—COINTELPRO and the destruction of the Black Panther Party. We seem to have forgotten everything we ever learned about revolution: that it's about the people. It's about making qualitative and quantitative changes in the conditions of our people. Revolution is not about gaining name or organizational recognition at the expense of building a foundation for a movement that will lead us to victory. In order to create the conditions for revolution, we must go back to basics and deal with the fact that revolution is protracted. It doesn't happen overnight. Therefore we have the time to make sure we lay the correct foundation and build a strong movement based on work. This is the only real way we can build the necessary support to free our political prisoners and prisoners of war.

A final word, to our political prisoners: We used to know that prison was a microcosm of society. That is, we recognized the truism that the conditions of the people who came through the doors of the prison reflected the state of the society without. Think back to what was happening on the streets at the time you were incarcerated. Think back to the activities that were going on among the prisoners in the institutions. Now compare that to what the people coming into the prisons today are talking about and doing, and you can deduce for yourself the state of the movement. Just as we have a job to do out here, you have a job to do in there. Being in prison does not release you from your obligation to educate to liberate. Some of you seem to have forgotten that. What being in prison does is change the venue in which you organize. It changes the playing field.

I remember another class that took place in the Harlem office of the Black Panther Party. This lesson had to do with the Ten-Ten-Ten Program.[4] This was a lesson on organizing. We had to learn the Ten-Point Program and Platform of the Party. We had to learn the Twenty-six Rules of the Party. We had to learn the Eight Points of Attention and the Three Main Rules of Discipline. We had to learn the motto and primary objective, then internalize all of it. We had to learn and internalize it for the day when the offices would no longer be open and available to us. We had to learn it for the day when we would be on our own without other Panthers, so that we could carry out the tasks of the revolution. Once we internalized these teachings, we were ready to go out and organize. The theory was that if each one of us organized ten people, and those people organized ten people, and those people organized ten people, then by the time the third group organized ten people each, we would number ten thousand people. It's a time-consuming method of organizing, but it's tried and true. This was the approach to organizing that I used in my section when I was in the Party. During the time I was incarcerated in Goochland, Virginia, the people in my section in the community stood by me and sent me packages and cards. They were there waiting when I was released from prison in 1983.

Organizations come and go, but we have to create within our people the spirit of struggle. We have to build a movement to liberate our people. The issue of political prisoners is part of that movement that we are building, and in building that movement we must understand that this is not a separate issue. It is an integral part of that movement. It can't be put in front of the movement and it can't be an afterthought. It must be woven into the very fiber.

Notes

1. "A gallant warrior and revolutionary passes," *New York Amsterdam News* 94, issue 35, p. 6, August 28, 2003.
2. Mao Tse-tung's "Red Book": See chapter 6, "On the Question of Sexism Within the Black Panther Party," note 7, p. 62.
3. Abdul Majid (Anthony Laborde) is a political prisoner in New York State, one of the "Queens Two." He was arrested in 1982, badly beaten upon arrest, and later convicted of a 1981 incident in Queens in which a police officer was killed in a shoot-out. With his codefendant, Bashir Hameed (James York, who died in prison in August 2008), Abdul was tried three times because the first two juries did not find the Queens Two guilty. In 1985, the Queens Two were denied a new trial following an appeal claiming that the exclusion of Black people from the jury in their third trial violated their right to a fair trial.

   Herman Bell and Albert Nuh Washington are two of the New York Three, members of the Black Panther Party who were convicted of the 1970 killing of two New York City police officers. Jalil Muntaqim (Anthony Bottom) is the third. Nuh died of cancer in prison in 2000. Herman and Jalil remain in prison in New York State, having been denied parole several times, despite the support of the son and other family members of one of the policemen killed in the case. It took two trials to convict the New York Three; discrepancies in various pieces of evidence were never fully resolved.

   Liberation schools were community education projects of the Black Panther Party.
4. In the early days of the Panthers, Huey Newton and others went door to door in Oakland asking community members to name the goals they felt would better their community. From this process arose the Party's Ten-Point Program:

1. We want freedom. We want power to determine the destiny of our Black community.
2. We want full employment for our people.
3. We want an end to the robbery by the white man of our Black community.
4. We want decent housing, fit for the shelter of human beings.
5. We want education for our people that exposes the true nature of this society. We want education that teaches us our true history and our role in the present day society.
6. We want all Black men to be exempt from military service.
7. We want an immediate end to police brutality and murder of Black people.
8. We want freedom for all Black men held in federal, state, county, and city prisons and jails.
9. We want all Black people when brought to trial to be tried in court by a jury of their peer group, or people from the Black communities, as defined by the Constitution of the United States.
10. We want bread, housing, education, clothing, justice, and peace. And as our major political objective, a United Nations–supervised plebiscite to be held throughout the Black colony in which Black colonial subjects will be allowed to participate, for the purpose of determining the will of Black people as to their national destiny.

The other items Safiya names were internal rules of the Party. In an undated pamphlet, *Notes on the Black Panther Party, Its Basic Working Papers and Policy Statements*, Safiya wrote:

"These basic documents are the foundation from which all the theory and practice that flowed from the Black Panther Party outward was produced. It is impossible to receive a clear and undistorted picture of what the Black Panther Party was truly about without an understanding of the politics that guided it.

"In developing the guiding principles of the Black Panther Party, much effort went into studying revolutionary struggles going on around the world. Particular study was given to Mao Tse-tung in China, Kim Il Sung in North Korea, Carlos Marighella and the Tupamaros in Uruguay, Amilcar Cabral in Mozambique, and Fidel Castro in Cuba. In our own backyard, the Black Panther Party saw itself as the collective 'heirs of Malcolm X' who now stood ten feet tall facing the 'wrath of the racist pig oppressor.'"

11. Building Support for Political Prisoners of War Incarcerated in North America

Safiya wrote this essay in 1997, at about the time she was forming the Jericho Movement to Free US Political Prisoners, a national campaign which began with a march and rally at the White House in late March, 1998.[1] Unlike most of her writings and speeches for Jericho, however, this one focuses exclusively on the Black political prisoners, and she addresses much of her essay to the members of the Congressional Black Caucus.

We have political prisoners and prisoners of war incarcerated in prisons and jails across America. In the past two years, we have seen the execution of two avowed revolutionaries, Ajamu Nassor and Ziyon Yisrayah, in the state of Indiana.[2] We have Mumia Abu-Jamal, another revolutionary, on death row in Pennsylvania. Geronimo Pratt has been in prison in California for almost thirty years even though the government knows that he is innocent of the crime for which he was convicted.[3] The stories of COINTELPRO's involvement in the manufacturing, doctoring, concealing, and manipulation of evidence to ensure that revolutionaries are kept off the streets and behind bars are legion. Yet the vast majority of the leadership of the Black community turn a blind eye to the reality that political prisoners and prisoners of war exist in this country.

The vast majority of these brothers and sisters are products of movements and organizations that existed in the 1960s and 1970s. They belonged to organizations such as the Black Panther Party (BPP), Provisional Government of the Republic of New Afrika (PG-RNA), Revolutionary Action Movement (RAM), and MOVE. Some were not members per se, but were involved with smaller, equally dedicated, parallel organizations in their communities. They were moved by the conditions of the times into taking actions in defense of their communities and in support of the Black nation. All of them sacrificed their lives to improve the conditions under which we lived. Make no bones about it: the motivation of these brothers and sisters was not to secure wealth or property for themselves, but for the greater community. They believed in what they were doing and their motivation was *love of their people.*

The New York Three—Albert Washington, Anthony Bottom, and Herman Bell—are three former members of the Black Panther Party who are incarcerated in the state of New York serving a twenty-five-years-to-life sentence. They were convicted of the assassination of two New York City police officers. They have already served twenty-five years. The history of this case can be traced to the Nixon White House and a government counter-intelligence program (COINTELPRO) called NEWKILL. Even though there is evidence to show that the government manipulated, manufactured, and marshaled evidence in this case, these three men are still in prison.[4]

Geronimo Pratt, another former member of the Black Panther Party, has been in prison since 1969. That's when he was convicted of killing a white woman on a tennis court in southern California—at a time when the government had him under surveillance and knew he was in northern California at a Panther meeting. The government then destroyed the surveillance tapes so the evidence could not be used to support Geronimo's statement on his whereabouts. The trial took place during the height of animosity caused by the split in the Black Panther Party. As a result, the people who had been at the meeting with Geronimo were under orders not to testify in his defense. Over the years, former FBI agents such as Wes Swearingen have come forward and stated that Geronimo could not have committed the crime because he was in northern California, some four hundred miles away, at the time of the murder. Yet, twenty-seven years later, Geronimo is still in prison. This case can be traced to a program within COINTELPRO called PRATT.[5]

David Rice (Mondo we Langa) and Ed Poindexter are two members of a local Panther support group known as the National Committee to Combat Fascism (NCCF), out of Lincoln, Nebraska. They have been serving time in virtual obscurity for almost twenty-six years, having also gone to prison in middle America while the Black Panther Party was being split asunder because of internal contradictions and the covert actions of COINTELPRO.[6]

Sundiata Acoli was the codefendant of Assata Shakur, former member of the Black Panther Party and civil rights and human rights activist who began his work with the Freedom Rides.[7] I believe that the major threat Sundiata poses to the government resides in who he is and what he gave up in order to become involved in the struggle for liberation in this country.

A graduate of Prairie View University in Texas, Sundiata Acoli, then known as Clark Squire, went to work for NASA. A mathematician and computer analyst, Sundiata helped develop the program to put the first man on the moon. With a stellar life in front of him if he could only close his eyes to the plight of his people around him, Sundiata couldn't do it. He left NASA in search of freedom for his people and ended up in the Black Panther Party. He has already spent twenty-three years in prison.[8]

What Is the Problem?

The list of political prisoners is long and their sentences are even longer. The government of these United States would have you believe that these people are common criminals. The United States government waged an orchestrated campaign to demonize, vilify, and criminalize these people in the eyes of the community and the world prior to bringing them to trial and during the years of their incarceration. For the most part, they've done their job well—so well, in fact, that even the most progressive elements of our community hesitate even to speak the words "political prisoner" when they come together. When you bring those words up, they change the conversation.

Such things as the length of the sentences given these brothers and sisters; their treatment before, during, and after their trials and since their incarceration; the level and type of security they have been subjected to during their incarceration; the denial of parole; etc., are evidence that they are not being treated as common criminals but rather as political prisoners. Yet the government says they are not political prisoners—even though the same government will readily admit that it is the politics, discipline, and humanity of these prisoners that set them apart from the rest of the prison population. To paraphrase the words of Nelson Mandela, the people went into prison as dedicated and disciplined members of political organizations, and they still are.

The government of the United States would have you and the world believe that these women and men are gangsters and common criminals. Our task, our job, is to change this. Since they are being treated differently because of their political beliefs and affiliations, they must be recognized as political prisoners and prisoners of war.

How Is This to Be Done?

We have been working on an initiative for almost a year now to get the Congressional Black Caucus and, in the long run, Congress to hold hearings into the role of COINTELPRO in all these cases. The New Afrikan Liberation Front, the Free Mumia Abu-Jamal Coalition (New York) and the International Concerned Family and Friends of Mumia Abu-Jamal met with representatives of the Congressional Black Caucus (CBC) in February of this year. We made a proposal to them and some agreements were made to do work to flesh out this idea.[9] We believe that the Church Committee Hearings into Government Misconduct, which revealed some of the government's criminal activity that occurred under the name of counterintelligence, did not go far enough. The documentation opened under the Church Committee investigation spoke to manufacturing and manipulating evidence and framing people, as well as the other scurrilous activities of the FBI and the Department of Justice. What they didn't do was investigate the various cases and expose the government's role in specific cases. Just now, some of the allegations in specific cases are being borne out. For nineteen years, Dhoruba Bin-Wahad kept saying that he had been framed and that the government had withheld evidence that could confirm his innocence. No one listened and the years piled up. Finally, with his attorneys, he was able to prove his case and walk out of prison—nineteen years and three hundred pages of FBI documents later.[10]

We are asking that Black leaders:

Pick up the mantle with us and make the call strong
and loud for the continuation of the hearings into
COINTELPRO and its role in the imprisonment of these
Black and New Afrikan political prisoners and prisoners
of war.

Look at the attached list of political prisoners and prisoners
of war and begin to find out about them—what their
status is, what they need, and how you can support the
ones in your area.

Raise the issue of the existence of political prisoners and
prisoners of war.

Organize forums and speaking engagements in your area
so that we can more effectively make known to our
community that there are people who have been in
prison for years who were (and are) willing to sacrifice
their lives to make a better world for all of us.

Write to them; let them know you care.

Even though we might not all agree on everything, we all
agree that there's something wrong with our condition, and that
something has to be done about it. What we're all coming to
realize is that we need each other fighting on whatever level we
can to make a difference. It's taken us a long time to get to this
place, but now that we're here, let's build to win!

Free all political prisoners and prisoners of war!

Safiya Asya Bukhari
Vice President and Minister of Defense
Republic of New Afrika

At the end of the essay on building support for political prisoners, Safiya attached a list of political prisoners and their addresses. Only part of that list could be found. As Safiya was instrumental in forming and leading the political prisoner support organization the Jericho Movement, the current listing of political prisoners from the Jericho website (thejerichomovement.com) is printed here. Because political prisoners are frequently (and arbitrarily) moved from one prison to another, please check the Jericho website for the most current information.

From the time Safiya created her list up until fall 2009, when the Jericho Movement published the list below, seven of the people on Safiya's list had died. Their deaths behind bars serve as a reminder to everyone to step up support for the political prisoners and work hard toward their release. Safiya would express that much more eloquently if she were writing this now.

Those on Safiya's original list who have since died:

Thomas Warner (Pennsylvania; died 1998, suicide)
Albert Nuh Washington (New York State; died 2000, cancer)
Teddy Jah Heath (New York State; died 2000, cancer)
Merle Africa (Pennsylvania; died 1998, cancer)
Richard Williams (federal prison; died 2005, cancer)
Bashir Hameed (James York) (New York State; died 2008, cancer)
Eddie Hatcher (North Carolina; died 2009, AIDS)

Abdullah, Haki Malik (Michael Green) #C-56123, PO Box 3456, Corcoran, CA 93212

Abu-Jamal, Mumia #AM 8335, SCI-Greene, 175 Progress Dr, Waynesburg, PA 15370

Acoli, Sundiata #39794-066, FCI Otisville, PO Box 1000, Otisville, NY 10963

Africa, **Charles Simms** #AM4975, SCI Graterford, Box 244, Graterford PA 19426

Africa, **Debbie Sims** #006307, 451 Fullerton Ave, Cambridge Springs, PA 16403

Africa, **Delbert Orr** #AM4985, SCI Dallas Drawer K, Dallas, PA 18612

Africa, **Edward Goodman** #AM4974, 301 Morea Rd, Frackville, PA 17932

Africa, **Janet Holloway** #006308, 451 Fullerton Ave, Cambridge Springs, PA 16403

Africa, **Janine Phillips** #006309, 451 Fullerton Ave, Cambridge Springs, PA 16403

Africa, **Michael Davis** #AM4973, SCI Graterford, Box 244, Graterford, PA 19426

Africa, **William Phillips** #AM4984, SCI Dallas Drawer K, Dallas, PA 18612

Al-Amin, Jamil Abdullah #99974-555, USP Florence ADMAX, PO Box 8500, Florence, CO 81226

Azania, Zolo #4969, Indiana State Prison, PO Box 41, Michigan City, IN 46361

Barnes, Grant #137563, San Carlos Correctional Facility, PO Box 3, Pueblo, CO 81002

Bell, Herman #79-C-0262, Sullivan Correctional Facility, PO Box 116, Fallsburg, NY 12733

Block, Nathan #36359-086, FCI Lompoc, 3600 Guard Road, Lompoc, CA 93436

Bomani Sababu, Kojo (Grailing Brown) #39384-066, USP Hazelton, PO Box 2000, Bruceton Mills, WV 26525

Bowen, Joseph AM-4272, 1 Kelley Dr, Coal Township, PA 17866

Bowers, Veronza #35316-136, USP Atlanta, PO Box 150160, Atlanta, GA 30315

Buck, Marilyn #00482-285, Unit A, Camp Parks, 5701 Eighth St, Dublin, CA 94568

Burton, Fred "Muhammad" AF 3896, SCI Somerset, 1590 Walters Mill Rd, Somerset, PA 15510

Campa, Rubén #58733-004 (envelope addressed to Rubén Campa, letter addressed to Fernando Gonzáles) FDC Miami, PO Box 019120, Miami, FL 33101

Chubbuck, Byron Shane (Oso Blanco) #07909-051, USP Lewisburg, PO Box 1000, Lewisburg, PA 17837

Conroy, Jacob #93501-011, FCI Terminal Island, PO Box 3007, San Pedro, CA 90731

Conway, Marshall Eddie #116469, Jessup Correctional Institution, PO Box 534, Jessup, MD 20794

Dunne, Bill #10916-086, USP Big Sandy, PO Box 2068, Inez, KY 41224

Fitzgerald, Romaine "Chip" #B-27527, Centinela State Prison, FC-2-110, PO Box 921, Imperial, CA 92251

Ford, Patrice Lumumba #96639-011, USP Coleman 1, PO Box 1033, Coleman, FL 33521

Gazzola, Lauren # 93497-011, FCI Danbury, Rte #37, Danbury, CT 06811

Gilday, William # W33537, MCI Shirley, PO Box 1218, Shirley, MA 01464-1218

Gilbert, David #83-A-6158, Clinton Correctional Facility, PO Box 2001, Dannemora, NY 12929

González Claudio, Avelino #357422, MacDougall-Walker CI, 1153 East St, South Suffield, CT 06080

González, René #58738-004, FCI Marianna, PO Box 7007, Marianna, FL 32447-7007

Guerrero, Antonio #58741-004, FDC Miami, PO Box 019120, Miami, FL 33101

Hayes, Robert Seth #74-A-2280, Wende CF, Wende Rd, PO Box 1187, Alden, NY 14004

Hernández, Alvaro Luna #255735, Hughes Unit, Rte 2, Box 4400, Gatesville, TX 76597

Hernández, Gerardo #58739-004, USP Victorville, PO Box 5500, Adelanto, CA 92301

Hilton, Freddie (Kamau Sadiki) #0001150688, Augusta State Medical Prison, Bldg 13A-2 E7, 3001 Gordon Hwy, Grovetown, GA 30813

Hoover, Larry #86063-024, Florence ADMAX, PO Box 8500, Florence, CO 81226

Ka'bah, Abdullah Malik (aka Jeff Fort) #92298-024, USP Florence ADMAX, PO Box 8500, Florence, CO 81226

Kambui, Sekou (William Turk) #113058, Box 56, SCC (B1-21), Elmore, AL 36025

Khabir, Maumin (Melvin Mayes) #09891-000, USP Terre Haute, PO Box 33, Terre Haute, IN 47808

Kjonaas, Kevin #93502-011, Unit I, FCI Sandstone, PO Box 1000, Sandstone, MN 55072

Koti, Mohamman Geuka 80-A-0808, 354 Hunter Street, Ossining, NY 10562

Laaman, Jaan Karl #10372-016, USP Tucson, PO Box 24550, Tucson, AZ 85734

Lake, Richard Mafundi #079972, Donaldson CF, 100 Warrior Lane, Bessemer, AL 35023

Langa, Mondo we (David Rice) #27768, Nebraska State Penitentiary, PO Box 2500, Lincoln, NE 68542

Latine, Maliki Shakur # 81-A-4469, Clinton Correctional Facility, PO Box 2001, Dannemora, NY 12929

López Rivera, Oscar #87651-024, FCI Terre Haute, PO Box 33, Terre Haute, IN 47808

Magee, Ruchell Cinque # A92051, C-2 107L CSATF, PO Box 5242, Corcoran, CA 93212

Majid, Abdul (Anthony Laborde) #83-A-0483, Elmira C.F., PO Box 500, 1879 Davis St, Elmira, NY 14902

Manning, Thomas #10373-016, USP Hazelton, PO Box 2000, Bruceton Mills, WV 26525

McDavid, Eric 16209-097, FCI Victorville Medium II, PO Box 5300, Adelanto, CA 92301

McGowan, Daniel #63794-053, USP Marion, PO Box 1000, Marion, IL 62959

Medina, Luís #58734-004 (address envelope to Luis Medina, letter to Ramón Labañino), FDC Miami, PO Box 019120, Miami, FL 33101

Muntaqim, Jalil (Anthony Bottom) #77-A-4283, Auburn CF, PO Box 618, Auburn, NY 13021

Odinga, Sekou 09-A-3775, Shawangunk Correctional Facility, PO Box 700, Wallkill, NY 12589

Paul, Jonathan #07167-085, FCI Phoenix, 37910 N 45th Ave, Phoenix, AZ 85086

Peltier, Leonard #89637-132, USP Lewisburg, PO Box 1000, Lewisburg, PA 17837

Pinell, Hugo "Dahariki" #A88401, SHU D3-221, PO Box 7500, Crescent City, CA 95531

Poindexter, Ed #27767, Nebraska State Penitentiary, PO Box 2500, Lincoln, NE 68542

Powell, Reverend Joy #07-G-0632, Bedford Hills CF, PO Box 1000, Bedford Hills, NY 10507

Rodríguez, Luis V. #C33000, Mule Creek State Prison, PO Box 409000, Ione, CA 95640

Shabazz Bey, Hanif (Beaumont Gereau), #295933, Keen Mountain CC, PO Box 860, Oakwood, VA 24631

Shakur, Mutulu #83205-012, USP Florence ADMAX, PO Box 8500, Florence, CO 81226

Shoats, Russell Maroon #AF-3855, SCI Greene, 175 Progress Drive, Waynesburg, PA 15370

Torres, Carlos Alberto #88976-024, FCI Pekin, PO Box 5000, Pekin, IL 61555

Torres, Francisco 2307534, out on bail; can be reached at: Committee for the Defense of Human Rights, PO Box 90221, Pasadena, CA 91109

Tyler, Gary #84156, Louisiana State Penitentiary, ASH-4, Angola, LA 70712

Wallace, Herman #76759, Elayn Hunt Correctional Center, 6925 Hwy 74, St. Gabriel, LA 70776

Waters, Briana 36432-086, FCI Danbury, Rte 37, Danbury, CT 06811

Watson, Gary #098990, Unit SHU17, Delaware Correctional Center,1181 Paddock Rd, Smyrna, DE 19977

Woodfox, Albert #72148, Camp D, Eagle 1, Louisiana State Penitentiary, Angola, LA 70712

Zacher, Joyanna #36360-086, FCI Dublin, 5701 8th St, Camp Parks, Unit F, Dublin, CA 94568

Notes

1. See chapter 20, "Q&A on Jericho 98," p. 206. See also thejerichomovement.com.
2. Ajamu Nassor (Gregory Resnover) and Ziyon Yisrayah (Tommie Smith): political prisoners executed by the state of Indiana, January 1997.

    Police raided the home of Ziyon Yisrayah and his co-worker Ajamu Nassor in 1980, shooting and throwing teargas bombs, one of which caused a couch in the front room to catch fire. The raid was conducted against the two men for their roles in objecting to the treatment of the Black community by the police. Yisrayah was injured in the raid, and one white cop was killed. Suppressed in the trial was the evidence that the murdered officer had been shot in the back, and that the bullet that killed him did not come from either of the guns fired in self-defense from inside the house. Both Yisrayah and Nassor were sentenced to death for killing the officer. The state of Indiana killed Ajamu Nassor on December 8, 1994, and Ziyon Yisrayah on July 17, 1996.

    Prisoners in Indiana protested as Ziyon's execution date approached. According to Shaka Shakur, one of the prisoners, "The top half of D cell house, approximately 150 prisoners of all nationalities, ate their afternoon meal in complete silence to protest the planned premeditated murder of an innocent man." Ten New Afrikan prisoners were later punished for their role in the protest, which was characterized by prison officials as a riot. Six of the men received additional sentences of up to four years as a result.

3. Geronimo ji Jaga (Elmer Pratt) was released from prison in June 1997, soon after this article was written. Indeed, the evidence of his innocence had been in the possession of the government and it was only a concerted legal and political campaign that forced the disclosure of this evidence and the overturning of Geronimo's murder conviction. In 2000, the state of California and the city of Los Angeles paid Geronimo a $4.5 million settlement for their wrongdoing and his unjust imprisonment for twenty-seven years.

4. For information on the New York Three, see chapter 14, "CBS Tries the New York Three," p. 156. Albert Nuh Washington, about whom Safiya writes in several chapters of this book, died in prison in 2000 of liver cancer. He was sixty-four years old.

The other two members of the New York Three, Herman Bell and Jalil Muntaqim (Anthony Bottom), have been refused parole several times, despite the recommendation of members of the family of one of the police officers (Waverly Jones) killed in the offense that they be released. Every parole request has been met with intense opposition and public campaigns by law enforcement and the widow of the other slain officer, Joseph Piagentini. Both Herman and Jalil were indicted in 2007 in the "San Francisco 8" case; New York City police commissioner Ray Kelly was quoted in the *New York Times* as saying that the new case "dealt a blow to the legacy" of the protest groups that grew from the Black Panthers. The charges against them have since been resolved by pleas to lesser charges, with no additional prison time. NEWKILL was FBI computer language for an investigation of Black radicals suspected of connection with police killings in New York.

5. See note 3.

6. According to a statement by the group Nebraskans for Justice (and signed by several state politicians, including an ex-governor), "In April of 1971, Omahans David Rice (Mondo we Langa) and Ed Poindexter were each convicted of first-degree murder and sentenced to life in prison for the death of Omaha Police officer Larry Minard. Minard was killed on August 17, 1970, when a dynamite-filled briefcase exploded as he and two other officers investigated a tip from a 911 call that a crime was taking place at 2867 Ohio Street in Omaha.

"Initially, state authorities sought only the conviction of Duane Christopher Peak, a fifteen-year-old who was peripherally involved in the activities of the National Committee to Combat Fascism (NCCF), an Omaha group that spun-off from a local chapter of the nationally prominent Black Panthers organization. Rice and Poindexter were executive officers in the NCCF. For years, both men were engaged in legal, political activities protesting police conduct in the Black community of North Omaha.

"Peak implicated Rice and Poindexter in the bombing and served no time for his involvement. At a preliminary hearing on Sept. 28, 1970, Peak shocked prosecutors by exonerating Rice and Poindexter. After a break for the noon hour, by eyewitness accounts, Peak returned to the hearing visibly shaken, wearing sunglasses, and changed his entire story from the morning, implicating Rice and Poindexter."

During the trial, key evidence was suppressed as well.

Amnesty International named Rice and Poindexter prisoners of conscience. Despite being recommended for parole by the state parole board, both men remain incarcerated. Early in 2007, new evidence emerged and it is possible that Poindexter's case will be reopened—meaning Rice's would likely have to be as well.

7. Freedom Rides were bus rides to southern cities taken by Black and white northerners as an expression of protest against segregation in the early 1960s. Riders were often attacked by the Klan and other racists, and many Riders were badly injured and jailed. The courageous rides sparked outrage and action from many others in support of the civil rights movement.

8. Sundiata has now been behind bars for thirty-six years. He was denied parole by the state of New Jersey once; he is incarcerated in federal prison, although his conviction was in the jurisdiction of New Jersey. Sundiata is now seventy-three years old and a prolific writer. See sundiataacoli.org.

9. For recent information of these efforts, see freemumia.com.

10. The Church Committee refers to the Senate Select Committee to Study Governmental Operations with Respect to Intelligence Activities, instituted in 1975, and chaired by Senator Frank Church of Utah. The committee was charged with investigating a wide range of US government intelligence agencies. In 1976 the Committee issued a report (archived online at pbs.org/moyers/journal/10262007/profile2.html and elsewhere) describing many of the illegal actions employed by the FBI

against the Black Panther Party and other radical organizations. The documentation of these tactics by a Senate committee lends emphasis to the arguments made by Safiya and others that it is unjust to imprison Black radicals for decades while those who carried out murders under COINTELPRO serve no time and suffer no criminal persecution.

11. Dhoruba Bin-Wahad was released from prison in New York State in 1990.

12. Talks on the Black Panther Party and the Black Liberation Struggle

In September 1991, organizers in Chicago held a conference commemorating the 1971 uprising at Attica prison in New York State. Safiya traveled to Chicago for this "Attica Remembered" conference, giving speeches, leading workshops, and providing interviews at community radio stations and bookstores. The following encompasses two of those presentations: a radio interview conducted by Tyehimba Jess for WHTK radio, and a talk at a Black community bookstore called Freedom Found Books. Both of these, fortunately, were preserved in audiotapes. Because the two talks covered much of the same material, they have been combined here. In the first half, Safiya discusses some weaknesses and problems in the Black Panther Party. The second half concerns the Attica rebellion itself.

Akil Al Jundi, a leader at Attica as well as in the work to reveal the truth about the rebellion and the state assault against it, was present at Safiya's talk in the bookstore. Akil, who died in 1997, added to Safiya's comments his own about the importance of community organizing.

The Black Panthers: Going Underground, Arrest, and Imprisonment

After witnessing how the police—and the system they represented—treated Black people who were trying to organize for basic community demands, I decided I was going to dedicate my life to making sure that I would never again be treated as a second-class citizen. And from that day forward, I have been a member of the Black liberation movement. That's when I joined the Black Panther Party.

I was in the Harlem office of the Party from 1969, when I became a Panther, to 1974, when I went underground. In the interim, in addition to all our community work, the Party had called for a national revolutionary constitutional convention.[1] There had been, during this time, many internal problems in the Party. The Party was not perfect. Anytime you have an organization becoming as strong and internationally known as quickly as the Black Panther Party was—and it was young people, and a lot of egos developed because the media was always there; the white man was always there with the money that you weren't used to getting—you're going to have problems. The people in the Party allowed liberalism and egos to become more important than what we were working for. The principles were supposed to give you the guide to deal with problems. But those things went by the wayside because the leaders justified what they did by saying, "We're the leaders; we started it; we are more important than the individuals." And that is not so. One thing we should have been clear about is that the struggle is more important than the individual. The people and advancing the struggle are more important than any individual. And the organization, which is necessary for the struggle to move from one level to another, is definitely more important than the individual. That got turned around.

By 1971 there was so much internal bickering in the Party and so much deviation from principles that there was a split. And while we were dealing with those internal contradictions and that fratricide, the government was making a move on us through the counterintelligence program, which they called COINTELPRO. We were not aware of it at the time. We did not know that a lot of the things we saw as internal contradictions were actually being manipulated by the government. And every little weakness or mistake that they saw was used and preyed upon. COINTELPRO was designed to neutralize the Party. It was an all-encompassing program from coast to coast. On December 4, 1969, it culminated in the death of Fred Hampton in Chicago, and in that same year, Geronimo Pratt was incarcerated in California, shoot-outs went on in New Orleans and Detroit—all across the country the Party offices were under attack. And one of the things we were saying in the Party is that the Black Panther Party always stood for self-defense. So in order to protect ourselves and the community, it was necessary for us to defend ourselves. And by being inside the offices and being sitting targets we were not really defending ourselves, we were making it easy for them. So it was decided to secure the offices, the Party, and the community workers by going on the offense, with the objective to defend and liberate the Black community and to make it possible for the political apparatus to continue.

In that period it was also necessary to defend the community. In New York City alone, police brutality had risen to such a height that more and more youth were being killed—out and out murdered in the streets of New York. There was no way that, as principled people and as revolutionaries, members of the Party could sit back and not make a move to defend the people and get the police off the backs of the community. While we were dealing with our internal contradictions, we had a principled responsibility to defend our community. The Party had put ourselves out there as defenders of the community, and there was no way, as people who were dedicated to our community, we could allow this to happen.

These things led to a lot of brothers and sisters who were members of the Party and accused of membership in the BLA being captured and forced underground and some being killed. And we had so many political prisoners that it was necessary for us to find a way to avoid siphoning off Party money and Party time trying to defend them. One of the things I was trying to do was to form what was called the National Committee to Defend Political Prisoners. It was my responsibility to make sure the captured comrades were taken care of, that they received letters, the legal defense was handled, etc. And in dealing with that aspect of it I became a target of COINTELPRO. I was placed on the known-militants list—I was called the number one Black militant, which is really ridiculous, because I never saw myself as number one anything, other than that my commitment to the struggle was total. Later I got a copy of my FBI file and saw some of what they had, which was ridiculous.

All this was going on simultaneously. By 1973 I had been traveling all over the country, setting up offices, making sure the political work was being done, handling trials, making sure people had defense lawyers and that organizing was done around their defense effort. In New York we had the New York Five, which became the New York Three—three are still incarcerated today and two have been released from their charges. This is their twentieth year in prison. We also had Henry Sha Sha Brown, who was charged with the assassination of a police officer and whose trial ended in acquittal, and he still spent fifteen years in prison and just got out about four years ago. We had the New Haven Three in Connecticut, and one of them just got out six months ago. Richard Dhoruba Moore just got out last year after nineteen years.

The split led to the demise of the Black Panther Party. And that also led to the isolation, and to the death, in two or three years' time, of at least thirteen people, and the arrest, capture, and conviction of two or three score more, coast to coast—and the majority of those people are still in prison today.

All this was going on at the same time in New York. And there were still a lot of people they were not able to capture. The work was still going on in the community. Every time they thought they had broken the back of the struggle something else happened. So what they began to do was have roundups. They would give out subpoenas to the grand jury. My eventual arrest and my going underground were precipitated by getting subpoenaed to appear before the grand jury to testify. The subpoena came with immunity from prosecution, which gave me no option but to go underground rather than go before the grand jury.

What immunity from prosecution means is this: if you received a subpoena to go before the grand jury, you could appear and then invoke the Fifth Amendment, saying, "I refuse to answer a question on the basis that it might incriminate me." With immunity, you can't invoke the Fifth Amendment. You can't be prosecuted on the basis of anything you say. So if you go before the grand jury, you either answer the questions or you don't answer the questions, at which point you can be arrested for contempt. It can be civil contempt or felony contempt. You are forced to testify and give information against other people.

When I was subpoenaed, in the spring of 1974, Twymon Myers had recently been assassinated in New York. Patrick Murphy, who was then superintendent of police in New York, had made a special trip to Washington to have Twymon put on the FBI's Ten Most Wanted List. At the time that he was assassinated in November 1973, he had been on the Ten Most Wanted List for about six months. He had been shot, out in front of a building where he had been staying, by a combined FBI–New York State police–New York City police force. They shot him eighty times, and shot him in his head. That night they had a rally in front of the Forty-fourth Precinct to celebrate that they had finally captured him.

One reason why I was subpoenaed to give evidence against the BLA was that, after making the decision to stay above-ground and work through the political apparatus, to try to keep the Panther offices open, I was considered the source of the majority of information that came out about the BLA. I was the one who released the press releases or the communiqués the BLA sent. So they thought that if anyone had any information about the BLA, I probably had that information. They made a decision to subpoena me, and I made a decision not to testify. I went underground. I was underground for about nine months before I was captured in Norfolk, Virginia, in January 1975, with Masai Ehehosi. Our comrade, Kombozi Amistad, was killed in the incident.

We had already decided that if we got captured we would take the position of prisoners of war. All of us were citizens of the RNA (Republic of New Afrika). The government of the United States had no right to try us. The people in Virginia, the community, supported us because of that position.[2]

But we were tried anyway. The whole thing—jury selection, trial, conviction, and sentencing—all took place in one day. The harshest part was not the trial or the sentence. It wasn't the incarceration. It was the way they treated Kombozi. They stomped him to death and then cremated him to make sure there was no evidence of what they had done. When his mother got there, they just gave her his clothes, because they had already cremated him. They did that. And then they charged us with his death. For thirty days we were facing the death penalty. They wouldn't allow Masai and me to communicate. We had already watched the cops raid the funeral of Twymon Myers with machine guns, come to the cemetery at Butler, New Jersey, where he was being buried, and we didn't know whether we'd come out of the cemetery alive. They'd already killed so many. They'd already shot twenty-eight Panthers. They didn't understand that it wasn't death that was to be feared; it was life as a slave that was to be feared.

I was sentenced to the Virginia State Penitentiary, and that's a men's prison. I was the only woman ever sentenced to that prison, and I was told to do every day there, but they didn't keep me there. They took me there to give me a number, but then they took me to the Virginia Correctional Center for Women. So now I am reminding you, this was a state case. But it was a federal caravan that took me to prison. I found out later that they had also made clear to the prison that they were supposed to make monthly reports on what was happening with me.

They took me into the quarantine hall. When the people running the quarantine hall realized who I was, I was taken straight to maximum-security segregation.

That's being in the hole, in isolation. I was there twenty-one days, and they said it was because there were no empty rooms in the quarantine hall. But the room where they held me in the quarantine hall while they looked for male guards to take me to segregation was an empty regular cell. So that made no sense. As soon as I got into maximum security I began to investigate the rules of the institution. At that time, they were not used to having women in prison in the South who were political, who knew their rights—their quote, unquote, rights—and who knew the law. They were used to having docile women who had no understanding of what was happening. They didn't know how to deal with me. Their way of dealing with a political woman was to isolate her. They told all the other women that I was trouble and to stay away from me and so on. They expected me to be wearing combat boots and the works. That I would be uncivilized. That's what they expected. What they got was me. They didn't know how to deal with me, because they expected me to throw down at every drop. What they didn't understand was that I knew I was totally surrounded, that I had to use my mind, my brain, instead of brawn, in the situation that I was in, in order to survive it.

In prison we continued to organize, because we were taught that the struggle is everywhere. Wherever there are people of color there is a place to organize. We moved to consolidate and organize with other organizations behind the walls. We did what we couldn't do in the streets, because of the repression there. We used our prison time as a moment to reinforce what we were doing, to lay foundations and build foundations and write, to educate the people about what was happening, and to organize against the conditions in prison.

I began working on parenting and keeping the families together, especially for the long-term offenders.[3] I began fighting for a decent law library, decent job training for the women, religious freedom—things that had never been dealt with in the women's institution. Working with women who didn't have correct legal help. Those are issues I got involved with. These things had not been dealt with inside women's prisons.

In December 1976, I escaped. I was recaptured in February 1977 and brought back to the institution. They put me in maximum-security segregation, and I spent the next three years and seven months in maximum-security segregation. Prior to that, the most time anyone had gotten in maximum-security segregation was six months.

Isolation in maximum security was hard. Sometimes I felt like I was losing my mind. I developed a case of claustrophobia during that time, and I still have residual effects of that, but I recognize it so I can deal with it. Because once you understand what's happening to you, you can work with yourself to try to overcome it.

I'm a Muslim and to keep myself together, I got into my faith and made *salat* (prayer) in order to get outside of myself and have some external force working. To maintain my sanity, I took correspondence courses in electrical engineering and technology. I felt I needed to have some kind of sense of order, and math tends to do that for me. I worked on establishing long-term programs for women in prison. I kept up contact with what was happening in the street. I worked with the women in prison, helping them with their cases—anything to maintain my responsibility to the community and at the same time to maintain my sanity. One of the things they try to do quickly in prison is to break you. And if they're able to break you, to destroy your sense of self-esteem, then they've got you. I tried to maintain that sense of self-esteem.

The biggest struggle for me in prison was to make them understand that I'm me. And I think that's true for Black people in general. If they can get you to deny who you are—to say it's too much trouble being me, so I'll do what you want me to do— then they've got you. Since my whole struggle on the street was to be who I am and to be accepted—no, to be recognized—for who I am as a person, and for who we are as a people, and for who I am as a Black person, I'm not going to go inside the walls and allow them to take that from me in there.

I made work release in 1983 and parole in August of that year. When I went to the parole board, I couldn't admit to guilt for a crime. I didn't consider struggling for the liberation of Black people to be a crime.

I never denied my political beliefs and associations. That's an issue: how to make parole without denying those. They asked me about violence. I said I don't believe in violence for the sake of violence, but everyone is capable of violence under the correct conditions. I said I would only take up violence to defend my home and family. Of course, they didn't realize that by "family" I meant my comrades, my codefendant who was killed, and all Black people.

I said my beliefs have not changed, but how I go about pursuing them has changed. We have to make changes within ourselves, educate the community. We have to change those negative things we have in ourselves before we can join together.

I think that's important. I think about the film, *The Battle of Algiers*, where before they go out to do battle with the French, they have to clean up the drugs and crime in their community. Get rid of the drug pushers. We have to do that. We have to go back into our community and clean up the drugs. So when you go out to struggle you don't have to worry about what's behind you. All the successful struggles begin with cleaning up the internal problems. Until you do that, you'll never have a successful struggle.

The basis of the movement now is still the same as it ever was. The primary objective remains the same: to establish political power for Black people. The Black movement is so factionalized today that it's ridiculous, with everybody wanting to be the leader. We're going nowhere. We're dying, by leaps and bounds. We're losing our youth and everything else. The prisons are overflowing with us, women and children and men. All the infighting between organizations is leaving the people out there with nowhere to go. So for those of us who are sincere about struggle, about turning this whole mess around, our primary, our immediate, objective is to do something about this factionalism, to come together in some form of unity and organize, so that we can collectively move forward and come back to dealing with organizing our people toward our freedom, to see that we're not annihilated in the next ten years.

It's not easy. We never said it was going to be easy.

But you know one thing I've learned—and I've learned it from watching other folks, the reactionaries—is it's got to start in the home. We neglect that home thing. They teach their children to hate us from the dinner table, from the crib. We have to start teaching our children from the crib, at the dinner table, that *never again*. After Germany, after the six million were killed in the Holocaust, the Jews said, "Never again," and look where they're at now. After the forty million Black people died in the holocaust of the Middle Passage, Black people have not yet said, "Never again." At some point, collectively, we have to say, "Never again will we be victimized the way we were in the past." The victimization of Black people in this country has to stop. And we have to stop doing rash actions and instead build foundations from which to move.

The Black Panther Party does not exist as the Party anymore. We do believe that in order to move our struggle forward, there's a need for a political party. Together we can build a party. But in the interim, Panthers are out there, and people who are committed to build the struggle are out there.

Attica

The Black Panthers were involved in the prison movement because we realized that prison was a microcosm of the society. One thing that was very clear to us was that the most down, the most revolutionary brothers and sisters, at that point, were in prison. As Ho Chi Minh wrote, "When the prison doors are open, the real dragon will fly out."[4] So we were very involved in the prison struggle.

There is a background to the Attica uprising. In the early 1970s, there were prison uprisings all over the country. I had been down to Columbia, South Carolina, where there was an uprising in the state prison, and the prisoners had asked me to come in and negotiate. When I got back to New York, George Jackson had just been assassinated in California on August 21, 1971. That was one of the precipitating moves. A year earlier, in August 1970, George's little brother, Jonathan had gotten killed trying to liberate some brothers in the courtroom in Marin County, California. Then George Jackson had been killed when they had tried to set him up inside San Quentin. And then came Attica.

It was not expected. We didn't expect that it would be Attica. I thought it would be Dannemora's Special Housing Unit 14 that would go up, because they were actually beating the prisoners inside there.[5] The D block in Attica was not where we thought the uprising would come from. But you had a very different crew that had amassed itself inside Attica at that point. And they were very strong brothers.

The conditions inside Attica were deplorable—the brutality, the food, the lack of education, the racism. The Ku Klux Klan was running rampant inside the prisons in New York State at that time, and the prisons had cut back on visiting and all the programs.[6] The lockdowns were starting as well.[7]

During the takeover of Attica prison in D Yard, there was a conscious effort on the part of the brothers not to mistreat the guards. They handled it in a very principled and disciplined way so that the state would see that they were serious. They even set up security details among themselves to make sure that nobody was mistreated. And a whole bunch of people from outside—lawyers, journalists, activists—had gone inside and were trying to negotiate. But the media were saying that the prisoners were cutting the guards' throats, and that was one of the pretexts on which then-governor Nelson Rockefeller ordered the state troopers to go in there and wage the assault on September 13.

At the time of Attica, I was working out of the Harlem Black Panther Party office. I was editor of the *Right On! Black Community News Service*, our paper; after the split, the Huey faction of the Party kept the Black Panther paper. One of the demands of the brothers in Attica was to have asylum in a non-imperialist country. My role was to investigate the possibility of non-imperialist countries that would accept them. I was on the phone constantly until Nelson Rockefeller issued the order to go into Attica for the massacre. Cuba, North Vietnam, and North Korea had said they would accept the brothers. The state had a choice, rather than kill those brothers, let them go. They wouldn't have had to spend X amount of dollars to keep them in prison. They wouldn't have had to let them go free—they could have sent them to another country. They wouldn't have had the blood of September 13 on their hands. But they didn't send them.

After the massacre, there was a funeral and a march in the streets of New York. We met at Brother Herbert Daughtry's church in Brooklyn, the House of the Lord Church, on Atlantic Avenue. The Brooklyn chapter of the Black Panther Party, the brothers and sisters who worked out of that office, had organized the churches, the schools, and the community—they were organized to do the work. We had educated the community; the connection was there, and they raised the funds to buy the caskets, to get caskets donated, to bury those brothers who were killed in Attica. The Party was involved and considered it our job to do that, because those people were our heroes. The prisons of America were the universities of the revolution.

When some of the other brothers who'd been in D block came home, they kept up that principled behavior, the behavior that had made what went on during the uprising so stirring. You could see that the politics were there, the principles were there, and the determination was there. They kept it up. The uprising wasn't just a momentary thing. It was part of them.

One of the things I've been involved in is trying to make sure that we begin to have an economic base so that we can make the best legal defense possible available to anyone in our community who is victimized by the legal system. The other thing is to try to make sure it doesn't happen in the first place. Because it's hard to get people out of prison once they are in. While you're waiting for someone to find out you really didn't do what they've charged you with doing, you could get a case while you're in there. So you can get killed before you get out of there. Or psychologically damaged for life.

Our Black young men have enough going against them without the psychological trauma of being incarcerated at twelve, thirteen, fourteen, fifteen years of age, and that's the age at which our young Black men are going to prison today. The other thing is to deal with rooting out the systemic racism that infests our justice system. We can't get a fair trial in this system for Black people, because we're already stereotyped; whatever we're accused of, we did it. If you got indicted, you did it. And if you got killed for doing it, then you did it. And if you didn't do it this time, you did it another time. So if you didn't do it this time, you're caught for what you did last week or the week before, so now you're doing time for that. And that's true no matter who you are in America, if you're Black.

If you don't realize that there are political prisoners, or you don't realize that Black and other oppressed people in this country are in a state of war, then you get victimized over and over again. And the second time around, we have to struggle differently, to learn from the past and change our tactics. Right now, I am trying to do a lot of speaking to make people understand what happened in the past, why we can't allow it to continue, and why we have to speak out against it now.

Kids aren't learning it, because we're not spreading the history ourselves. In Africa they had griots. So we have to be the modern-day storytellers.

Notes

1. Led by the Panthers, some ten thousand to fifteen thousand activists convened in Philadelphia in September 1970 at the multicultural Revolutionary People's Constitutional Convention. For a discussion of this event and its impact on the Party's future, see George Katsiaficas, "Organization and Movement: The Case of the Black Panther Party and the Revolutionary People's Constitutional Convention of 1970," in Kathleen Cleaver and George Katsiaficas, eds., *Liberation, Imagination, and the Black Panther Party: A New Look at the Panthers and Their Legacy* (New York: Routledge, 2001).

2. According to a report on KPFA radio at the time, at her arraignment Safiya said: "I refuse to take part in any proceedings in this court. I refuse to answer any questions. If you have provisions to deal with prisoners of war, then I will talk to you. But otherwise, I will not." She declared herself to be in a unit of the BLA and a citizen of the Republic of New Afrika.

3. Safiya was one of the prisoners who founded a program called MILK (Mothers Inside Loving Kids) as a way to prevent the separation of children from their incarcerated mothers.

4. From a poem by Ho Chi Minh, leader of the Vietnamese liberation struggle, founder of the Indochinese Communist Party and the Viet Minh, and first president of the Democratic Republic of Vietnam in 1945. Ho died in 1969.

5. Safiya is referring to a section of the notoriously brutal Clinton Correctional Facility, located in the town of Dannemora, New York, less than an hour's drive from the Canadian border.

6. The Klan was active among prison guards in New York State during

that period. Among the guards and other staff who were Klan members was the head of the reading program at Eastern Correctional Facility at Napanoch, New York, who was later shown to be the Grand Dragon of the New York State Klan.

7. In this period, lockdowns of prisons—locking all prisoners in their cells and prohibiting any movement in the institution—became a common response from the authorities to any demands by prisoners for their rights.

13. Lest We Forget

This essay, printed as a pamphlet, now long out of print, expresses some of the most basic tenets of Safiya's politics. Even more, the words in "Lest We Forget" resonate with the passion, the ache, the longing, behind her life's work.

On its cover, the twenty-eight-page pamphlet, published sometime after 1981, attributes "Lest We Forget" to Safiya A. Bukhari; the price of the pamphlet is given as two dollars. Behind the type is a dense layout of photos of thirty-two of the people profiled in the pamphlet—all members of Black liberation organizations who lost their lives in the years from 1968 to 1981. When most of the deaths occurred, activists had not been aware of the FBI's counterintelligence program that was behind many of the killings. COINTELPRO came to broad public awareness only in the mid-1970s; by 1981, we were all still trying to put all these deaths in perspective and figure out how to respond.

In her introduction, Safiya writes of "the determination of our people to wait no longer for the realization of people of African descent as human beings in the eyes of mankind." This could describe the basis for her lifelong commitment to the cause of justice for Black people, including her unwavering work to support and free political prisoners. The descriptions of some of the Panthers are similar to those in an article, "Fallen Comrades," in the February 1991 issue of the *Black Panther, Black Community News Service*. That article bears no byline, so it is not clear whether Safiya wrote it.

Constantly people of color are confronted with the reality that death is our ever-present companion. We've had to live with the conditions that make us more prone to high blood pressure, diabetes, high infant mortality, strokes, heart attacks, etc., for so long that we see these things as part of our heritage. It has become commonplace to hear that someone known to us or related to us was killed in an argument, gambling, or trying to take someone off. Even more commonplace is our spending our lives in the living death of prison.

We're not shocked or surprised by this. In fact, we've become complacent with this as the status quo. We've begun to plod along, waiting for our number to come up. On a very real level we are the walking dead: people without a future and with an extremely chaotic past. We have been aimlessly wandering through life, purposeless, directionless—slaves to other people's whims, ideas, and desires.

Throughout history, voices rose out of and above the quagmire and declared themselves men and women. Human beings with souls, who wanted to know how it felt to be free and live outside the shadow of death. Cinqué, Nat Turner, Gabriel Prosser, Harriet Tubman, Denmark Vesey—men and women who lived and died to the tune of "Oh, freedom, Oh, freedom, Oh freedom in my heart. Before I'd be a slave I'll be buried in my grave and go home to my Lord and be free."

There is no equivocation when we recall those heroes. Why? Because it's safe to remember them. They are far removed from our day and time, so we can glory in their battles and victories vicariously with no threat to us.

While we are busy recanting the glory of our long dead heroes, new heroes are going forth into battle to carry our struggle for dignity, freedom, independence, and humanity one step closer to reality in the spirit of Claude McKay's "If We Must Die":

> If we must die, let it not be like hogs
> Hunted and penned in an inglorious spot,
> While round us bark the mad and hungry dogs,
> Making their mock at our accursed lot.
> If we must die, O let us nobly die,
> So that our precious blood may not be shed
> In vain; then even the monsters we defy
> Shall be constrained to honor us though dead!
> O kinsmen! We must meet the common foe!
> Though far outnumbered let us show us brave,
> And for their thousand blows deal one deathblow!
> What though before us lies the open grave?
> Like men we'll face the murderous, cowardly pack,
> Pressed to the wall, dying, but fighting back!

The past thirty years have seen some doors crack for Blacks and other people of color in America. These changes didn't occur in a vacuum. They were political moves in an attempt to undermine the rising tide of Black unrest and our demands for civil and human rights. No concrete changes in the very real condition of Black people occurred. We're still at the bottom of the totem pole.

With the advent of the twentieth century the Black man in America began to take a decided shift away from quiet acquiescence to our plight. We had begun, in massive numbers, to say, "No More." Our leaders—Marcus Garvey, Elijah Muhammad, Martin Luther King Jr., and Malcolm X—articulated the determination of our people to wait no longer for the realization of people of African descent as human beings in the eyes of mankind.

The twentieth century became the time to take a stand. Four hundred years of racist oppression and economic exploitation were enough. Not one more century. Not one more generation without a collective, organized resistance. "Either/or" became the battle cry. America was put on notice: the choice is the ballot or the bullet!

Realizing that no concessions would be gained without a fight, brothers and sisters determined to lay down their very lives, if it became necessary, to achieve our freedom. The following is a chronicle of those unsung heroes who have given the only thing that was theirs to give—*their lives!*

A People's War of Liberation is like the points of a starfish. When a soldier (guerrilla) dies, another grows and takes his or her place in the struggle, or in the body of the army.

Here are some of those fallen:

Arthur Morris. Member of the Southern California chapter, Los Angeles Branch, of the Black Panther Party. Arthur was the first member of the Black Panther Party to die in the struggle for Black liberation.[1] ASSASSINATED March 1968.

Bobby James Hutton. Affectionately known as Lil' Bobby Hutton, born April 25, 1950. He was the first person to join the Black Panther Party. He joined when he was sixteen when the Party was founded in 1966. He served as finance coordinator. He was one of the Panthers arrested on May 2, 1967, at the Sacramento legislature protest where Bobby Seale read the Party's position on self-defense for oppressed people (Executive

Mandate No. 1). Bobby was murdered two days after the assassination of Martin Luther King Jr., by dozens of Oakland police. He was unarmed, but with utmost courage, sacrificed his life so others might live. ASSASSINATED April 6, 1968.

Steve Bartholomew, twenty-one; **Robert Lawrence**, twenty-two; and **Tommy Lewis**, eighteen. They were riding in a car when they noticed they were being followed by a Los Angeles police squad car. They stopped at a gas station so that any incident could be witnessed. The squad car stopped also. As Steve was getting out of the car a volley of police gunfire killed him instantly. The Panthers returned fire and Robert was killed. Tommy died later at Los Angeles Central Receiving Hospital from peritonitis (severe intestinal inflammation) caused by stomach wounds and loss of blood. ASSASSINATED August 25, 1968.

Nathaniel Clark. Member of the Los Angeles Branch of the Black Panther Party and a student at the University of California, Los Angeles. Killed as he slept. ASSASSINATED September 12, 1968.

Welton Armstead. Member of the Seattle, Washington, Branch of the Black Panther Party. Known as Butch. Welton was seventeen years old when he was killed. ASSASSINATED October 15, 1968.

Sidney Miller. Twenty-two days after the Seattle police murdered Welton Armstead, a white Seattle businessman murdered Sidney Miller, twenty-one years old. He was shot point blank in the head as he was leaving a West Seattle grocery store. The owner said he "thought" Sidney was about to rob the store. ASSASSINATED November 7, 1968.

Frank Diggs. Los Angeles chapter, Black Panther Party, forty years old. Frank was shot to death and left in an alley on the outskirts of Los Angeles by unknown assailants. ASSASSINATED December 30, 1968.

Alprentice "Bunchy" Carter. Came from the streets of LA, where he was "the Mayor of the Ghetto." He became the organizer and driving force for the Southern California chapter of the Black Panther Party, the first chapter of the Party outside the Bay Area. Before coming to the Party Bunchy had been a member of the Slausons, one of the largest gangs in LA. The sum total of his life experiences imbued Bunchy with a revolutionary fervor and commitment, which he expressed as follows:

> Black Mother, I must confess that I still breathe
> Though you are not yet free. . . .
> For a slave of natural death who dies
> Can't balance out two dead flies.
> I'd rather live without the shame
> A bullet lodged within my brain
> If I were not to reach my goal
> Let bleeding cancer torment my soul.

Bunchy was shot from behind and killed on the steps of UCLA while organizing and educating Black students around self-determination and student control of the Black student unions in preparation for community control. Though the fingers that pulled the trigger on Bunchy were members of Ron Karenga's US organization,[2] in the final analysis, Bunchy's death is the responsibility of the racist American government. ASSASSINATED January 17, 1969.

John Jerome Huggins. Born in New Haven, Connecticut. John and his wife, Ericka, became members of the Southern California chapter of the Black Panther Party soon after its doors opened. Together with Bunchy Carter, John, as deputy minister of information, provided the leadership needed as that chapter grew. The assassination of Bunchy and John, on the steps of UCLA, by members of the US organization was part of the COINTELPRO strategy to foment a war between the Black Panther Party and the US organization so they would kill each other off. Bunchy and John ASSASSINATED January 17, 1969.

Alex Rackley. Member of the New York chapter, Harlem Branch, of the Black Panther Party. Alex was killed by George Sams, a police agent who infiltrated the Party. He was shot through the head and heart in New Haven, Connecticut. The New Haven Police Department also had an informer on the scene at the Sams-engineered and -ordered execution, but no effort was made to prevent it. ASSASSINATED May 21, 1969.

John Savage. In the aftermath of the assassinations of Bunchy and John, relationships between the Black Panther Party (BPP) and US grew increasingly tense. On Friday, May 23, 1969, John Savage and another Party member, Jeffrey Jennings, were walking toward the Party office in San Diego, California, when they met a US member named "Tambozi." As they walked past, Tambozi grabbed John Savage by the shoulder, jammed a .38 automatic to the back of his neck and pulled the trigger. John, age twenty-four, died instantly. ASSASSINATED May 23, 1969.

Sylvester Bell. Less than three months after the

assassination of John Savage, US struck again. Sylvester Bell became the fourth member of the Black Panther Party murdered in cold blood by Karenga's men. Sylvester's murder came at a time when the LA trial of US members for the assassination of Bunchy and John had just begun—an attempt to intimidate witnesses at the trial. Sylvester was thirty-four years old. ASSASSINATED August 15, 1969.

Larry Roberson. On the morning of July 14, 1969, Larry Roberson, twenty years old, and Grady "Slim" Moore, members of the Chicago Branch of the Black Panther Party, noticed police harassing a group of elderly Black men, forcing them to line up against a wall, and they went to investigate. An argument ensued and without hesitation the police pulled their guns and started shooting. Larry was critically wounded in his stomach, thigh, and leg. (Grady Moore escaped uninjured.) Larry managed to wound two of his assailants. He was taken to Cook County Hospital and placed under police guard. He was harassed, threatened, and periodically beaten. He died in the hospital. Because Larry placed himself between the oppressor and his people without thought for his own life, Fred Hampton said, "Larry Roberson was too revolutionary proletarian intoxicated to be astronomically intimidated." ASSASSINATED September 4, 1969.

Walter "Toure" Pope. As soon as he was released by the California Youth Authority from Tracy, California, Walter joined the Black Panther Party. Toure, twenty years old, was singled out for constant harassment by the Los Angeles Police Department because of his effectiveness as distribution manager of the *Black Panther*

Black Community News Service in Southern California. In three months he increased the circulation from fifteen hundred a week to over seven thousand a week. Walter was brutally gunned down in broad daylight as he left a store where he had just dropped off some newspapers. According to eyewitness reports, the police suddenly came upon him and opened fire. Toure never had a chance. ASSASSINATED October 18, 1969.

Spurgeon Winters. "Jake" was an honor student in school and a revolutionist. He worked on the Chicago chapter's Breakfast Program and the free health clinic and was part of the education cadre. He was killed when one hundred policemen opened fire on him and Lance Bell, who was wounded. Three policemen were killed and seven wounded in the attack on the deserted building where the two took refuge. Jake was nineteen. ASSASSINATED November 13, 1969.

Mark Clark. Mark was a defense captain for the Peoria, Illinois, Branch of the BPP. He made frequent trips to Chicago to confer with the leadership of the Party's chapter there in order to help him organize in downstate Peoria. Mark made one such trip in December of 1969 and stayed at Fred Hampton's apartment. Chicago police raided Fred's apartment on the morning of December 4. Mark was murdered by the raiders as they crashed through the apartment door. He was shot through the heart. Several other occupants were wounded by indiscriminate police gunfire. Mark Clark was twenty-two. ASSASSINATED December 4, 1969.

Fred Hampton. The name Fred Hampton has secured a permanent place in the annals of people's struggle, because, sadly enough, this was one of the hundreds of thousands of Black deaths America chose to publicize. A young outspoken critic of America's treatment of Black and poor people, Fred's dedication to the cause of freedom led him and others to organize in Chicago. The organizational and speaking abilities of Fred Hampton won for him national attention. Political persecution of Fred Hampton included numerous false arrests. He was convicted of a seventy-dollar ice cream truck robbery in 1969, but community pressure forced his release. Such persecution culminated on December 4, 1969 at four o'clock in the morning, when a raiding party of Chicago police invaded Fred's apartment and shot him several times as he slept. He was twenty-one years old. The Black community lost a beautiful warrior for human dignity, but Fred often said, "You can kill a revolutionary, but you can't kill the revolution." ASSASSINATED December 4, 1969.

Sterling Jones. Fred Hampton and Mark Clark were only days in their graves when the Chicago Police Department struck again. On Christmas Day, Sterling Jones, seventeen, a member of the Illinois chapter, responded to a knock at his family's apartment door. As Sterling opened the door, he was shot directly in the face by an unknown assailant. The bullet killed him and his assailant fled into the night. ASSASSINATED December 25, 1969.

Jonathan Jackson. On August 7, 1970, a young Black man entered the Marin County Courthouse in California. The events that followed came to be called the August 7 Movement. Jonathan had walked into the courthouse where San Quentin prison inmate James McClain was defending himself against charges of assaulting a prison guard. Also present were two inmates serving as witnesses on behalf of McClain. They were William Christmas and Ruchell Magee. Jonathan interrupted the court proceedings, stating, "We are revolutionary justice," then gave weapons to McClain, Christmas, and Magee. They all left the courtroom. Several jurors, the prosecutor, and the judge were also taken. Within minutes the van that Jonathan and party had gotten into was riddled with bullets from the guns of San Quentin guards and other state agents, who disregarded the lives of not only Jonathan Jackson and the three inmates, but also those of the jurors, judge, and prosecutor. When the shooting ended, Jonathan Jackson lay dead, as did William Christmas, James McClain, and the Marin County judge. George Jackson summed up his brother's heroic actions in this way: "Man-child, Black man-child with a machine gun in hand, he was free for a while. I guess that's more than most of us can expect."

Carl Hampton. Brother Carl was the chairman (coordinator) of the People's Party II, a revolutionary organization in Houston, Texas. Carl was the motivating force of the small organization, which followed the example and the policies of the BPP. At the time the Party was not organizing in the South, so Carl, seeing the need for a party that would serve the people's needs and desires, started the People's Party, which sold the BPP newspaper. Culminating a series of incidents on July 28, 1970, Houston police surrounded the Dowling Street area where the People's Party II office was located and attacked the entire community. Carl was killed at two a.m. in defense of the community.

Fred Bennett. Pieces of the body of Fred Bennett were
found in April 1971, in a mountainous region near
Oakland, California. Fred had been the coordinator
of the East Oakland branch of the BPP and had been
a Party member for three years, having joined in early
1968. Fred's body was mutilated when police claimed
they "found" him. They held on to Fred's body without
announcement for more than two months. ASSASSINATED
February 1971.

Ralph Featherstone and **Che Payne.** Killed by a car bomb
outside a Maryland courthouse where Rap Brown was
scheduled for a hearing. ASSASSINATED March 9, 1970.

Babatunde X Omarwali. A member of the Illinois chapter
of the BPP, Babatunde was a shining example of our
many revolutionary brothers who have turned from
being used as Black cannon fodder by the US military
to become dedicated soldiers in service to the oppressed
community as Black liberation fighters. Babatunde
joined the Party in Chicago after serving two years in
the US Army, and he quickly became one of the Party's
best organizers. In the summer of 1970, he had just
returned to Chicago from the Cairo-Carbondale area
after organizing a National Committee to Combat
Fascism (NCCF) office there. On July 27, twenty-
six-year-old Babatunde's remains were "found" lying
across railroad tracks in a deserted area of the city by
Chicago police. They claimed that Babatunde had been
attempting to destroy the tracks and that the bomb went
off prematurely, killing him. Although mutilated beyond
recognition, the body of "Black Panther Babatunde X
Omarwali" was positively identified by the Chicago
police. They could do so because it was the police

themselves who murdered him and placed his body on the railroad tracks. ASSASSINATED July 27, 1970.

Robert Webb. Deputy minister of defense of the BPP. Spent years organizing coast to coast, building the discipline and security of the Party and community in preparation for liberation. When it became apparent that there were corrupt forces operating within the BPP, Robert took a stand for principles first. That stand was to bring about his death on March 8, 1971.

Sam Napier. Circulation manager, BPP. Lived and breathed the Black Panther newspaper. He would constantly intone, "Circulate to educate to liberate." Sam was another casualty of the internal split of the BPP. Fanon talked of the contradictions in *Wretched of the Earth* when he referred to colonial war and mental disorders. Oftentimes we lose sight of who our real enemies are and give vent to our emotional responses. In the deaths of Robert Webb and Sam Napier, the people's liberation struggle lost two of its staunchest supporters. Psychologically, COINTELPRO scored a bull's eye. Sam died April 17, 1971.

George Jackson. George Jackson spent the last eleven years of his life behind prison walls, seven of them in solitary confinement. During his imprisonment, George attained an extraordinary level of revolutionary political consciousness. He was appointed field marshal of the Black Panther Party. He was an eloquent writer. He authored two important books: *Soledad Brother* and *Blood in My Eye*. The latter was completed shortly before his assassination. On August 21, 1971, nameless guards of California's San Quentin prison assassinated George Jackson. They said he was trying to escape, but the brothers inside said that George gave his life to save the lives of others. The people of the oppressed communities of the world know that the San Quentin prison officials carried out a premeditated plan to silence a voice that was so full of revolutionary humanism they could no longer bear it.

Harold Russell. The first Black Liberation Army member to be slain. The BLA—the people's liberation army—boldly declared themselves to be soldiers fighting against the oppressive regime of the US government. Harold was killed in a shoot-out on 122nd Street between Seventh and Eighth Avenues in Harlem, New York. Prior to becoming a member of the BLA, Harold had been a member of the Brooklyn Branch of the BPP. SLAIN IN COMBAT spring 1971.

Sandra Pratt. Wife of Geronimo. Known as Red to her comrades and friends. The death of Sandra was especially heartfelt because of its senselessness, bestiality, and brutality. The sister was pregnant with new lifeblood for the people's struggle. The reactionary forces that slew the sister mutilated her and placed her body in a mattress cover and dumped her in an intersection in Los Angeles. ASSASSINATED fall 1971.

Frank Fields. Known to his comrades as Heavy, a member of the Olugbala tribe of the BLA. Open war had been declared between the US government and the BLA. Frank was killed in one of the FBI's search-and-destroy missions in Florida. SLAIN IN COMBAT December 31, 1971.

Ronald Carter. The response of the government to the BLA was to close ranks and consolidate their forces. For the first time they realized that every act of aggression they launched upon the Black community would be met with an act of revolutionary justice. The FBI launched a nationwide manhunt for BLA soldiers and ordered them killed on sight. Ronald was killed in one of these confrontations in St. Louis, Missouri. SLAIN IN COMBAT February 15, 1972.

Joseph Waddell. Joseph Waddell, or "Joe-Dell," joined the BPP in September 1970 while in the city jail in High Point, North Carolina. Before going to jail, he had functioned as a community worker. Joe-Dell was transferred to Central Prison in Raleigh, North Carolina, and because of his revolutionary posture, he was frequently beaten by prison guards. On June 13, 1972, twenty-one-year-old Joseph Waddell was pronounced dead by prison officials. They said the cause of death was a heart attack. Joe-Dell was physically healthy before his death and had never suffered from heart trouble before. Prison inmates close to Joe-Dell said he was the victim of prison authorities, who had probably drugged or poisoned him to induce the attack. Joe-Dell's internal organs were removed by prison authorities before they released his body to his family.

Anthony White. Known affectionately and in struggle as Kimu Olugbala. Kimu had been captured and seriously injured in the process, but his spirit had not been broken. While incarcerated at the infamous Tombs (the Manhattan House of Detention for Men) in New York he escaped to rejoin his comrades in struggle. On Monday, January 22, 1973, Kimu was killed in a shoot-out with New York police, choosing death over slavery. SLAIN IN COMBAT January 22, 1973.

Woodie Greene. Known in struggle as Changa Olugbala.

All we need to know about Brother Woodie is that he was a warrior in the people's army. He was a young man who'd once been bound and gagged and caged in the white man's zoos (jails), and had vowed never to return. He was slain in the same shoot-out that saw the death of Kimu. SLAIN IN COMBAT January 22, 1973.

Mark Essex. Mark became involved in the struggle for Black liberation while still within the US military apparatus. He served as a dental technician in the navy. Upon his release his first stop was at the Harlem office of the BPP. He wanted to learn as much as possible to take home with him to Emporia, Kansas. Mark died valiantly holding off enemy forces in Louisiana. SLAIN IN COMBAT spring 1973.

Zayd Malik Shakur. Known as Dedane Olugbala, Zayd was the minister of information of the New York Black Panther Party. He spent months and years educating the people to what must be done to secure our freedom and liberation. On May 2, Zayd died the way he lived—in combat, resisting the forces of oppression. He was killed in a shoot-out on the New Jersey Turnpike, in which Assata Shakur and Sundiata Acoli were captured. Zayd was a soldier in the people's liberation army. SLAIN IN COMBAT May 2, 1973.

Twymon Myers. "The elusive Twymon Myers" is what he came to be known as—to the oppressors. To the people he was friend, comrade, and defender. Twymon was no superstar; he just did what had to be done and faded into the night. He cared about everyone, especially the children. He believed that the only way to achieve freedom was to be willing to fight and die for it. If it wasn't worth fighting for, it wasn't worth having and you didn't really want it. On November 14, 1973, a combined force of New York police and FBI agents surrounded Twymon on a Bronx street and opened fire. Eighty bullets riddled his body. As he lay dead a police officer stood over him and shot him again in the head. The police rallied in front of the Forty-fourth Precinct in celebration. Twymon Myers was a warrior we can all be proud of. SLAIN IN COMBAT November 14, 1973.

Alfred Butler. Known in struggle as Kombozi Amistad. Became a member of the BPP in his youth and functioned out of the New Rochelle, New York, office. Kombozi later transferred to the West Coast from whence he went underground to carry the struggle to the next level—the armed struggle—as a member of the BLA. It was in his capacity as a soldier in this formation that he was SLAIN IN COMBAT in Norfolk, Virginia, January 25, 1975.

Timothy Adams. Known to his comrades in arms, friends, and family as Red. Red was critically wounded in a battle with the enemy after attempting to liberate fellow comrades from the infamous Tombs in 1973. For many years he was confined to a wheelchair as a result of these wounds, but his spirit was undaunted. Even though his death came years after the battle, it was directly related. His life, his struggle to overcome, and his death were a source of inspiration to us all.

Melvin Kearney. Known in struggle as Rema Olugbala, he was a member of the BLA. Rema was killed in a courageous attempt to escape from the Brooklyn House of Detention, when the rope he was climbing down broke. He was twenty-two years old. Even against the overwhelming odds posed by the prison officials, Rema never lost his combative spirit. DIED IN COMBAT May 25, 1976.

TO MARTYR REMA OLUGBALA, BLA

I make love at a fraction of an inch
outside my window bars
I make love with freedom
And she invites me to be with her
and she's right outside my window bars
My love is great
I cherish her
and she's right outside my window bars
I dance with death
But my mind is set . . .
FREEDOM!
We're going to get it on a fraction of an inch
outside my window bars
I love you, freedom
I dance with death.

John Clark. Andaliwa was a thirty-year-old Black revolutionary who gave his life in an attempt to escape to freedom. He died in a shoot-out between prisoners and guards inside Trenton state prison in New Jersey. In that shoot-out, three guards were injured. John carried on the struggle behind the walls. SLAIN IN COMBAT January 19, 1976.

Mtayari Shabaka Sundiata (Samuel Smith). Became a citizen of record in the Republic of New Afrika in 1968. Mtayari worked among the youth in the Ocean Hill–Brownsville section of Brooklyn. In 1970 he was incarcerated as the result of a shoot-out with the police. Upon his release, he joined the ranks of the BLA. It was in this capacity of a people's warrior that he was SLAIN IN COMBAT October 23, 1981.

To those of us who have dedicated our lives to the liberation of Black people, who have dared to say, "We shall have our freedom or the Earth will be leveled by our attempts to gain it," death is a common occurrence. It is something we had to accept, for we knew that in waging struggle to free ourselves from the chains of slavery our choices were small—either to be jailed or assassinated—but we had nothing to lose and everything to gain.

We know that where there is struggle there's sacrifice. The death of our comrades was a sacrifice, for in our struggle some deaths are lighter than a feather and others are as weighty as a mountain. Every one of these deaths is weighty as mountains, for these comrades not only practiced the principles of revolutionary warfare, they taught others to do the same. In their lives and in their deaths they said:

> I may—if you wish—lose my livelihood
> I may sell my shirt and bed,
> I may work as a stone cutter,
> A street sweeper, a porter.
> I may clean your stores
> Or rummage your garbage for food.
> I may lay down hungry,
> O enemy of the sun,
> But
> I shall not compromise
> And to the last pulse in my veins
> I shall resist.
> You may take the last strip of my land,
> Feed my youth to prison cells.
> You may plunder my heritage.
> You may burn my books, my poems,

Or feed my flesh to the dogs.
You may spread a web of terror
On the roofs of my village,
O enemy of the sun,
But
I shall not compromise
And to the last pulse in my veins
I shall resist.
You may put out the light in my eyes.
You may deprive me of my mother's kisses.
You may curse my father, my people.
You may distort my history,
You may deprive my children of a smile
And of life's necessities.
You may fool my friends with a borrowed face.
You may build walls of hatred around me.
You may glue my eyes to humiliations,
O enemy of the sun,
But
I shall not compromise
And to the last pulse in my veins
I shall resist.
O enemy of the sun
The decorations are raised at the port.
The ejaculations fill the air,
A glow in the hearts,
And in the horizon
A sail is seen
Challenging the wind
And the depths.
It is Field Marshall Dedan Kamathi (Mau Mau)
Returning home

From the sea of loss.
It is the return of the sun,
Of my exiled ones,
And for her sake and his,
I swear
I shall not compromise
And to the last pulse in my veins
I shall resist,
Resist—and resist.[4]

Notes

1. According to the article "Fallen Comrades," mentioned above, Morris was also the brother of Alprentice "Bunchy" Carter and "was shot and killed by agents of the US government."
2. US (United Slaves) was a Black cultural nationalist organization founded in 1965. The FBI preyed on divisions between cultural and political groups within the nationalist movement. See chapter 8, "We Too Are Veterans," note 1, p. 86.
3. These lines are based closely on the poem "Enemy of the Sun," by Palestinian poet Samih al-Qasim.

14. CBS Tries the New York Three

In 1979, Robert Tanenbaum, the district attorney who prosecuted the New York Three, published *Badge of the Assassin*.[1] The book purported to tell the story of the case, but instead presented a sensationalized, fabricated version, smearing the Black Panther Party. Tanenbaum later acted as a producer of the made-for-TV movie based on the book.

The TV movie aired during a period when the New York mainstream media were engaged in a campaign to rehabilitate the image of the New York Police Department following waves of protest at police killings of unarmed Black and Latino people. At least one TV station ran regular segments during the eleven o'clock news, showing viewers how tough the job of the police was. One segment, for example, showed a reporter performing some of the exercises involved in police training. Followed by a camera, the reporter patrolled a dark alley or basement corridor. Suddenly a figure would jump out at him from a corner, and the reporter had to make a split-second decision whether to shoot or hold fire. Then the lights would come up on the cardboard figure, revealing either a thug brandishing a pistol and about to shoot, a teenager holding a radio, or a mother carrying a tiny infant. A supervising officer would then inform the reporter either that he had just killed an innocent civilian or that he himself was now dead. The message to the viewers was that the job of the police is so difficult that cops should be forgiven for killing innocent civilians from time to time— and that such killings are purely accidental.

In *CBS Tries the New York Three*, a video produced in 1988 by Paper Tiger TV, Safiya (she was shown as Safiya Bukhari-Alston in the credits), Brian Glick, and the New

York Three—Herman Bell, Jalil Muntaqim, and Albert Nuh Washington—respond to *Badge of the Assassin*. Glick, a Boston-based lawyer and human rights activist, joined Safiya, along with Herman, Jalil, and Nuh (in video clips shot in the various prisons where they were then being held), to discuss the purpose of *Badge of the Assassin* and the truth about the case and the Black Panther Party. This is an excerpted transcript of *CBS Tries the New York Three*. The video intersperses photomontages, music, and clips from the CBS movie between the segments of talk.

SAFIYA [*voiceover*]: What you're seeing is CBS TV's dramatization of state prosecutor Robert Tanenbaum's book about the killing of two police officers on May 21, 1971, in New York. Herman Bell, Anthony Bottom, and Albert Washington, three activists from the Black Panther Party now serving twenty-five years to life, are portrayed as the murderers. This CBS docudrama, which was first aired in 1985 and continues to run on national television today, is a carefully crafted lie. The truth is that the New York Three were wrongly convicted in a retrial and that government agencies are the real criminals.

BRIAN GLICK: The three were convicted in 1976 in a trial that was rigged from the start. To begin with Albert Washington: There was no evidence of any kind against him. Contrary to what you saw in *Badge of the Assassin*, even the prosecution admitted there was no evidence to show that Washington was at the scene of the crime. The only reason he was convicted was that the judge manipulated the jury by telling them that the evidence that was put in against Bottom and Bell actually applied to Washington—and that evidence was no good, as it turned out.

HERMAN BELL [*videotaped in Shawangunk Correctional Facility*]: As a child I watched people working in the fields picking cotton, plowing with mules, that sort of thing, and then from time to time they would get hold of me and make me do a little work. Maybe I'd pull a few bales of cotton, do some stacking. I watched the people working that way under the hot sun.

ANTHONY JALIL BOTTOM [*videotaped at Wallkill Correctional Facility*]: I was raised in New York, in a middle-class, a working family. When I was growing up I was never really in need of anything. My mother and my stepfather provided for me and my sisters and brother. But of course I was part of the times. I was involved in the sixties movements. I was a member of the Black Student Union—I was one of the leaders of the Black Student Union in junior high school and high school. So the conditions of the times—what was going on in the streets—affected me.

SAFIYA BUKHARI-ALSTON [*identified on screen as "community organizer"*]: In *Badge of the Assassin*, Tanenbaum portrayed these three individuals as raving, maniacal thugs who were not about liberating Black people, who were not about anything but taking human lives.

HERMAN: Malcolm X was on Susskind's show,[2] and I was sitting in the living room watching the TV, and the interview came on, and Susskind was condemning the African people for committing atrocities against the white missionaries. He painted this in such a light as to make the Africans completely guilty and responsible—in other words, they were doing things senselessly—and Malcolm corrected him in terms of focusing on the history, the context of it. Without Malcolm's historical explanation, I would have had to accept everything Susskind had said.

JALIL: I had no major dream for myself other than being a part of the movement, being part of the struggle. And it seemed as if every time I backed away, I would meet an old friend who was now involved in the Black Panther Party, and that would influence me to get involved with the Party. There was no way for me to get around it. From high school, I was involved.

SAFIYA: One of the things that was really, really important to us as members of the Black Panther Party was that we understood that our role was to defend the Black community—to bring about changes, to stand up for the first time and finally, after four hundred years of oppression, to say that we are tired, we are people, and we wanted to be treated as such.

[*A voiceover summarizes the Black Panther Party Ten-Point Program: "We want land, we want bread, we want housing, we want clothing, we want education, we want justice, we want peace, and we want a Black plebiscite in the UN where the Black colonial subjects will participate in analyzing and projecting politically upon the racist atrocities that have been committed to the Black people of this nation."*]

SAFIYA: And the Black Panther paper was circulated to 100,000 and 150,000 within this community. Nationwide it was sold weekly in the community, and the Ten-Point Program and Platform of Twenty-Six Rules were in every edition of the Black Panther newspaper.

We had a position on drugs that was so strong that it was understood that no Party member could use narcotics; no Party member could be under the influence of narcotics if we wanted to do Party work; and if a Party member was caught shooting up they were automatically expelled from the Party, no matter what position they held, no matter how well known they were in the community, or anything else. No one was above this rule.

The teenagers, the youth, in their after-school hours they worked in the community, they worked with the welfare mothers, they worked with the children, they worked in the liberation schools. They weren't out in the community assaulting the old people and stealing pocketbooks. Because that was understood, that no Party member could steal anything from the masses, no Party member could lie or cheat or assault the masses. So on a very real level, the statistics of crime in the Black community when the Black Panther Party was in operation, was in existence, in the community at large, in general, were very low. Whereas today, you can't walk the streets at night, you are scared to walk the streets in your own community.

And this is what the government saw as a threat, because we wanted control of our community, and we had that kind of control in our community. When Jalil says he was a product of his time, he was a product of what was happening, he's talking about the fact that what was cool was to be a member of the Black Panther Party. If he was going to be involved and have pride in his community, he had no choice but to be active in the Black Panther Party. That was where it was at in those times. Today, where it's at is being in the streets.

JALIL: The Black Panther Party in my opinion was the most profound Black experience in this country, other than three individuals—Marcus Garvey, Malcolm X, and Martin Luther King. After them comes the Black Panther Party. And what we represented in the community was a sense of dignity, a sense of strength.

HERMAN: The Breakfast for Children Program really was fascinating to me because I felt good that I could participate in a program that was able to fulfill some of the community's vital needs. We would go to the various houses to pick up the youngsters before they would go to school. Once they got involved in the program and had been participating for a while, if we showed up ten or fifteen minutes late they would say in a huff, "What took you so long? Why weren't you here?"

ALBERT NUH WASHINGTON [*videotaped in Wende prison*]: The parents used to come down and help. It was ironic, because a lot of times they would come down and help basically because they also wanted something to eat. We used to get donations of food from merchants in the community. Actually, we never really reached our full potential.

BRIAN GLICK: The potential of the Black Panther Party was never realized largely because of secret FBI and police attacks on the Party, part of a secret program that they called COINTEL-PRO, for "counterintelligence program." It was only after the movements of the sixties had essentially been defeated that we learned that they'd been victimized by CIA-style covert operations. The kind of things we know the CIA has done in Nicaragua, Chile, and all around the world were actually done in this country, at home, by the FBI and police against all the movements of the sixties. Secret FBI documents that were later found directed FBI agents across the country to "disrupt, misdirect, discredit or otherwise neutralize"[3]—neutralize in the Mafia sense—the entire Black movement, from Martin Luther King straight through to the Black Panther Party. FBI agents were ordered to do everything they could to cripple and destroy the Party starting in 1968. One FBI document argued that "the Negro youth and moderate"—this is another quote—"must be made to understand that if they succumb to revolutionary teaching they will be dead revolutionaries." Following this document the FBI incited Black street gangs into violent attacks on the Black Panther Party, and they themselves, the FBI and the police, raided Panther offices across the country, smashed up the equipment, tore up the files, broke the windows, dragged Panthers out into the streets naked, beat people up, threw them in jail. And in some cases they actually killed Panther leaders, particularly Fred Hampton, a very important Panther leader in Chicago. The FBI and police organized essentially a death squad execution, breaking into his apartment in the middle of the night and gunning him down.[4]

Now this did two things. On the one hand, it very much weakened the Party internally. On the other, it built very broad public support, because people were outraged. And then, to exploit the weaknesses and to undermine the support, the FBI and the police stepped up psychological warfare against the Party. They used infiltrators and forged documents and made anonymous threats to disrupt the Party's work and split the Party apart.

They worked to discredit the Party—this was a very central thing—and demoralize it, to alienate its supporters. They used stories that their collaborators in the TV and newspapers planted for them. They spread false rumors; they forged whole publications. The whole country was filled with leaflets that said they were from the Black Panther Party that had been written and distributed by the FBI. People in the community were told that the food in the Breakfast Program that we've heard about was poisoned, and churches and merchants who cooperated with the program were harassed and intimidated by the FBI. In one case there was a coloring book that had been proposed for use in the Breakfast Program that the Panthers had rejected, saying this is racist, this is violent, this is not what we want, and the FBI gets hold of it, the FBI makes it more racist, more violent, and puts it out all across the country and tells people, "This is what the Panther Breakfast Program is."[5]

Now a key part of all this, of the COINTELRPO plan, was getting people arrested, prosecuted, and jailed on false charges. There was an FBI document that said that Panthers should be arrested on every possible charge and held without bail so that they would be in jail all through the summer and all through the year. There was another document that instructed that since the purpose of COINTELPRO is to disrupt the Panthers, "it is immaterial whether the facts exist to substantiate the charge."[6]

These false charges were used to keep important Party activists out of the Party and out of the community and to divert resources and energy into defending them. Millions of dollars [had to be] spent on bail. But most important about all of these charges was the way the government and the media worked together to criminalize the Black Panther Party, to fool the people of this country into believing that the Panthers actually were criminals and thugs. This is the role of *Badge of the Assassin*. And it is in this context of the FBI and the police and the media working together to criminalize the Party that we can understand the case of the New York Three and this false, lying, distorted CBS and prosecution so-called docudrama.

JALIL: Through the course of the trial, the attorneys made motions to bring up the issues of COINTELPRO and the judge denied it. He said in effect that we did not have any proof that we were victims of COINTELPRO. The truth of the matter is that we did not have the proof—the DA had all the proof.

GLICK: Some of the main witnesses in the case were FBI agents. The FBI paraded in there as paragons of integrity, the untouchables, and the prosecution got the judge to prohibit the defense from saying anything to the jurors about COINTELPRO. These agents were under orders to lie to convict Black Panthers. And most important of all, it turns out that the main witnesses against the New York Three were secretly bribed by the police and the FBI, intimidated and threatened.

One crucial witness, a former coworker of the New York Three named Ruben Scott, was tortured.[7] They shoved an electrified cattle prod repeatedly into his testicles as they interrogated him about the New York Three. Then, when he was brought up here to testify, this witness asked for a private confidential meeting with the judge. He went in there and he said to the judge, "The testimony that they're having me give isn't true, isn't what happened. I'm about to lie because I'm scared." And what did the judge do? The judge called the prosecutor to warn him about what Scott had said and turned him back to police custody without giving him any protection, without notifying the defense, turned him back to police custody and let them work him over for five weeks until they got him into line to give the testimony that they wanted him to give. Now since that time, Ruben Scott has finally served his time in jail, he's come out, and he's signed one affidavit after another saying very clearly, "This crucial testimony was false."

Any one of these issues I've discussed would be enough, in an ordinary case, to reopen a conviction and get a new trial. All of these issues and other ones besides were raised in legal papers that we filed in a New York State court where the New York Three had originally been convicted. It was brought before the very same judge that we've been talking about. That judge threw out all of our claims, saying we didn't need a hearing on any of our claims because he, the judge, was there and he knows what really happened.

The New York appeals court refused to even listen to the case and we're now bringing it into federal court.[8]

We think this case is important not just because of its history, but because the kind of attacks made under COINTEL-PRO didn't stop in the 1960s. They continued all through the seventies and eighties. They have been used against all the movements in this country, and especially against those working against US intervention in Central America, where former agents have admitted they infiltrated for the FBI into CISPES—the Committee in Solidarity with the People of El Salvador—and tried to seduce an activist nun to get black-mail photos for the FBI, and put out phony publications, and exchanged information with the death squads in El Salvador. In order to combat that today, we need to keep on exposing what the government does. And a case like the New York Three is one part of that fight to expose the truth of what the government does. It's also a part of a struggle to reclaim the true history of the 1960s. The government and the media have conned us into blaming the victims for what was done to them under COINTELPRO. It's left us with a legacy of cynicism and despair. In order to move forward into the 1990s what we need to do is turn this around and make clear what really happened in the sixties.

SAFIYA: These brothers—and countless others who are in prison and have been in prison since the sixties and throughout the sixties until today—have sacrificed upward of seventeen years of their lives in the struggle for the liberation of Black people.[9] They've been away from their families, they've been away from their children. The children have grown up and the prisoners have become grandparents. Their sacrifice is for the progress that has been made in the Black community and among oppressed people. And the community has moved forward. The community has moved forward and these brothers have remained behind bars. It's important that we, in some measure, show our support for the sacrifice they've made by getting involved in the effort to free these brothers and to see that justice is done.

HERMAN: If we don't get support from people in the streets then I will be fifty-five or fifty-six years old before I get to go to the parole board and I'll just be in here, rotting away in here, as will my two codefendants Jalil and Nuh.[10]

JALIL: I believe in the power of the people. With that power we can be out of prison in eighteen months.

NUH: Contrary to what's shown in *Badge of the Assassin*, I'm not one who takes pleasure in the suffering of another human being. First of all for religious reasons, because I'm a Muslim. In the Koran we're taught not to defile our enemies. This is a thing that the movie doesn't go into, but then I guess it wasn't a movie about me.

Notes

1. Robert Tanenbaum and Philip Rosenberg, *Badge of the Assassin* (New York: Henry Robbins, 1979).
2. Susskind's show was *Open End*, later titled *The David Susskind Show*, and was a debate and discussion program that ran on WNEW-TV from 1958 to 1987. Malcolm X appeared on the show in 1962 and again on February 2, 1965—just weeks before his assassination.
3. These are actual quotes from FBI documents.
4. These facts have been fully documented in litigation awarding damages to the survivors and to the Hampton family. See Jeffrey Haas, *The Assassination of Fred Hampton: How the FBI and the Chicago Police Murdered a Black Panther* (Chicago: Lawrence Hill Books, 2009).
5. Documentation for this and the other facts Glick lists can be found in, among other places, his book, *War at Home: Covert Action Against US Activists and What We Can Do About It* (Boston: South End Press, 1989).

6. For this quote, from a September 16, 1970, FBI memo from FBI director J. Edgar Hoover, see Ward Churchill and Jim Vander Wall, *The COINTELPRO Papers: Documents from the FBI's Secret Wars Against Dissent in the United States* (Boston: South End Press, 2002), 148.

7. In 1973, Ruben Scott was tortured by police in New Orleans for several days in the presence of New York City detectives. In radio and TV interviews, as well as in the affidavits Glick mentions, Scott describes the torture and his subsequent repudiation of his confession and testimony. These facts were confirmed as legal findings in court proceedings in 1975. Scott's perjured testimony formed the basis of a 2003 California prosecution of the "Panther 8," also known as the "San Francisco 8."

8. For the outcome of this appeal, see chapter 18, "Safiya Interviews Albert Nuh Washington," p. 196.

9. Today, Herman and Jalil have spent thirty-seven and thirty-nine years in prison, respectively. Nuh Washington died in prison in 2000.

10. Herman Bell is now sixty-two years old.

15. Talking About Assata Shakur

In 1983, activist and journalist Sally O'Brien began hosting a weekly talk show called *Where We Live* on New York City's WBAI radio. The show frequently reported on political prisoners. Soon after Safiya's release from prison in 1983 she appeared on *Where We Live* several times to talk about the case of the New York Three—Albert Nuh Washington, Herman Bell, and Jalil Muntaqim.[1] Within the next few years, Sally recalls, she asked Safiya to co-host the show. Safiya agreed and continued co-hosting the show until her death. The show still airs every Thursday night at eight on WBAI/FM, New York.

The following is a partial transcript of a *Where We Live* interview Safiya did sometime in the mid- to late 1990s with Mark Holder, her comrade from the Black Panther Party who had served time in prison for a 1972 conviction (later overturned). He and Safiya had worked together in the Harlem office of the Party.

In order to encourage people to support political prisoners, Safiya often tried to make the personalities of the prisoners come alive for audiences. She sought to dispel the corrosive myths spread by police and mainstream media— myths intended to dehumanize the prisoners and portray them as dangerous criminals. In this interview, Safiya and Mark Holder work together to bring Assata Shakur into relief for the audience. Assata (Joanne Chesimard) had escaped from prison in 1979 and by 1986 she was known to be living in exile in Cuba. Throughout these years Assata was being hunted and vilified by the US government (this continues today). In the course of the interview, especially when they interrupt one another, both Safiya and Mark Holder laugh frequently, adding warmth to the reminiscences.

SAFIYA: I'm Safiya Bukhari and I'm here with Mark Holder. In 1970 Mark Holder was fifteen years old. He was my subsection leader in the Harlem office of the Black Panther Party. We're here to talk about our first encounter, our first meeting with Assata Shakur, then known as Joanne Chesimard. It's the winter of 1970. Tell us who you are and what you're doing.

MARK HOLDER: I'm a subsection leader in the Harlem branch of the Black Panther Party. What I was doing is providing leadership for the field cadres who were assigned to fieldwork out of the Harlem office—community organizing. I was responsible for the general education and training of new cadres in terms of the basic principles and the Party's political positions—making sure they were acquainted with the basic tenets of our ideological positions.

SB: This is 1970, this was your first encounter, the time you first encountered Assata Shakur. Tell us about that first meeting.

MH: The first time I met Assata Shakur was in the office on 2026 Seventh Avenue in Harlem. I remember being in the office one day and seeing that there was a new sister who was interested in joining the Party. At some point it was decided that she would go out into the field to do some door-to-door leafleting and organizing in that particular section. And I was assigned to take her to the field and show her the ropes, so to speak.

SB: Tell us about that experience.

MH: What first struck me when I met Assata was that she was a very attractive young college student, and I think I succumbed to some of the stereotypes or some remnants of sexist attitudes in men's attitudes and viewing of sisters because I remember thinking, This is a young sister who looked to be maybe . . .[2]

SB: Fragile?

MH: Yes, fragile, feminine, so to speak, someone who would need not only my guidance but maybe my protection. And I was in for quite a surprise, actually.

I remember we went to the East Harlem area of the community to do door-to-door street canvassing, giving out leaflets and talking to people about the Party, inviting them to our PE [political education] classes. Along the way I remember every time we passed an area that may have been congregated by street people, I felt a need to shelter and protect Assata from certain influences or dangers that I imagined she might have been intimidated by. I quickly found out that my attitude was not only incorrect but very unfounded, because everywhere we stopped, as soon as we came on the scene, the people weren't even interested in me anymore, and the sister was holding court. Everywhere she went she immediately gained an audience and was able to engage the people in a very earthy, grassroots basic level. She was able to talk to the elderly people of the community; she was able to talk to the young folks; she was able to talk to the hustlers, and the street people, regardless of what scenario, what grouping of people we came upon, she was able to engage them from a point where they were comfortable listening to her. She was very articulate, she was very convincing, and I quickly realized that this was not, as I may have initially thought, a timid, inexperienced woman who needed my protection and guidance. This was a very sophisticated, accomplished, confident woman who was able to deal with the people from a point of compassion, and to be very convincing.

Assata was the kind of person that, without a lot of direction and counseling, you could assign her a task, and she had the initiative and creativity to go out and accomplish the goal.

SB: What was she assigned to do?

MH: She was a college student at the time, and she was assigned to be the coordinator from the Harlem chapter with the Black student movements, to be the liaison between the Black Panther Party and the various student groups that were operating in the New York City area. I did some work with her because at the time I was a high school student myself, and the high school movement and the college movement were very closely connected. I remember attending a few meetings and organizing sessions for some political initiatives that we were involved in. I remember a couple at Borough of Manhattan Community College. I remember through her, meeting people like Yoruba Pablo Guzmán, who was the student coordinator from the Young Lords Party, and other student leaders from the various colleges and campuses. Assata always seemed to be articulate and able to express herself, very studied in terms of the history—African and African American history. She had obviously studied political ideology before she had joined the Party. Most of the people who had joined the Party pretty much got their political education in the Party through our political education programs and classes. But she came to the Party with a certain sophistication and knowledge of revolutionary ideology, political history, the history of the world's struggles. So she was able to fit right in more actively in the various programs, including the student movement. She always seemed to be someone that people respected. She always seemed able to quickly and accurately analyze a situation and offer very concrete and commonsense solutions or ideas to carry out ideology. And that was key. She wasn't an intellectual in the sense of one who just spouted ideological phrases. She was a practitioner. Assata was the type of person who was able to interpret the ideology into concrete programs and steps and actions that could be taken to motivate and organize people. That's what I remember.

SB: For our listening audience, just to clarify: We're talking about 1970 when Assata was in the Party, so we're talking in the past tense. In future discussion we are going to bring this up to the present. But I just want to make sure everyone understands that we're not talking as if she isn't with us anymore. I want to make sure that if you even think that we're thinking in those terms, I want to disabuse you of that idea. We're not.

You talked about Assata as the political woman. Talk about Assata the person.

MH: Assata is a very lively, outgoing, passionate person. There's nothing meek or timid about her. At the same time, she puts people at ease. She deals with people from compassion. She is able to deal with people in a way that is uplifting. Assata's the type of person you would say is the life of the party. One thing I remember is that she liked music. I liked being around Assata because she always had good music. We used to play tapes back in those days . . .

SB: The eight-tracks?

MH: No, this was after the eight-tracks, this was cassette tapes and vinyl records. She introduced me to jazz and a lot of other music. And the old classics of R&B like Nat King Cole.

SB: That's not R&B!

MH: OK, blues. She had very good taste in music. And she was the type of person who liked to laugh, liked to smile, have a good time. During these times, for those who may not know, the Black Panther Party and the Black community were under serious repressive conditions and it was very easy to become embittered, or to become paranoid. A lot of people basically walked through life very rigid, very stiff, very cautious, very uptight. Assata was never like that. Assata was always very upbeat, smiling, very encouraging, no matter what the conditions were. I can't ever remember Assata being depressed or defeated by anything physical, like bad weather. I remember one incident when we were doing some community work in the Bronx and it was a chilly, rainy day. All day long I wasn't doing anything but whining about how cold it was, how wet it was, and she just seemed to ignore it. Not only did she just seem to ignore it and encourage me to continue to do the work . . .

SB: She didn't just say, "I encourage you to continue to do the work." I know she told you in no uncertain terms to get on with it, didn't she?

MH: Yes, but her manner wasn't brash or harsh. She just carried herself with a certain sense of enthusiasm and passion about what she believed in that I would say was infectious—it enabled you to embrace that type of feeling and respond accordingly, as opposed to being commanding or dictatorial or robotic. It was nothing like that. She would make a joke and smile and do a dance in the rain talking about how fun it was. That was her way of getting things done in the face of adversity.

SB: At some point she became the person in charge of the medical cadres.

MH: She did become the medical cadre, and her responsibility was threefold. One was to monitor and institute basic standards of health for the members of the Party, the cadres, and to monitor their health, because at the time, being in the Black Panther Party was not an easy job. There was very little sleep. Sometimes you worked twenty-hour days, no matter how cold, wet, or hot it was. To say the least, the living conditions were not exactly extravagant. So there were a lot of problems of fatigue.

SB: Malnourishment, a lot of colds.

MH: Yes. Bronchitis, some people with asthma, sleep deprivation...

SB: Miscarriages.

MH: A lot of the women were suffering miscarriages because there was just a basic lack of care and attention paid to certain basic medical needs. At the time we felt that the only thing that was important was revolution. We used to have a saying—do you remember it?—that a revolutionary is like an ox to be . . .

SB: . . . driven by the people.

MH: And we literally . . .

SB: . . . drove them to death . . .

MH: . . . drove ourselves to breaking points. So at some point it was realized that this was counterproductive, unhealthy, and destructive to the Party and to the individuals themselves, so they tried to correct this problem by starting a health program, of which Assata was coordinator, to monitor and try to take care of the health needs of the office. One included monitoring people's sleep, how much sleep you had, making recommendations that a person should be given lighter duties when they got to the point of fatigue. We were encouraged to take vitamins. A serious effort was made to prepare nutritious meals on a collective basis and to have people come into the office together in the evening to have a good meal.

Assata was also concerned with community health programs. That was another aspect of the Party's programs of creating socialist institutions in the community, like our free medical clinics. We had one in Brooklyn on Sutter Avenue; we were working on one on Claremont Parkway in the

Bronx. She worked with the people who were creating those programs.

She was also very close to some of the people that were involved with the Lincoln detox program in the Bronx.[3] I met a lot of those people, like Mutulu Shakur,[4] through her. She was instrumental in recruiting the participation and assistance of the visiting nurse services of Harlem who started a program—they were involved in community health and safety concerns through the Red Cross and I think some church groups and I remember she organized an initiative through which they came to our office and trained the cadres in first aid and CPR. The environment of the times was very antagonistic with the state forces and physical confrontations becoming more and more a reality, so we thought it was relevant for people to be trained in first aid and CPR for lifesaving purposes.

SB: This was about the mid- to late sixties to mid-seventies?

MH: Late sixties going into seventy-one.

SB: Can we back up a minute, because we talked about Zayd Shakur and you were there when Zayd was there, and he was killed on the New Jersey Turnpike in the shoot-out that resulted in Sundiata Acoli's incarceration and Assata's incarceration and her subsequently being in exile in Cuba. Assata was very close with Zayd. Can you tell us a little bit about Zayd? Make him real for us for a minute here.

MH: Zayd was my political mentor.

SB: And he was short like you, too.

MH: Yeah, we got along just fine. Zayd was . . .

SB: "El Mosquito."

MH: Yes, that was him; that was his nickname. Zayd was another one who was very upbeat, very encouraging. I would describe Zayd as a schoolmaster, someone who would be the principal of a school. He was a teacher. He befriended you and educated you. Zayd, in my opinion, had the most sophisticated, developed political understanding and knowledge of the people I encountered in the Party. In fact Zayd was the one who usually led at least the leadership political education classes and program because he had a very sophisticated . . .

SB: . . . [He was] deputy minister of information.

MH: Yeah, that was his title. And it was no mistake. Zayd took me under his wing. I was fifteen at the time. For days on end he would keep me with him. I guess what he was trying to do was make sure that I, a young person who was looked at by leadership, I guess, as having some leadership potential, got some . . .

SB: Got it right.

MH: Yeah.

SB: Got it right. I think that's it. So it was not by just any coincidence or chance that it was Zayd who brought Assata and turned her over to you.

MH: Things didn't happen by accident in the Party. There were people in the Party who had a sophisticated understanding and grasp of revolutionary ideology and principles, and who attempted to put those principles in practice in the method by which they carried out the programs and policies of the Party and the way they educated and carried new people through the process of revolutionary education. And Zayd is definitely one that comes to mind who was able to do that and did that very effectively. And I would say we were blessed to have had the tutelage of people like Zayd.

SB: I really wanted for people to get a glimpse into Zayd because later on when we talk about what happened on the turnpike and how Zayd, in Assata's own words, attempted to protect them and in essence gave his own life to protect them . . .

MH: The picture, the image you have of Zayd—first you have to understand, Zayd was maybe all of 5'5" ...

SB: And skinny.

MH: Maybe 120 pounds? Very articulate. He was the epitome of the college professor, the schoolmaster; Zayd was never one who spoke harshly or had an aggressively antagonistic attitude about anything.

SB: When he got excited his voice got higher.

MH: Squeaky. But myself, and I'm sure everyone else who knew Zayd, had the same reaction when that incident came over the media. I was incarcerated at the time, it happened ...

SB: ... May 3, 1973 ...

MH: ... about six months after I was arrested. I was lying in my cell in whatever jail I was in and they used to pipe the radio in over the PA system. And the news flash came over. The initial shock and horror of it was ... being a Panther, after a while you were accustomed to certain things. The contradictions between the Party and the state had a long time before that become very antagonistic—repeated shoot-outs, frame-ups, murders of Panthers. So at a certain point you were pretty much acclimated or conditioned to expecting these things. After all, we had already seen the murder of Fred Hampton and massive shoot-ins at offices from New Orleans to LA to Philadelphia. All these things had already happened, so the state trying to murder a Panther was no great surprise to anybody at this point. But to hear that Zayd of all people was involved in what they called a gun battle—I just couldn't believe it. First of all I couldn't imagine Zayd in a situation ...

SB: ... where a gun battle would erupt.

MH: Where a gun battle would erupt. The Black Panther Party was a political organization, a revolutionary organization.

The Black Panther Party believed in armed self-defense and the Black Panther Party was an armed organization. Certain members of the Party were trained in arms to protect the Party and its programs. But Zayd was not . . .

sb: He was deputy minister of information! . . . [*both laughing*]

mh: . . . a person you ever saw or would associate with that aspect, the defensive aspect, of the Party. Zayd was the quintessential educator, *the* intellectual of the Party. So to hear that he was involved in some kind of armed conflict, I just knew—and others thought this too—that it had to have been just an out-and-out hit, like a death squad type of action. That was our initial impression.

sb: Now we go back again. We've come up to the end of seventy, beginning of seventy-one. I remember all the news clippings saying Assata was seen everywhere and doing everything, and every time there was a woman—or someone they thought was a woman—involved in anything they thought it was Assata. Do you know at what point she made the decision that she wanted to function underground, or that she was forced underground?

mh: Most people were forced into the underground. Very few, none that I can recall, made a conscious decision that they were going to choose a life of being a fugitive, being on the run, being underground. Usually that was the result of some initiative by the state—either an indictment on some kind of trumped-up conspiracy, or grand jury; sometimes it was the result of aggressive surveillance and harassment of people's families; various reasons forced people to make the decision that they didn't feel that they could continue to function politically in an aboveground manner because they had become a target of the state, the police, and that their effectiveness was pretty much neutralized out in the open.

And many people feared, rightfully, that their lives were at stake—that the state was willing, and was in the process of organizing and planning, peoples' assassinations.

SB: There is one more thing. Let me just bring this in for you. You also remember that the split [in the Party] was going on at the same time that the state repression was going on. We don't want to leave out that part.

MH: Yes, there was a twofold repressive circumstance that forced people to take certain precautionary defensive measures to carry out their political work in a clandestine fashion. The antagonism between the so-called West and East Coast factions of the Black Panther Party had become outright militaristic so there were certain dangers all around—particularly for those people in leadership positions. Specifically in the case of Assata—Assata was very close to Zayd and to some of the codefendants in the Panther 21 trial. Right after the split in the Party for various reasons, some of the Panther 21 made a decision that they were not going to continue going to court and run the risk of being railroaded. There were signs and signals that the state was preparing to plan certain preemptive actions against them—assassinations—and there were death threats being waged and launched against these people. A tactical decision was made that these people would go underground. So what that meant was jumping bail and not going to court again.

At this time the Panther Party was very thoroughly infiltrated by agents of the Special Services, BOSS, in New York, and by the FBI, so they had a certain degree of intelligence as to who was close associates, who frequented certain locations.[5] By this time it was pretty well known that Assata traveled in circles with [the people who went underground]. So after they failed to show up to court one morning, here comes the fugitive squad with the search warrants, and of course Assata had an apartment at this time on 131st Street . . .

SB: No, it was further up . . .

MH: Yeah, 138th Street and Amsterdam Avenue—it was right on the corner there, right across from City College—and that was one of the first apartments that was raided in the days right after they failed to show up in court. Threats were made by the NYPD (New York Police Department) that these people would not be taken alive. So after this point, heavy surveillance and harassment were leveled against her family—her mother, ex-husband, her aunt, close friends— they were put under surveillance, harassed, told that all kinds of bad things would happen to her. This created a climate of fear. I'm sure that led to her decision that her effectiveness as an aboveground political organizer had been neutralized and that to continue to try to do work as an organizer would play right into their hands—that they would set her up, possibly murder her. So I'm sure that helped lead to her decision to go underground so that she could continue to do revolutionary work in another fashion.

SB: Now we're in the thick of it. Let's get to 1971. Assata's been forced underground. The Panther 21 trial is coming to a head. Dhoruba Bin-Wahad and Michael Cetewayo Tabor have jumped bail; Afeni Shakur is back in prison along with Joan Bird, and Afeni's pregnant with Tupac. We're setting the stage for a climate of terror. Just from the headlines, in May 1971 the Panther 21 were acquitted, by this time you also had [several killings of police officers,] and why? People would ask, Why? Well, [to begin to answer that], we've also had all these incidents in the community, where the unarmed youth in the community—Ricky Boden, Clifford Glover, Rita Hay-worth—have been killed by police [*MH adds some of these names*]—the community's under siege; the Party's under siege; there's a split going on; there's the Bureau of Special Services, the Joint Terrorist Task Force—there's a whole hysteria. They have COINTELPRO going on . . .

MH: Yes, this marked the massive program nationally of the militarization of local police forces, the forming of paramilitary SWAT special weapons units, the integration of the intelligence sections of the FBI and the local police, closely coordinated with the paramilitary rapid-response teams that they used first against the Party and other political entities and then eventually against the communities themselves in order to suppress and pacify and intimidate anybody from even thinking about not just rebelling but even protesting.

SB: At this point, you had been forced underground, Assata had been forced underground, and all this stuff is going on. Did you have any contact with her in those days? I just want to know attitudes—if there were any personality changes occurring.

MH: I was in very close contact with Assata when we were underground. Assata remained the sweet, compassionate, outgoing, lively, life-of-the-party-type person who was always encouraging, always thoughtful, always thinking, always providing solutions to problems no matter how acute the dangers of the rigors of the circumstance were. Assata was always able to come up with a common sense solution that tended to minimize risk and maximize gain. That was the strength of Assata. I remember during this period of course we were underground and so the need to acquire certain self-defense skills became more and more acute. I remember a couple of incidents where I was assigned responsibility of giving her certain physical self-defense training, because I had the background in martial arts, and I remember going to the park and going through basic self-defense techniques and then one time I said, let's see how this stuff works; let's spar—and she damn near kicked my butt. We were very close and her personality never changed. She remained—what I remember about Assata is her smile, her laugh—she was always full of jokes. We had a sister-brother type of relationship.

SB: Big sister–little brother.

MH: Yes, big sister–little brother. And she would always tease me like a big sister would and play jokes on me and laugh at my youth and my innocence. I learned a lot from Assata about life—about a young person growing up and assuming adult responsibilities at a very young age. She was very instrumental in that socialization process for me.

SB: I was initially given an assignment also to take her into the community. And what struck me is what Che means when he says, "A true revolutionary is motivated by great feelings of love," and I think when I think about how she deals, how love is her motivating factor, I'd apply that. If you're motivated by hate and revenge and guilt and any of those other things, it's a hardening thing, and it's temporary.

Mark, did you have anything—I want to thank you for this opportunity to talk about Assata—but do you have any personal message to add?

MH: I would just like to tell Assata, of course I know she knows this, I still love you and the people love you. Stay strong and keep smiling.

Notes

1. For information on the New York Three, see chapter 14, "CBS Tries the New York Three," p. 156.

2. Ellipses throughout this article represent moments when Safiya and Mark Holder talked in unison, or finished one another's sentences, together constructing events and memories.

3. This was an experimental and very effective program at Lincoln Hospital in the Bronx, New York, to use acupuncture instead of methadone to treat drug addiction. Along with the Black activists mentioned here, members of the Puerto Rican group the Young Lords were also involved with the detox project.

4. Mutula Shakur played a key energizing role in the Lincoln detox program and other community health initiatives. "Dr. Mutulu Shakur is a New Afrikan (Black) man whose primary work has been in the area of health. He is a doctor of acupuncture and was a co-founder and director of two institutions devoted to improving health care in the Black community. . . . In March 1982, Dr. Shakur and 10 others were indicted by a federal grand jury under a set of US conspiracy laws called 'Racketeer Influenced and Corrupt Organization' (RICO) laws. These conspiracy laws were ostensibly developed to aid the government in its prosecution of organized crime figures; however, they have been used with varying degrees of success against revolutionary organizations. Dr. Shakur was charged with conspiracy and participation in a clandestine paramilitary unit that carried out actual and attempted expropriations from several banks. Eight incidents were alleged to have occurred between December 1976 to October 1981. In addition he was charged with participation in the 1979 prison escape of Assata Shakur, who is now in exile in Cuba" (mutulushakur.com/about.html). Mutulu Shakur is currently incarcerated in the Federal Bureau of Prisons high security prison in Florence, Colorado. He is also the stepfather of the late Tupac Shakur.

5. See chapter 2, "Testimony: Experiences in the Black Panther Party," note 7, p. 32.

16. Free Mumia Abu-Jamal!

Mumia Abu-Jamal came to the attention of progressive people around the country between 1981, when he was convicted of killing Philadelphia police officer Daniel Faulkner, and the early 1990s. His case was (and remains) a dramatic example of government repression against those who speak out for justice. Mumia has also become widely—internationally—known for his commentaries on issues of social justice and for his books. His most recent book, a groundbreaking investigation of the phenomenon of jailhouse lawyering, was published in March 2009.[1]

Safiya knew Mumia in the early days of the Black Panther Party, when he came to New York from Philadelphia.[2] While she was in prison, Safiya learned of his case and corresponded with him.[3] She poured enormous energy and emotion into support for Mumia. Pam Africa, a leader of the International Concerned Family and Friends of Mumia Abu-Jamal, lights up when asked to talk about Safiya's work. "She radiated love," she says. "I often received late-night phone calls from Safiya, or made one to her, every time a political prisoner or one of the families needed anything." Pam Africa also remembers that Safiya attended to every person who tried in some way to participate in the support movement. "She took time to help and encourage each individual. Once, when a young brother wanted to perform a song for Mumia at an event, his nerve began failing him as he started to sing. Safiya quietly stepped up, put her arm around him and joined in the singing until he regained his composure and could carry on."

In 1992, Safiya co-founded the Free Mumia Abu-Jamal Coalition (New York City) with political activist and journalist

Sally O'Brien and, later, Suzanne Ross. As Safiya said at an event in New York in 1999, "I was working on the New York Three case—I was one of the few working on it—and I literally got a waiver from the New York Three to start working on Mumia's case before many people were doing work on it." Safiya's concern, as remembered by Suzanne, who is now director of the coalition, was to enable as broad a group of people as possible to become involved in the fight to save the life of Mumia Abu-Jamal. Suzanne remembers:

> Safiya felt that Mumia's case was particularly pressing, since he was on death row, and she cared deeply about him. She also felt that because of his international fame his case could be "used" to build a movement for all the political prisoners. She read every legal document we ever received about Mumia's case, and read it faster than anyone else did. She was on top of every development and had her own legal assessments of the attorneys' strategy and performance. Safiya was such a quick thinker and fighter that it was exciting to strategize with her. When we were trying to get the Justice Department to conduct a civil rights investigation of Mumia's case, we got a letter saying it was too late, that the statute of limitations had expired—except in cases where there was evidence of a conspiracy, they added parenthetically. [Safiya immediately] said, "So that's what we have to argue, that there was a conspiracy." And so we did, leading and waging an international campaign. Safiya collaborated with [attorney] Joan Gibbs on writing the legal arguments.

On June 1, 1995, Pennsylvania governor Tom Ridge signed a death warrant for Mumia, setting August 17 at ten p.m. for his execution. At the time, lawyers were preparing to file papers seeking a new trial for Mumia. On August 7, a stay of execution was issued by the district court. Rallies were held all over the country throughout the summer of 1995, first protesting the warrant and then marking the stay. On August 12, Safiya addressed such a rally in Philadelphia, joyful but arguing that people should not stop fighting for Mumia's freedom, and that a stay of execution was only a temporary reprieve. Here is the extemporaneous speech she delivered as the crowd repeatedly responded with roars of approval.

Free the land! Free Mumia! All power to the people! As salaam alaikum![4] Right on! And whatever else.

On Monday, when I heard about the stay of execution, I was in Cuba. In Cuba, the people are behind us 100 percent in the struggle to free Mumia Abu-Jamal. And one of the things they were concerned about, and that I am concerned about, is whether we recognize that we have not freed Mumia. This is just a temporary victory that can go away at any time if we forget to carry on the work of winning a new trial and freeing Mumia Abu-Jamal.

I'm glad to see all of you out there, and the exuberance of the work that's being done, and the breadth and reach of the coalition, and the unity around this issue. But I want to say that the system is diabolical. Mumia is still in Judge Sabo's courtroom, and as long as he's in Judge Sabo's courtroom, Sabo can take back that stay anytime he wants to.[5] We have to be cognizant of the fact that we have not won this war yet. We have a reprieve, but we have to be very aware that August 17 has not passed. There's a warrant out there with Mumia's name on it that says, "Execution on the 17 of August." Until the seventeenth passes, that warrant can still be put into effect. We have to be clear on this. We have not won yet. We cannot lay down our arms. We cannot go back in our bedrooms and sleep soundly. We cannot stop the vigilance. We have to be very astute, to understand that this system does not want Mumia back on the streets. We have a break now, so that we can look at it and continue to push forth the issue. We can still go out there and educate the people. We have to still go out there and make the politicians accountable. We have to still go out there and make the people in the boardrooms accountable. We have to put in effect an economic boycott and hit them where it hurts—in their pockets. We have to make sure they understand that we are not appeased by a stay, that we understand that until Mumia is home out here on the streets with us, carrying on the work of organizing, we have not won the war.

We have to understand that this is just a precursor of what is to come. The struggle has to continue. We have to go out there, and for all those people who have not taken a position on the freedom of Mumia Abu-Jamal, they have to take a position. No one is excepted from this responsibility. We have to recognize the fact that when the National Association of Black Journalists has its conference on August 16, it's still the day before August 17.[6] We cannot let up the work. We cannot be pacified by a stay of execution. We have to get a new trial.

So the struggle has to continue. We cannot forget the fact that August 17 is still out there, and Sabo is still the hanging judge. We forced him to give us a stay. We forced him to do something he has never done before—to give a stay of execution. Do you think he is going to take that lying down, quietly? Do you think we're going to slap him in the face and he's not going to come back fighting? We have to make him understand that he cannot do anything but give Mumia a new trial.

So when I say, "Free Mumia," I am saying, Go out there and work. Go back to where you came from with a new determination to make sure the word goes out. Don't just say, "I went to a demonstration in Philadelphia, and I got to see everybody." Go back out there and work, and free Mumia!

Notes

1. Mumia Abu-Jamal, *Jailhouse Lawyers: Prisoners Defending Prisoners v. the USA* (San Francisco: City Lights, 2009).

2. "Safiya, who, as Sister Bernice, was my boss when I was at the Ministry of Information in the Bronx, was a sho' nuff, no limit soldier. And as the bourgeois media wanted to do pieces on our lighter-complected sistas of the BPP, nobody gave Safiya her props, when she did it all—often above and beyond what most brothers were willing to do." Mumia Abu-Jamal, quoted with permission in *PROUDFLESH: A New Afrikan Journal of Culture, Politics & Consciousness*, at proudfleshjournal.com/issue5/abu-jamal.html.

3. In a July 2002 interview, Safiya said, "Mumia got sentenced to death while I was still in prison. It was really a shock, a Panther on death row" (interview with Imani Henry, *Worker's World* newspaper, August 8, 2002).

4. Islamic greeting meaning "peace be with you."

5. Judge Albert Sabo had been a sheriff before becoming a judge. He was notorious for his enmity to defendants and was known as "the hanging judge." In his obituary of May 10, 2002, the *Philadelphia Inquirer* stated, "According to a 1992 *Inquirer* article, he was the judge in 31 cases that resulted in the death penalty—the most in the state. One in six people sentenced to die in Pennsylvania were sentenced in Judge Sabo's courtroom. No other judge in the country had put as many people on death row."

6. The National Association of Black Journalists (NABJ) convened their annual conference in Philadelphia in August 1995. The NABJ website ("30 Moments in Journalism," NABJ.org) announced, "Abu-Jamal, a freelance radio reporter and outgoing president of the Philadelphia Association of Black Journalists, is sentenced to death for the 1981 murder of a police officer. PABJ [the Philadelphia Association of Black Journalists] maintains 'considered support' for him and his right to a fair trial. After years of appeals, Abu-Jamal's execution is set to happen during the 1995 NABJ convention in Philadelphia, but a stay is granted just before. Disappointing many who want it to join an international chorus to 'free him,' NABJ joins other journalist groups in supporting [only] his free-speech rights. Prison officials had banned him from doing media interviews."

17. COINTELPRO and the Case of Mumia Abu-Jamal

This is Safiya's foreword to the pamphlet, *Wages of COINTELPRO: The Case of Mumia Abu-Jamal.*[1] *Wages of COINTELPRO* has been republished in *Cages of Steel: The Politics of Imprisonment in the United States*, but the foreword is not included in that version.[2] The original pamphlet is out of print.

Safiya was a member—and founder—of the coalition.[3] In this essay, she reviews the history of FBI surveillance and harassment of Mumia Abu-Jamal since his teens. In so doing, she reminds us that it is entirely possible that Mumia—like Fred Hampton before him—was targeted by the FBI because they saw him as a potential "Black messiah" (in the actual language used by J. Edgar Hoover, outlining the goals of FBI techniques geared to undermine or destroy Black leaders). The wide popularity and power of Mumia's writings and recordings from death row lend weight to this suggestion.

Mumia Abu-Jamal, former member of the Black Panther Party, MOVE supporter,[4] internationally renowned revolutionary journalist, husband, father, grandfather, is on death row in Pennsylvania. On Thursday, June 1, 1995, Pennsylvania governor Tom Ridge signed a warrant of execution and ordered Mumia to be put to death by lethal injection on August 17, 1995 at ten p.m.—despite knowing that Mumia's legal team was filing his postconviction relief appeal (PCRA) on Monday, June 5, 1995.

The ostensible reason the Commonwealth of Pennsylvania plans to execute Mumia Abu-Jamal is for the death of police officer Daniel Faulkner, the night of December 9, 1981. Mumia was arrested on the scene, tried, convicted, and sentenced to be executed for Daniel Faulkner's death. The real reason for Mumia being on death row is his political beliefs and affiliations and the fact that his life was a testimony to his political beliefs. Mumia did not just verbalize what he knew to be the inequities and oppressive nature of Philadelphia specifically and this society in general. Mumia internalized the problem and then used his journalistic skills and political education to pull the cover off the corrupt government in Philadelphia, its police, and its police state and expose them for who and what they were/are.

Mumia understood the purpose of journalism. He understood that he had a responsibility to tell the truth and expose corruption and injustice to the people. The people could not be expected to act on this corruption without the facts. Mumia not only exposed the corruption but also uncovered the facts and made them known to the people in a manner that the people had no problem understanding. He also spoke out in defense of the people who had no one else to speak for them. A case in point was that of the MOVE organization, which had been under attack by the government of Philadelphia and the Philadelphia Police Department. Women and men in the MOVE organization had been continually victimized by the police department—to the point that the brutality suffered by the women had led to miscarriages and stillborn babies. One MOVE sister had been beaten to the point that the baby in her arms died as a result. No one but Mumia would report these atrocities.

But Mumia's standing up for truth did not start just with MOVE. The record of his quest for truth and speaking out began in 1968, when he was fourteen years old and was arrested protesting Governor George Wallace while Wallace was campaigning in Philadelphia. This was the same George Wallace who refused to integrate the schools in Alabama. After Mumia was beaten at this protest, he helped form the Philadelphia chapter of the Black Panther Party. By the time he was sixteen years old, he had found his niche: journalism. He knew which side he stood on in the struggle between the oppressed and the oppressor, and from that day forward he has worked to educate the people and expose by example the nature of the state.

This constant barrage of information exposing the Philadelphia Police Department's history of police brutality and police violence made him a thorn in the side of the Philadelphia Police Department and someone to be dealt with. The Black Panther Party, which had helped him develop his journalism skills, in addition to his political education, had been destroyed by the FBI's COINTELPRO war against it and the inability of members of the Party to internalize some very basic principles of protracted struggle. There were a lot of Panthers left out there on their own without organizational backing and support, who were now vulnerable to the police departments of their various cities and states and to the FBI because of their political stances while they were members of the Black Panther Party.

Mumia's FBI records very clearly indicate that the surveillance that he was under did not cease with his resignation from the Black Panther Party or the split and subsequent demise of the Black Panther Party. An FBI memorandum dated December 3, 1970, from SAC (FBI acronym for *special agent in charge*), Philadelphia, to the director of the FBI stated,

COOK (Mumia's name at birth) left the Black Panther Party in mid-October 1970, having resigned. He was not the object of Party discipline. He, along with several other individuals long associated with the Party, ceased their Black Panther Party affiliation. COOK has returned to high school, but still associates with [another ex-

Panther] and his new organization, dubbed the "Black United Liberation Front." . . . Thus far they have secured an office . . . and published a leaflet denouncing the Philadelphia Police Department.

On April 4, 1972, in another FBI document from SAC, Philadelphia, to SAC, Albany, it is stated that after Mumia had registered for school at Goddard College in Plainfield, Vermont, the FBI attempted to harass and victimize Mumia through determining whether he was attending school on any type of grant involving federal money. What is interesting to note here is not only that Mumia is no longer associated with the Black Panther Party but also that he is now attending school and the FBI still has him under surveillance and is still harassing him. This clearly tells us that the threat that Mumia—as well as anybody else who has become politically aware—poses is not lessened by their ceasing to belong to a political grouping, because the threat is that of being an aware and politically conscious oppressed person. The government could not allow people to become aware of what the real problem is in this country and how they have been used as cannon fodder in their wars, scapegoats for their exploitative capitalist failures, and victims of their racist policies and how they have been murdered in the government's rush to define its failures on the domestic front in terms of controlling street crime and violence.

Mumia knew and understood these dynamics and he spoke, wrote, and organized the people of Philadelphia to know and understand what was happening. It was for this reason that the state and federal government, in the person of the FBI, did not lose sight of Mumia. It was for this reason that continuously, from the time he was fourteen years old until the present, Mumia has been under constant surveillance.

This surveillance continues even though he has been in prison since December 9, 1981, and on death row since July 1982. An FBI memorandum dated February 27, 1991, from the FBI in Philadelphia to the director of the FBI sought to establish a link between Mumia on death row and the machine gun attack on the American Embassy in Bonn, Germany, on February 13, 1991.

These FBI documents more than anything provide convincing evidence to establish the fact that Mumia's being on death row has everything to do with his political beliefs and affiliations, his devotion and championship of the human rights of Black and other oppressed peoples, and his commitment to revolutionary justice.

In this struggle for revolutionary justice Mumia's weapon of choice has always been the pen. Pulling the shade off and exposing the unjust and their injustices to the eyes of the world was what he did—and he did it so well that he was a major threat to them. Frank Rizzo called him that "new breed" of activist journalist and said that there would come a time when Mumia's activism would work against him.[5] Rizzo added that he waited patiently for a time when a way could be found to silence the "Voice of the Voiceless."[6]

Nowhere in these FBI documents, during any of the surveillance, is there a connection between Mumia and any act of violence. There is, for the entire world to see, a clear and well-documented case of political surveillance and persecution. The FBI, in conjunction with the police departments of cities and states all over this country, has been involved in a conspiracy to remove Black Panthers, former Black Panthers, and revolutionaries of all persuasions from the streets of our cities and lock them away from society. In their own papers they have stated that they would manufacture evidence if none existed to substantiate cases against such people. This is what they've done in the case of Mumia Abu-Jamal.

The state has manufactured a case, stacked the deck with the hanging judge Albert Sabo, terrorized witnesses, denied Mumia adequate assistance of counsel, used his political history as a weapon against him, and sentenced him to die. They did this not because of the death of police officer Daniel Faulkner, because they know that Mumia did not commit this murder. They did this to silence a revolutionary voice. The death of police officer Daniel Faulkner presented them with the opportunity they had been waiting for—to silence Mumia—and they ran with it.

Ward Churchill, in his piece, "The Wages of COINTELPRO: The Case of Mumia Abu-Jamal," paints a clear picture of the frame-up and at the end points us in the direction of what we have to do. But we should know already what we have to do. We have to stop the runaway train that the state is on toward the execution of Mumia Abu-Jamal. We have to do this . . . we have to do this . . . we have to do this . . . *by any means necessary!*

Notes

1. Ward Churchill, "Wages of COINTELPRO: The Case of Mumia Abu-Jamal" (pamphlet, now out of print: New York/Philadelphia: Coalition to Free Mumia Abu-Jamal/International Concerned Family and Friends of Mumia Abu-Jamal, 1996).
2. Ward Churchill and Jim Vander Wall, eds., *Cages of Steel: The Politics of Imprisonment in the United States* (Washington, DC: Maisonneuve Press, 1992).
3. For more on Safiya's relationship to Mumia and her work on his case, see the introduction to chapter 16, "Free Mumia Abu-Jamal!," p. 184.
4. MOVE is a Philadelphia-based organization founded by John Africa (since deceased) that strives to live by natural law. The organization was targeted by police and dramatically attacked several times; several members of the organization, including children and infants, were killed in these assaults. The most widely known assault was on May 13, 1985, when a house inhabited by MOVE was incinerated by a percussion bomb dropped on it from a police helicopter at the direction

of then–Philadelphia mayor Wilson Goode. Six adults and five children were killed and the fire was left to burn, destroying homes on the entire block (in a predominantly Black neighborhood). MOVE has eight members currently serving long sentences as a result of a 1978 confrontation initiated by police. This group is called the MOVE Nine; one of the original defendants, Merle Africa, died in prison in 1998. Pam Africa, a MOVE member and leader of the international support movement for Mumia Abu-Jamal, remembers that after Merle's death, Safiya mentioned Merle and memorialized her every time she spoke at any gathering.

5. Frank Rizzo was the former chief of police of Philadelphia.
6. Mumia is widely—and deservedly—known as the "Voice of the Voiceless" for his unstinting articulation of views and needs of oppressed communities.

18. Safiya Interviews Albert Nuh Washington

On February 24, 2000, as co-host with Sally O'Brien of the
weekly hour-long WBAI radio program *Where We Live*, Safiya
took a call from political prisoner Albert Nuh Washington and
connected Nuh to that evening's show.[1] At the time, Nuh was
terminally ill with metastasized liver cancer. Safiya, Sally, and
Israel Ajima, a third host, interviewed Nuh. Excerpts from
this interview are included here because they elucidate the
relationship between Nuh and Safiya; in other writings she
refers frequently to Nuh as her mentor. Nuh was also the
person who introduced Safiya to Islam.

Before the interview begins, snatches are audible of a
telephone conversation between Safiya and Nuh about the
status of his case—including the fact that a final appeal has
just been denied. Then Sally asks Safiya to introduce Nuh.
In Safiya's response, you can detect her grief and anger
at the denial of the appeal and Nuh's impending death.
She becomes slightly impatient, as if feeling that after so
many efforts, such extensive work, nothing fundamental
is changing: Nuh remains in prison and other dearly loved
comrades have died behind the walls. In this period, it
seems clear that Safiya's heart was becoming increasingly
burdened not only with such grief, but also with frustration
and rage at the apparent inability of the support movements
to win release and justice for the political prisoners. Safiya's
introduction of Nuh exhibits how overwhelming such feelings
could become: An impeccable organizer, she seems to forget
here that some listeners might not be familiar with the case
of Nuh.

Two months after this interview, on April 28, 2000, Albert
Nuh Washington died of cancer without being released from

prison. His name and Safiya's are now joined in the Safiya Bukhari–Albert Nuh Washington Foundation initiated by Safiya's daughter Wonda Jones.[2]

Safiya Introduces Nuh (at Sally's request)

SAFIYA: Do I really have to introduce Albert Nuh Washington to our listening audience? We've been talking about him for years, and especially at this time, over the past few months, we've been keeping the listening audience updated on the situation with him. And it's really a treat for me to introduce my mentor, my comrade, my friend Albert Nuh Washington.

SALLY: Welcome, Nuh, and because we can't assume that new listeners know about your case, can you please explain how long you've been incarcerated and what you were convicted of?

NUH: I'm one of the New York Three—the other two are Herman Bell and Anthony Jalil Bottom—and we've been in prison for twenty-eight and a half years. We were convicted for the murder of two New York City police officers back in 1971. And we just recently lost our last legal battle. [We had gone to court to show] that the district attorney had made a deal with one of the witnesses to testify, and in turn the witness had perjured himself. [But] the courts refused to look at this. The last time we went in on a perjury of a witness they said that the perjury didn't make any difference. So I guess, politically speaking, you can lie and it has no effect on the case even though the people [in the jury] are thereby denied hearing the whole truth. And so people are making a judgment based on erroneous information and on the words of perjurers. We did get an earlier hearing on other evidence, but the judge said that even though there were serious errors, they weren't enough to overturn the conviction.

They went through a lot of legal gymnastics. The law states that if you put in documentation and that there's any reasonable possibility that this is truth, then you're entitled to an evidentiary hearing. So we put in the documentation and they said that we hadn't proved it. Of course we didn't prove it, because you didn't give us the evidentiary hearing.

Nuh Answers Questions About the Black Panther Party

NUH: The BPP was scary to the US government, because you had a whole group of people who are oppressed, and then you had a group—the Party—that was directly preaching to them. And the government, the counterintelligence organizations, have dealt with these things around the world, and then they see them cropping up in their own backyard.

I think a lot of people fail to recognize that the Black Panther Party was one of the first Black militant organizations that was totally organized and that had principles and made efforts to maintain its integrity. If you look at the history of other countries where parties for liberation were formed, you find that they went through thirty or forty years of learning, learning how to struggle. The Black Panther Party within four to five years had made great advances. But because of the pressure brought to bear by the government, the Party was unable to use all these tools that it had. And we didn't have the personnel educated enough to take us through these little traps [set by the government's counterintelligence program]. If you study China and the Chinese Communist Party, they went through things with the Kuomintang and they had internal struggles and these things were ongoing for many, many years.

So when you look at that history of the Black Panther Party, you have to put it in a historical context.

Mistakes are part of struggle. Setbacks are part of struggle. You have to approach struggle with the idea that it's going to be hard and long. And therefore you have to arm yourselves with the tools to get you by. You can't let personalities or personal agendas get in the way. You have to figure out how to build unity within the Party based upon principles. People have to learn to struggle with each other without thinking that disagreements constitute a personal attack.

So all these things come into play. The interactions among people are very complex. In order to maintain certain unity, principles have to govern. Anything else leads to chaos and confusion.

Nuh Comments on the Current Period

NUH: There's an old saying, "No investigation, no right to speak." Being locked up a long time gives me a very narrow perspective of what's going on in the community.

But while I don't know exactly what's going on, I know what I hear from comrades and friends: They're optimistic about today's youth, they see a lot of potential there, so that means the spirit of the Black Panther Party survives. And those who were a part of it have an obligation to share this knowledge, and I hope they haven't wasted the past twenty-five or thirty years without analyzing, because it's one thing to talk about the glory days, but now you have to give the younger people, OK, this is where we went wrong, and this is how to avoid this. No easy fights, no easy victories. From what I hear they're very optimistic about the young people, and that makes me optimistic and happy.

Concluding Thoughts

SAFIYA: One thing before we lose you, Nuh [*Nuh's phone time is about to run out*], in terms of your time on the air tonight, our audience would like to know how you, Nuh Washington—you, the person—are doing and how you are holding up under what's going on with you.

NUH: Back in November I found out that I had cancer that had spread from my liver to my spine. I was treated with some radiation to shrink the tumor on the spine, and that took away a great deal of pain that I was in. Since then I'm still kind of weak, but I've gained a few pounds, and I take every day as a blessing. I strive to improve myself each day, to do a little more, and my attitude is that I expect to feel good. So I'm going to live each day to the fullest and strive with all my might and spirit to hang out as long as I can, just like anybody else, and continue and try to contribute to the general struggle for liberation.

I would like to thank all the people who have written to me. Your cards and well wishes have been greatly appreciated and I'm very touched by them. It's hard to write back individually because even though I feel good, it still takes a lot of energy for me to sit down and write. So I'm thankful for the opportunity to tell all of you how thankful I am for all the cards and letters. They have reached me. And what's even more heartening is the fact that people have the attitude that they respect the sacrifices made by the Black Panther Party and the Black Liberation Army. When you're in the twilight of your life, to know that there are people who think that you did something worthwhile is in itself very encouraging and warming.

[*Nuh's phone time expires and the call is disconnected. A few minutes later, Safiya comes back on the air. Sounding as if she is fighting tears, she says the following:*]

SAFIYA: Nuh called me back to ask me please to let everyone—especially the brothers over at Shawangunk [where Nuh had been incarcerated before he was moved, for medical reasons, to Coxsackie]—know that he received your good wishes, and hang in there. He's a little tired right now, because being on the air really takes a lot out of him. He was happy to have the chance to thank everyone and to let people know in his own words how he's doing. And he's still struggling, not just on the personal front but on the political front also.

Notes

1. For more on *Where We Live*, see the introduction to chapter 15, "Talking About Assata Shakur," p. 168.
2. See the preface, p. ix.

19. Letter for the Parole of Jalil Muntaqim

In July 2002, Anthony Jalil Bottom (Jalil Muntaqim)[1] appeared before the New York State parole board for the first time (he has appeared three times since then). In preparation for his hearing, Jalil asked community members to write letters of support. As one of the people helping him gather those letters, I reminded Safiya that hers was past due. She told me that she was having a difficult time writing her letter, because she felt painfully torn between a wild hope that he would win his release and cold fear that he would not. A few days after that discussion she sent me a copy of the letter she succeeded in writing. In the letter, Safiya summarizes some of the developments in her own life.

May 5, 2002

To Whom It May Concern:

I write this letter in support of Anthony Jalil Bottom's application for release on parole. I've procrastinated this long in hopes that God would guide my hand and give me exactly the right thing to say that would make a difference. Thus far, I have received no such guidance and time is running short, therefore I can only write what I know about Jalil and what I know to be his intentions should he be released on parole.

My name is Safiya Bukhari-Alston. I've known Jalil for well over thirty years. I knew the young brash political Jalil. I knew the young, incarcerated, worried father Jalil. The son and brother Jalil who could do nothing while his mother and sisters went through changes or were victimized. I know the grandfather Jalil. The depressed Jalil. The sad Jalil. The angry Jalil who could do nothing but watch while a friend died in jail.

I don't know the one dimensional Anthony Bottom #77-A-4823. There is no such person. Jalil is a complex person. He's a human being, moved by his feelings, beliefs, and what he perceives to be the right thing to do.

At nineteen years old, prior to his arrest, Jalil worked and helped support his family. He had been taught responsibility and took that responsibility seriously. He wasn't into drugs or any of the other social ills that were so prevalent in our community. Jalil, like so many of us who were products of that generation, felt a responsibility to make a difference in our community. The Rev. Dr. Martin Luther King Jr. had just been killed, and Malcolm X, "El Hajj Malik Shabazz," had also been shot down. We all felt that if these great men could give up their lives for what they believed in, then we had a responsibility to do something. The rallying cry of Malcolm X, "We shall have our freedom. We shall have it, by any means necessary," became our mantra.

While he was on trial, Jalil became a father. Even from behind bars, he never abdicated his responsibilities as a father. He tried to be the best father he could be. He tried to be involved in every aspect of his daughter's life. I remember when she was fifteen going on sixteen, going through some major crises of confidence. She didn't believe she had anyone she could talk to, anyone who loved her. Jalil arranged for her to come out to New York and spend the summer so they could visit and have some quality time together. It turned out to be very important for both of them.

That same conscientiousness he displayed towards his daughter extends toward all the members of his family. Jalil and his mother are very close. He's the firstborn, and was born when she was very young. He's very protective of her, and she feels like a part of her is missing. She moved to Georgia and bought a house, which she plans to turn over to him upon his release. In a very real sense they have been doing this time together. He feels the pain that she is enduring because of him, and he is haunted and driven by it.

Which brings us to today. His youth was dedicated to his people and the community. He placed his people and community in front of his responsibility to his family. As a consequence of his devotion to his people, his family suffered. For a number of years now, his plans have been to bring some joy and happiness into the lives of his family, especially his mother and daughter. That is his primary goal at this point in his life.

I can say this unequivocally because it was my goal on my release from prison. Prior to my release on parole in 1983, I made a promise to my mother that I would be there for her. I have done that. I have been home for almost twenty years now. I have earned my college degree. I have finished raising my daughter and, for the last fourteen years, worked as the director of administration of a multi-office law firm. I'm not saying that the desire to make a difference for my people is not still there. I'm saying that we have all matured and are rational enough to realize that it takes more than one or two people to bring about necessary change.

Jalil is a dreamer, but he's also practical. He's older, and what keeps him going today is the desire to be there for his family. It is my hope that, in considering whether or not to grant parole to Anthony Bottom, you will consider the three dimensional person.

Thank you for taking the time to read my letter. I hope I have said something worthy of reflection.

Sincerely,
Safiya Bukhari-Alston

Notes

1. Jalil Muntaqim is one of the New York Three (see chapter 14, "CBS Tries the New York Three," p. 156) and has been denied parole twice since 2002, always for the same reason: "the seriousness of the conviction." From 1971 to 2006, Jalil was incarcerated in New York State prisons; the visits with his daughter that Safiya mentions in this letter are prison visits. In 2007, Jalil was transferred to the San Francisco jail to face thirty-six-year-old charges of conspiracy and the killing of a police officer as part of the San Francisco 8 (freethesf8.org). At the time of the killing, Jalil was in prison.

   As described by the defense committee, "Eight former Black community activists—Black Panthers and others—were arrested January 23, 2007, in California, New York, and Florida on charges related to the 1971 killing of a San Francisco police officer. Similar charges were thrown out [more than thirty years ago] after it was revealed that police used torture to extract confessions when some of these same men were arrested in New Orleans in 1973.

   "Richard Brown, Richard O'Neal, Ray Boudreaux, and Hank Jones were arrested in California. Francisco Torres was arrested in Queens, New York. Harold Taylor was arrested in Florida. Two men charged— Herman Bell and Jalil Muntaqim—have been held as political prisoners for over 30 years in New York State prisons. A ninth man, Ronald Stanley Bridgeforth, is still being sought. The men were charged with the murder of Sgt. John Young and a conspiracy that encompasses numerous acts between 1968 and 1973.

   "Harold Taylor and John Bowman (recently deceased) as well as Ruben Scott (thought to be a government witness) were first charged in 1975. But a judge tossed out the charges, finding that Taylor and his two co-defendants made statements after police in New Orleans tortured them for several days employing electric shock, cattle prods, beatings, sensory deprivation plastic bags and hot, wet blankets for asphyxiation. Such 'evidence' is neither credible nor legal.

   "At the end of July [2009], Herman Bell and Jalil Muntaqim were sentenced to probation and time served, after Herman agreed to plead to voluntary manslaughter and Jalil to conspiracy to voluntary manslaughter. All charges were then dropped on Richard Brown, Hank Jones, Harold Taylor, and Ray Boudreaux, with the prosecution admitting it had "insufficient evidence" against them. Charges had already been dropped against Richard O'Neal last year" (freethesf8.org).

20. Q&A on Jericho 98

This interview was conducted just before the Jericho 98 march and rally in Washington, DC, March 27, 1998. It was published in *Crossroad*, the newsletter of the Crossroad Support Network.[1] The newsletter is described as "a non-sectarian newsletter produced by and for New Afrikan Prisoners of War and Political Prisoners . . . dedicated to contributing to and continuing an ongoing discussion around identity, purpose, and direction for Afrikan-descended people who want a higher level of human life."[2]

This is the first in a series of interviews, articles, and speeches Safiya gave about Jericho 98. In 1997, at the urging of Jalil Muntaqim, one of the New York Three, Safiya and former political prisoner Herman Ferguson initiated the work for Jericho (Iyaluua Ferguson, Herman's wife and comrade, and others played significant roles as well). In a 2004 letter, Jalil wrote:

> Jericho [had] originated with the RNA-PG (Republic of New Afrika–Provisional Government) marching in front of the White House in the late 80s. However, after 1993, these marches ceased, so in 1996, I first called for the Jericho March on the White House, but it was agreed that it was too soon. Then Herman [Ferguson], Safiya, and I had a meeting to develop the means to organize the Jericho 1998 March on the White House, and everything evolved from there. The Jericho 98 March was sponsored by the New Afrikan Liberation Front and RNA-PG. Under Safiya's leadership, Jericho organizing committees developed across the country and in Germany, Italy, the Basque region of Spain, England, etc.

Herman Ferguson says, "The first time I met Jalil it was because Safiya was going up to see him and told me to come along. Organizing for the march took us through some changes. Safiya was such a hard worker, with a lot of commitment. Her energy was infectious. So many memories—getting up at midnight to take a bus to get to DC at five or six a.m., then wait until it was late enough to start calling on people, organizing, then get the bus back to New York that night. We really had to pour it on."

Cleo Silvers remembers organizing with Safiya in Harlem at the Million Youth March in 1998. "Safiya used her sternest exterior to keep the police from moving us from our literature table on 118th Street," she remembers. "That was her exterior, to keep us from being hurt. She was really warm, kind, and loving."

Sally O'Brien worked with Safiya on Jericho as well. In a tribute shortly after Safiya's death, Sally summed up Safiya's energy this way: "There were no tools left unused in her fierce drive. She left a legacy of action behind words."

This essay lays the basis for much of the thinking behind the Jericho Movement and march in 1998. The rally held symbolism: activists would fight the battle of Jericho and the prison walls would come tumbling down. The 1998 rally gathered some thousands of participants in the march to the White House.[3]

The interview has been excerpted here to avoid repeating material in Safiya's other speeches and writings on political prisoners.

Q: Why do you say Jericho is more than just a march?

A: The march on the White House is just to have a massive number of people raising a demand and putting the government on notice that we're not going to continue the status quo in relationship to our political prisoners and prisoners of war. So it's just the beginning of a long struggle to win amnesty and freedom for our political prisoners, and to build an apparatus that will enable us to make sure that our political prisoners—and the question of political prisoners—is not lost in the overall struggles of the movements. It's designed to get them legal help, to let people know that they're there; to make sure that they're accorded the treatment of political prisoner and prisoner of war status.

Jericho will free up people from various organizations to go back into the community to do the work of organizing our communities for liberation. We feel that we should have done this thirty years ago, so that our political prisoners would have an apparatus and those who were involved in the struggle don't get lost in the shuffle. People would know that if they become involved in political work and activities, they will not be left alone to rot in prison without support networks, without their families being taken care of, without medical care and all those other things that should be accorded to people who get involved in struggle and end up in prison. So this is an attempt to correct a lack of movement within the movement itself, to build structures for people who go to prison—from this point on as well as from the past—so that organizations won't be tied down in it and use all their resources in court proceedings.

The campaign to neutralize our struggles through the use of the criminal justice system was a documented campaign by the federal government, part of COINTELPRO. We can document it and take it back to 1968, in their FBI memorandum talking about imprisoning people even though the evidence is not there to support the crime that they're being charged with. The government made a determination to use the criminal justice system to criminalize the struggles of oppressed people and incarcerate them, to break the backs of organizations financially, and to take away those people who made up the cadre of those organizations. And they did it well, because some of these people fell in the sixties and are still in prison today.

The attack on the movement—the concerted attack by the government on the various movements and the decision to imprison leadership and drain our resources through all the trials—made a lot of us into defendants. A lot of our actions went into keeping courtrooms packed and keeping funds going to make sure that the money is there to pay lawyers. That made it almost impossible for us to continue the organizing around decent housing, quality education, homelessness—all those issues that were part of our struggles in the community, that helped us educate our people to what the situation is. Invariably, the leadership was taken off to prison and building the support mechanisms around these cases kept us from working around the everyday issues affecting our people.

Jericho will put together one apparatus around the issue of political prisoners. It will free up the organizations to go back into the communities to do the work of educating and organizing our people. Until now, the organizations either made the decision to organize in the community—and therefore neglect the issue of political prisoners—or else they made the decision to do the support work around the political prisoners and therefore neglected the work in the community. There has not been a way to fuse both areas of work. Jericho allows you to have two or three people out of your organization whose work is around political prisoners. They're working on a national basis with an apparatus designed to do that work, so you're maximizing the work that's being done. That allows the rest of the organization to deal with the issues that will further the movements in the communities. We intend to have a conference following the Jericho march to bring all these Jericho organizing committees together to determine and strategize how to take this from a concept to a reality.

In COINTELPRO the FBI also said that they wanted to make sure that the youth understood that it was better for them to be a drug dealer—or anything—than to be a revolutionary. The crux of that is that our youth are now involved in anything other than revolutionary activities. They look at the fact that we didn't do anything about our warriors, our fighters, our members of organizations who went to jail because of their political activities. We left them there. So they internalize the idea, whether anybody told them or not, that if you get involved and you go to prison, then you're stupid, because ain't nobody doing nothing about getting you out of prison, and nobody supporting you while you in there. Now the people don't even know you're there and what you're there for.

Q: How do you decide which prisoners are on the Jericho list?

A: We need to break the barrier, internationally, on the fact that political prisoners exist in this country. The United States government consistently denies that political prisoners exist. As long as that barrier is not broken, we'll still have our people languishing in prison and not being accorded political prisoner status and treatment under international law as governed by the Universal Declaration of Human Rights.

We have to put our strongest foot forward in order to do this. We have strategies and we have tactics. People who went to jail as a result of their work on the street, their involvement in liberation struggles on the street, whose cases from the very beginning started from that point of view and who are still there, are different from those who became political after their arrest.

Jericho is designed to raise the issues of these political cases. From the very beginning they were political. Once we push those through and get the US government to acknowledge and the world to recognize the fact that these people are political prisoners, then we can open the door and bring other people through. Then we can bring in the cases of those people who became political in prison. We have to have a scientific approach. We can't be waylaid by personalities or emotions.

This is very important because the first thing the government will say if we put out a list with all these people on it who claim to be political prisoners—they will look at those cases and in the international arena they will make us look like laughingstocks. They'll pull out the case histories: "This person went to jail for raping the daughter of a neighbor," or "This person went to jail for robbing a mom-and-pop store," or "This person went to jail for shoplifting." And the cases are there and there was nothing political about their history in the community, and they can bring forth people to show that there was nothing political about their history in the community. Even though they became political in prison, the initial cases did not come from political activities on the street. And we know that there are people who became political in prison, but we also know that in order to break that wall of silence we need to begin talking about those other cases, the political ones. We could begin talking about that even if we only had two people on the list. But we have more than sixty people on this list that we can document as being political prisoners.

The first tactic is to break down the walls around these people who went to prison as a result of political beliefs and affiliations. Then we have the second phase, where we open the door for those people who became political behind the walls, whose sentences have been lengthened and made harder, who have been tortured and abused because of the political stands they have taken within the prisons. That is another element that we have to deal with. But we have to deal with it systematically and strategically, and we can no longer deal emotionally when it comes to moving our struggle forward.

The final phase is to target that prison-industrial complex that is used as a revolving door, as slave labor, where they can't deal with chattel slavery anymore on the streets, so they deal with the only form of slavery they can still get away with: "legitimate" involuntary servitude inside the prison camps as a result of convictions.

Q: You're a first vice president of the Provisional Government of the Republic of New Afrika (PG-RNA). Tell us why the PG-RNA felt it was important to build the Jericho campaign.

A: We've been having Jerichos for the past ten years as part of New Afrikan Nation Day. Wherever it is, we've been dealing with Jericho marches. But it hasn't been as widely organized as this one is. We feel, as the PG-RNA, that all our relationships with the US government take place on a foreign affairs basis. So when we talk about the freedom of our political prisoners and POWs, we take it from the point of view of one government approaching another with the amnesty question. We have to deal with negotiating their release under international law.

This year, President Clinton has been talking about the "race" question. Our minister of foreign affairs, Imari Obadele, is writing a letter for Jericho pointing out that we have to negotiate the release of our political prisoners before you can deal with the "race" issue. Because if you're saying that you want to resolve that issue, then let's start from the basis that over these past years, you have been keeping our people incarcerated. Not just citizens of the Republic of New Afrika, but also our allies among the indigenous people; the Puerto Rican people fighting colonialism; and our white allies, the American anti-imperialists. So we have to talk about freedom for these political prisoners.

We can't continue to let all these years pass without this issue being brought to the forefront. This is the thirtieth anniversary of the founding of the Provisional Government, so we are bringing that issue to the forefront. The PG has had a position on the freedom of our political prisoners and POWs for the longest. We felt that this was the time to raise the issue, not just with the US government, but before the Organization of African Unity and in Geneva before the UN Commission on Human Rights. We can no longer allow the status quo to continue as it has for the past umpteen years.

Q: Tell us about Jericho consolidating the individual cases and work on those cases.

A: Some of the political prisoners have defense committees with one or two people in them—usually the wife and the wife's best friend or something like that. Then you have some individuals like Geronimo ji Jaga and Mumia Abu-Jamal who have national committees. Then you have people with no defense committee, whose names are not even known, who just sit there rotting in prison. These little committees, every now and then you have them doing a lot of work, but we're still not making any movement. With Jericho, we felt that we can no longer do one or two political prisoners at a time and get them out of prison in seven- or ten-year intervals. We had to find a way that all the political prisoners can be dealt with; they can know that there is a unity of purpose here and that we move forward as a whole to get them out as a whole. And at the same time, if new people go to prison, there's something to deal with them from jump street.

Notice that we're not saying that those small defense committees should not be there. You're always going to have a need for people in local areas to deal with local cases. But at the same time, we need to maximize our resources, not drain resources around one individual. If we could move forward as a movement, that would be better than continuing to be fragmented and disunified and not making the most of the people we have at our disposal. That's what Jericho is all about.

Q: How have churches responded to Jericho?

A: There was a Jericho sermon preached in Louisiana, for example. It was dynamite! The preacher preached the Christian Jericho sermon, then talked about how Christians have abdicated their responsibility to free prisoners. He talked about Mumia, Geronimo, and about the Jericho that people have to wage now to go into the prisons to free the political prisoners, to free the captured.

The minister recognized this and enunciated it so well— the concept of Jericho and Joshua in the Bible and the Jericho that has to take place today. Part of Jericho is organizing the churches, to educate everybody. We've made a mistake in the past of just talking to those people who were already organized. Now we can't make that mistake again. As organizers we have to talk to everybody.

Q: What is the significance of organizing women in particular— for Jericho and for the struggle in general?

A: There are many things that went down in the past in terms of the role of women in our struggle. One thing that's very clear is that much of the work around political prisoners— like much of the rest of the work in our movement—has been done by women. Women are the people who are doing most of the work, but they have been vilified; they've been told that "their place is this," and they have been lacking in the self-esteem necessary to take their real place, their real responsibility, to be able to make those decisions necessary to move our struggle forward. We can't allow anybody to say to us that we can't make decisions, or that we're second place in this struggle.

No matter what's happening out there in the streets, women are involved. It's our sons and our daughters who are being victimized. So we have more at stake than anybody. We can't allow ourselves to be intimidated by the people, especially men, who say this is not our place, or tell us we can't do this, or that we have to listen to the decisions they make. The reality is that some of the bad decisions that have brought us to the place we are at have been made by men, because of ego and everything else. Women have to take responsibility. If we're scared to take responsibility because of some kind of relationship we have or may not have, then there's a problem. We have taken on, in our movements, the biggest enemy of human beings in the world: the US system of capitalism. Once we take on that system, and we're scared to take on our relationships, or face problems in relationships, or problems in how people deal with each other in an organizational framework, then there really is a problem. A small problem now is in danger of becoming a major problem later on, because it builds up animosity and lack of trust. So we have to take it on. Just to begin to address that issue as women frees us up to deal with the bigger issues.

Notes

1. "Interview with Safiya Bukhari, National Coordinator, Jericho 98 Campaign," *Crossroad* 8, no. 3, March/April 1998.
2. Prairiefire.org/crossroad.shtml.
3. For more of Jericho, see thejerichomovement.com.

21. Debate: Should We Grant Amnesty to America's Political Prisoners?

In 1998, two weeks before the Jericho march, Safiya participated in an hour-long debate on the question, Should we grant amnesty to America's political prisoners? The debate was taped and later shown on the Public Broadcasting System (PBS) in April 1998, as part of a series called *Debates Debates*, which aired from 1997 to the end of 2002. The show's webpage described it this way: "Experts participate in formal debates on public policy issues."

Two three-person teams debated the amnesty question. The "pro" side consisted of Ron Kuby, "civil rights lawyer"; Dr. Alan Berkman, "Columbia Presbyterian Hospital, New York"; and Safiya Bukhari, "National Jericho Program coordinator."[1] The "con" side consisted of Charlie Rose, "professor, Fordham Law School"; Ted Cruz, "former law clerk to Justice Rehnquist"; and Peter Thiel, "[of] the Independent Institute."[2]

This text contains excerpts of the debate transcript (which exceeds twenty pages). Kuby and Rose served as heads of their respective teams, delivering the opening and closing statements and introducing their team members, each of whom made an opening statement.

RON KUBY: Like all nations, the United States insists that it holds no political prisoners. But in America today there are over one hundred men and women incarcerated based upon their participation in some of the most profound confrontations in this past quarter century: Puerto Ricans who are in prison for fighting to free their country from colonialism; former Black Panthers who were put in jail when they met the illegal violence of the state with violence of their own; and activists who, in the late 1970s and 1980s, bombed American corporate and military targets to stop an illegal war against the people of El Salvador and Nicaragua. All these political prisoners fought for principles articulated in the United Nations Universal Declaration of Human Rights. They fought for equality and they fought for liberation. Ironically, as the United States denies that it holds political prisoners, it metes out especially harsh punishment to them. A leftist convicted of possession of explosives can serve fifty-eight years in prison; her apolitical counterpart gets probation. It's time that America moves towards peace and reconciliation with its own dissidents and offers amnesty to those prisoners incarcerated for "crimes" that were in fact acts taken out of deep moral conviction and were part of some of the most significant struggles in the past twenty-five years.

CHARLES ROSE: I'm a former executive assistant United States attorney for the Eastern District of New York, former adversary to Ron Kuby in many cases, now in private practice. There are no political prisoners in the US. These people Mr. Kuby terms political prisoners were all convicted of federal crimes. For example, Mr. Kuby talks about the Puerto Rican independence people. Those people, the FALN, were convicted of bombings.[3] Five people were dead. Four in Fraunces Tavern who had nothing to do with anything other than they were having lunch.[4] Even Mr. Berkman, one of the panelists, was convicted of being involved in bombing and possessing explosives.[5]

[Kuby introduces Dr. Alan Berkman as "medical director of an AIDS treatment program and a faculty member at the HIV center of Columbia University. He has just received a National Institutes *of Health grant to design AIDS treatment programs for mentally ill homeless people, and he is a former political prisoner, having served more than seven years in prison for crimes ranging from possession of explosives to treating a wounded fugitive."*]

ALAN BERKMAN: I just came back from South Africa, where I went to Robben Island and had a chance to stand in front of Nelson Mandela's cell, where he spent eighteen of his twenty-seven years in prison as a political prisoner, convicted in South African courts of conducting a campaign of sabotage. It was a painful experience, both because I almost died of maltreatment for cancer while I was a political prisoner in the United States, and because it brought home the ongoing reality for the people I know in this country who are political prisoners, who continue to be imprisoned after fifteen to thirty years. Am I saying that US political prisoners are similar to Nelson Mandela? Yes. In the most fundamental ways they are. People like Sekou Odinga, Sundiata Acoli, people like Carmen Valentin and Oscar Lopez of the [Puerto Rican Independence Movement], people like Leonard Peltier of the Native American movement, are as committed to the freedom and dignity of their people as Nelson Mandela has been. Should these people be given amnesty? Yes. We need truth and reconciliation just as South Africa has.

[*Rose introduces Ted Cruz as "an associate of the Cooper, Carvin and Rosenthal law firm in Washington, DC, and a former law clerk to Chief Justice William Rehnquist."*]

TED CRUZ: The obvious response to the question, Should amnesty be granted to America's political prisoners? is the response given by all of my friends and everyone I told about the topic of this show: What political prisoners? I'm here defending the startlingly counterintuitive position that violent criminals should be punished. Whether they're left wing, right wing, or absolutely wingless, if you commit a violent crime, you should be punished. I think all of us would agree that if one particular person is innocent, that person should be released. And there are procedures in the state and federal courts to do so. But the underlying principle is that anybody in this country who commits a violent crime, even if it's for some political manifesto that they swear their ideology to, should be punished. That's what our criminal system and our government are based upon, and it's what the citizens rely upon.

[*Kuby introduces Safiya Bukhari, saying, "she spent eight and a half years as an American political prisoner, and she's the director of the Jericho Project, designed to help win amnesty for political prisoners."*]

SAFIYA BUKHARI: Mr. Rose and Mr. Cruz contend that there are no political prisoners in the United States, based on the fact that the United States government only incarcerates people who commit crimes that break the laws under this system. But if that had been the contention in 1776, when the United States declared its independence, then all those people who commit crimes would today be in the jails not of the United States of America but of Europe. Fighters in the war of independence didn't win a revolution, change the system of this country, and become the United States on the basis of rhetoric or great political theologies and oratory. They did it with guns. They did it by sabotaging the government of England. Going to war. Committing crimes. Violating the laws of

England. So if that's the basis for determining there are no political prisoners, then by extension, nowhere in the world should there be revolutions. Nowhere in the world should there be liberation struggles. Nelson Mandela should still be in prison in South Africa. The United States needs to stop applying double standards. What comes to mind is that who has the power determines what is a crime.

[*Rose introduces Peter Thiel as "research fellow with the Independent Institute in Oakland, California."*]

PETER THIEL: We should not just talk about Black Panthers. Why don't we talk about a couple of other people? How about Timothy McVeigh, who bombed a federal building in Oklahoma? How about Paul Hill, the pro-lifer who shot an abortionist in Florida? How about the Unabomber, who went on a seventeen-year campaign against scientists, because he was committed to environmentalism? How about, for that matter, the World Trade Center bombers [of the 1993 bombing], Muslim fundamentalists who just wanted to kill people at random to build terror throughout the United States? All of these people were politically motivated. And they are not in jail because of their political motivations; they're in jail because of the violent crimes they committed. I want to also take issue with the South Africa comparison. The United States is not a fascist country, this is not Nazi Germany we're living in, and there are avenues for peaceful changes within this country. And that is why it's very different from the revolutionary war, when all the rights in the United States had been abrogated; it is very different from South Africa, where there were no avenues for peaceful change. There are, and we should use those.

KUBY asks Rose: Doesn't every nation on earth that holds political prisoners first define them as criminals? Nelson Mandela was defined as a criminal—he engaged in sabotage against the South African government—Gerry Adams in Northern Ireland was a criminal, even Jesus Christ was tried, convicted, and executed as a criminal. So isn't your dichotomy between political prisoners and simple criminal defendants a false dichotomy?

ROSE: No, because you're confusing other countries with the United States and our system of justice. I don't condone what happened in South Africa. In the United States the people that you term as political prisoners, are in prison because they committed violent crime. They were judged by juries, sentenced by judges. That is our system.

KUBY: But take the Puerto Rican independence fighters, for example. We're now in the one hundredth year of American colonialism in Puerto Rico. Puerto Rico was illegally occupied by a military force. In March 1997, the United States recognized that the people of Puerto Rico never had the opportunity to choose their own destiny in an election. If your nation is invaded and you take up arms against the invader, the invading country is going to punish you, but you are still a political prisoner—you're fighting for the liberation of your country.

ROSE: I do not agree that Puerto Rican independence should be had by bombing. There's a vote.

KUBY: You don't have the right to define the terms of struggle for oppressed people. Maybe in British-occupied Palestine Menachem Begin should have petitioned the English government instead of blowing up the King David Hotel. Maybe the Irish freedom fighters should have gone out and petitioned Parliament instead of planting bombs. But you don't have the right to dictate their terms of struggle, and it still is political.

ROSE: Most people in Puerto Rico do not want independence. A minority would vote for independence. Of those people who want independence, a miniscule number would choose to do it through death and violence.

BERKMAN: But the vast majority of the elected officials and the people of Puerto Rico support the release of the Puerto Rican political prisoners. Whether or not they would personally have decided on that course of action, they see them as patriots and part of their struggle. Also, internationally, the UN has never recognized any of the votes [on Puerto Rico's status] because under international anticolonial law, Puerto Rico would have to be decolonized first in order to have an honest or fair election, which the United States has never allowed to happen, which is why Puerto Rico still comes under the auspices of the decolonization committee of the UN.

You may not support the release of [the Puerto Rican political prisoners], but that's a problem of being in the majority in this country. The majority uses "democratic majority rule" to tyrannize a minority. But if you leave it up to the majority of Puerto Rican people, do you have any question that they would vote for the release of the prisoners?

THIEL asks Kuby: Who gets counted as a political prisoner? Why are the people who bombed the Word Trade Center not political prisoners? Why is the Unabomber not a political prisoner?

KUBY: The definition [of a political prisoner] is someone whose actions were taken in furtherance of the principles articulated in the United Nations Universal Declaration of Human Rights. That document speaks specifically of liberation movements; it speaks of equality among races and religions. So any individual who engages in a racist act—for example, a white supremacist who wants to reinstitute slavery or someone who wants to impose his religion on anyone—is excluded from that definition.

Start with the principles articulated in the UN Universal Declaration of Human Rights. Ask, Were these folks fighting for equality of all people, or were they fighting to establish a form of white supremacy? You can take, for example, Puerto Rican revolutionaries who were following the mandates of the [UN] decolonization committee, who were trying to free their country. Were they trying to overthrow the government of the United States and establish Puerto Rican dictatorship? Of course not. They were trying to get the United States out of their nation in compliance with the principles of the United Nations, which says, you can resist colonialism by any means necessary.

THIEL: So the only violence that's condoned is left-wing violence, violence in furtherance of left-wing causes.

KUBY: No, but it's probably only leftists who engage in acts of violence in support of equality and liberation. The right wing, virtually by definition, engages in violence in support of dictatorship, fascism, and inequality. [And they get shorter sentences.]

Contrast Susan Rosenberg, a white [leftist] woman who is serving fifty-eight years in prison[5] for possession of weapons and explosives, with Raymond Malvasi, whose case was also in the Southern District of New York. Malvasi blew up one abortion clinic, tried to bomb another, financed his bombing spree through robbing banks, and stored explosives in downtown Manhattan within two hundred feet of a school. He was prosecuted by the same government at the same time as Susan Rosenberg. He received seven years. Seven years in prison, and he was released after three. So Susan Rosenberg would be better off had she blown up abortion clinics. Right-wing, lunatic, anti-choice [defendants] don't need the political prisoner designation, because the government lets them right out of prison.

CRUZ: So someone goes out and murders somebody, but deep in their heart they're committed to the Universal Charter, then we should just ignore it?

KUBY: It depends who's being killed and for what reason. I'm not suggesting that this is Nazi Germany. But during the early 1980s, there was a secret, covert, and totally illegal war being conducted against the people of El Salvador and the people of Nicaragua by Oliver North and Ronald Reagan clandestinely, and when Congress tried to intervene, Oliver North and his friends lied to Congress about it. So we had the facade of democracy, but in practice when people tried to give voice to democratic principles, they were subverted by the very people you now extol as heroes. In that context, it's understandable that people would pick up a gun.

THIEL: The argument is not that America is perfect. The argument is that there is sufficient freedom, a sufficiently open society that there are avenues for peaceful change.

KUBY: And I'm not arguing that these political prisoners are perfect either. And I'm not arguing that they all did great things, and I'm not arguing that mistakes weren't made. I'm saying that given the historical and political context in which they were fighting, given the enormous amount of time they've already served in prison, it's time for reconciliation and amnesty.

BERKMAN: I want to return to the question of whether or not there's a democracy in the United States. One of the things we've always worried about is the tyranny of the majority.

In 1973, I was at Wounded Knee, where Native American people, who also have a long history of being tyrannized in the United States, tried to take back some of their land on their "reservation" in South Dakota, and were surrounded, as was I, by tanks, armored personnel carriers, machine guns—it was a war zone in the middle of the United States. And there was shooting back and forth, and people on both sides were killed. If there's a democracy in the United States, and Native Americans make up two or three million people, but are nations that were destroyed, why does the United States get to say, "We killed you, we eliminated most of your people, and now we get to vote on whether or not you get your rights as a nation." That's part of a "democracy" in this country as well. That's what people fight about.

BUKHARI: Ron talks about the secret war against Nicaragua. What about the secret war against dissidents right here in this country, the counterintelligence program? The same counterintelligence program that was used against the New York Three right here in New York, when they were on trial at 100 Centre Street for all sorts of activities that ended up, bottom line, with charges that they assassinated two New York City police officers. The counterintelligence program through which J. Edgar Hoover, in 1968, gave authority to the FBI to use any manner of activities in order to destroy the Black Panther Party, destroy the Black liberation movements in this country, [directed FBI agents to do that] even if they have to manufacture evidence or charges in order to get these people off the street. They could do this. And it was totally secret. It didn't come out until the late 1970s when the Church Committee said that this program, COINTELPRO, actually existed. What about that, the secret war against people inside this country who are involved in dissident activities?

CRUZ: To the extent improper things happened, I—and I expect most Americans—disapprove of them, and I don't deny that there are, on occasions, prosecutors who screw up and there are, on occasions, police officers that do things they shouldn't. I don't buy the argument of left-wing activists that there's this vast, overarching conspiracy of all the judges, all the politicians, all the police officers working together to oppress everyone.

BERKMAN: Nobody is saying that. The Church Committee—Church was a United States senator—had official hearings that documented this whole series of strategies from the FBI, directed by J. Edgar Hoover, to destroy the Black liberation movement, the Socialist Party, and the Native American movement. That was the FBI.

THIEL: Why should these people [the prisoners] not be treated as first-degree murderers? I mean, generally speaking, most of these things involve premeditated acts of violence.

BERKMAN: Let's talk about international law. I was a cellmate, in MCC [Metropolitan Correctional Center] in New York City, of Joe Doherty, who is a member of the Irish Republican Army, who was convicted, in one of the British secret courts in Northern Ireland, of killing a British army captain. Who escaped and came to the United States and was captured by the FBI. Every court of law that he went to upheld his right to not be extradited back to England and Ireland because there's a political exception to extradition treaties. And that international political exception recognizes that people have the right, even if they're not in uniform, to be soldiers in a liberation war, and uses that same International Declaration of Human Rights. We did not make up the definition. This is recognized under international law. But finally, the United States, because of their international political interests, dictated that Joe Doherty should be forced to be sent back to Ireland. But first he went through year after year after year where he was recognized—although he killed, in an ambush, a British army captain—that he was part of a liberation movement. For only a few political prisoners, I would say, is the issue of first-degree murder applicable. Many were responding to shoot-outs with the police that were initiated by the police, which gets back to COINTELPRO.

KUBY asks Thiel: Take a look at some of the liberation struggles in other nations at other times. You recognize, don't you, whether you support them or not, that the Jewish liberation movement in Palestine used force to expel the British, even blew up the King David Hotel, killed men, women, and children, Jews, Muslims, and Christians, right?

THIEL: I agree that there are lots of liberation movements that have used violence and in some cases it's legitimate. If I was a Jew in the Warsaw ghetto in 1943 and the Nazis were coming in to get me and exterminate me, I would have a right to shoot back, to defend myself. I think that would be perfectly legitimate. But we are not living in Nazi Germany today. We are not living in South Africa. We don't have a fascist government. There are other avenues for peaceful change, and that's why it is not necessary.

It makes a very big difference what time frame you're dealing with. When this happened one hundred years ago and all of the people involved are long dead, that's quite different from people coming after you.

BERKMAN: That's very convenient, for people in power to say: "Now we start all over again." For Native American people—having destroyed you, forget the fact that you have the right to your own territory—we'll decide, the majority now will decide for you. For Black people: Slavery was over one hundred years ago; lynching, that was the 1920s, let's see . . . segregation—I grew up in segregation. In the 1960s, with Malcolm X and Martin Luther King being killed, Black people might have the sense that any organized movement for their freedom and human rights would be destroyed by the US government. That was only thirty years ago. Now it's the subject of movies and hats. But for many people, it's their reality, and many of the Black Panther people we're talking about, including Safiya, very much came from that exact period of time where they felt they were totally at risk of being destroyed by the US government's illegal actions.

BUKHARI: The problem is that the white majority rule in this country—and that's what we have here—if they are in power, and they are in control, what will happen if they can hold out for X amount of years? Then we'll be dead and the situation is moot. And that's the situation that happened in Puerto Rico in 1898 when Spain was thrown out and the United States came in. And they held out one hundred years.

Your Constitution says it. People don't throw off governments for light or transient reasons. They have a right to change governments that don't work to ensure their freedom and their security. And these people are in that situation now. You talk about the Warsaw ghetto. There are ghettos in the United States right here. There are people without jobs. There are homeless people. And the vast majority of these people who make up these situations are not represented and defended by this government.

CRUZ asks Bukhari: Who is responsible for the oppression of political prisoners?

BUKHARI: It's not oppression of political prisoners; it's oppression of people who become political prisoners when they react against the oppression.

CRUZ: Well, I assume that you don't maintain it's just Republicans. So it's essentially everyone, all the prosecutors and all the judges?

BUKHARI: No. It's those people who make a profit off the exploitation of those who don't have. For example, right now in the prison-industrial complex, it's those people who don't have a problem with taking the jobs off the streets, putting the jobs in the prisons, and then sending the people off to prison to do the jobs at no wages or insignificant wages, so that they can make money off that cheap labor. It's those people that don't give adequate medical care to poor people who don't have the money to pay for the medical care. It's those people who are in control of the medical system.

THIEL: But who are these people?

BUKHARI: You know who the people are. You see them every day.

You think I see the whole world as a conspiracy, and that's not the case. When we talk about the cases of these political prisoners, we have to talk about the situation that led to these people being involved in political struggle. Maybe it led to organizing their communities, as I was—organizing around welfare issues, organizing around free breakfast programs because people didn't have food to feed their children before they went to school, organizing around homelessness and indecent housing issues. And then, because the situations were not being dealt with, we ended up moving from one level to another one.[7] You don't become political activists out of a vacuum.

CRUZ: I agree with you entirely that working for social causes and working to help the needy is a wonderful thing and should be done more. But do you see any difference between that and violent crime and murder?

BUKHARI: I'll just use myself as an example. I have a problem with violence for the sake of violence. The people I know all over the country as political prisoners have a problem with violence for the sake of violence. Violence is a last resort, when you've tried everything else. When we had ten-year-old Clifford Glover and all the other youth that were shot down in the streets of New York and the police would say that they had shot this ten-year-old in the back because they thought he was a robber, they'd shot him because they thought he'd just robbed something, and he's really on the way to school or to work with his father, and he gets shot down, and the cops get justifiable homicide; when Eleanor Bumpurs in the Bronx gets shot in her home because she's coming at the police with a kitchen knife, and she could have been dealt with without being shot and killed; when you have this kind of absence of respect for people because of the color of the skin, there is a problem.[8] And when you've tried every other way to deal with the desensitization of the police who occupy your community, then there's a problem. And you move to another level to try to deal with that. The level that I moved to was not picking up a gun and going out and shooting somebody. It was educating and organizing our people to put up a resistance. Then, when that didn't help, underground forces came into existence so that the police would know they could not come into our communities, shoot down our children, kill our grandmothers, without being met with another force of equal violence. And when that happened—you can check the records for yourself—when those people dealt with revolutionary justice, the amount of police murders in our communities went down by leaps and bounds. When that revolutionary justice ceased to operate because of a lot of the things that went down in the Justice Department, the level of police violence went back up. And that's what we have in the streets of New York today.

KUBY asks Rose: We've had a lot of discussion in the past hour about the nature of the war. Let's talk about the nature of the peace. You acknowledge as a prosecutor, don't you, that many, many people who commit comparable acts for right-wing purposes are serving a fraction of the sentence of leftists.

ROSE: That's probably statistically true.

KUBY: That people on the left who blew up an unoccupied military building are serving far longer than people who blew up abortion clinics, generally speaking.

ROSE: I don't know that there have been that many prosecutions of people who've blown up abortion clinics as opposed to, as we call them, left-wing bombings. But yes.

KUBY: So why can't we at least recognize that we have, as a government, treated leftists, because of their politics, because of their ideology, more severely than we've treated comparable bombers for right-wing motivations, and say, "All right, for those people who are no longer going to engage in violence, let them out of jail." What's wrong with taking these people, who have already served far longer terms than they would have if they were right-wingers, and saying, Look, the war is over. We want to stop the violence. Well, one way we stop the violence is by reconciliation and amnesty.

ROSE: I have no problem with that except when you're dealing with crimes of murder. For example, the Brinks robbery. There were two dead cops and one Brinks guard who are dead. How do they come alive? Who goes to them and says, I'm sorry? [These defendants] should be treated just like anyone else who consciously planned an armed robbery where people were murdered.

KUBY: But here's the problem. These actions—Brinks and the Fraunces Tavern bombing—didn't take place in some sort of vacuum. The precursor to Fraunces Tavern took place on January 11, 1975, when a CIA-trained Cuban counterrevolutionary blew up a cafeteria in Mayaguez, Puerto Rico, killed two *independentistas*, murdered one child, and maimed ten other people. In response, the FALN blew up Fraunces Tavern.[9] So it wasn't the Puerto Ricans who began blowing up American restaurants first. It was CIA-trained Cubans, who were never punished. Who were never punished. And look at COINTELPRO, the murders of Mark Clark and Fred Hampton, again by the police. It was out of that context that these acts of violence grew. I'm not suggesting that these acts [by the Left] are all justified. I'm suggesting that there's something fundamentally unfair about putting one side in prison for the rest of their lives and letting the other side go.

ROSE: Do you think for one minute that agents of the FBI who are working now, Louis Freeh, the director, who is probably one of the most honorable people I've ever met, aren't sad for what COINTELPRO was? I apologize for what COINTELPRO was.

KUBY: But one side goes to jail forever, the other side goes free, and I'm just saying let's have a little bit of equity. Let's all acknowledge we've all made mistakes, let's shake hands, and let's move together in the glorious endeavor of democracy. How about that?

CRUZ: It strikes me as altogether reasonable that an individual who states in the beginning that he has an intention to commit violent acts, then proceeds to carry out those violent acts, then continues to say that he intends to commit violent acts in the future and that he is committed to a lifelong course of violence against the innocent, I absolutely think that that person should be punished more severely.

BERKMAN: Right, and that describes almost nobody that I know, because people are not engaged in violence for the sake of violence. In fact you may notice that just as COINTELPRO is over, there's not been a big engagement by the Left in armed struggle over the last fifteen years either. People made judgments sometimes that were marred by the reality of police and FBI repression about when to engage in armed struggle, not because they had some lifelong commitment to violence. So if you leave aside your mischaracterization of these real people, should we not, in the spirit of reconciliation, [say,] "At some points some terrible things happened in this society, people on both sides reacted to it, and it's time to have truth and reconciliation"?

CRUZ: Violent criminals should be punished. Do you believe that someone who commits a violent crime but is deeply convinced in their heart of hearts and soul of souls that they're doing it to vindicate freedom, vindicate equality, should ever be punished?

BERKMAN: Your definition of political prisoner is not the same as mine. It's not a matter just of individual motivation. International law recognizes that "violent criminals" like Joe Doherty are political prisoners and should not be subjected to the criminal penalties or extradited back to the countries where they face criminal penalties—it recognizes that they are parts of political movements. Part of giving amnesty to political prisoners is saying to the Black community, for example, "Five hundred years after the discovery of America, and after years of slavery, we need to move forward." Part of moving forward is releasing the people who fought for freedom. Part of it, for Native Americans, is saying [the government] really did do terrible things. But Leonard Peltier is still in prison for fighting back about it. It's a political process. No one wakes up one day and says, for my political beliefs, I should go out and do this. That wasn't what I was part of; it wasn't what Safiya was part of; it's not part of what happened that put these people in prison. They were part of organizations, they were part of movements.

BUKHARI asks Thiel: I'll go back to when you say that all people who commit violent acts should be incarcerated and the book should be thrown at them. I'm going back to the Constitution. I continue to go back to the Constitution and the Revolutionary War because that's my basis in struggle. I believe in the Constitution, and I believe in the Bill of Rights, and I believe in the Declaration of Independence. For a long time I believed that the United States practiced what it preached. But then racism in this country, the haves and the have-nots in this country, became a reality to me. You say that violence, period—whether it's on the part of a great big bunch of people or an individual—is not something that we should deal with because we have a political way of resolving our contradictions. So how do you address the issue that the United States government does not want to engage in diplomacy with Saddam Hussein? Is that not violence, to drop bombs on hundreds of thousands of people at one time, when you created a situation to try to deal with another country? How do you justify the United States' refusal to [deal in diplomacy], and not deal with the situation inside this country that way?

THIEL: There's a very different situation when another country threatens the US, threatens civilians of Israel. That's a big issue with Saddam Hussein, as opposed to violent individuals within a free and open society who choose to engage in violence. I'll agree. Mistakes were made on our side. Mistakes were made on the side of conservatives. What people did to the American Indians was terrible.

BUKHARI: I'm not talking about conservatives. We're talking about a government that has changed hands from conservative to Democrat over and over again, and it continues to be the same thing.

THIEL: I'll make it more general. America has made mistakes. I will agree with that. But the question is, What do we do today? What do we do in practice in 1998?

BUKHARI: Amnesty and freedom for all political prisoners.

THIEL: Well, I would suggest that what we do is, we don't condone violence.

BUKHARI: On either part—the part of the government and the part of the people. You can't negotiate using violence because you have the means of winning, and then tell us that we have to negotiate by words only.

THIEL: This is the way the criminal justice system works. The government uses violence to restrain even more violence from breaking out. The government's violent in prosecuting criminals. But that's to restrain even more violence. And basically, if we can't do that, the whole civilized fabric of society will start to disintegrate.

BUKHARI: Even if the United States goes beyond its own criminal justice system and uses injustice to bring about justice? When it does not support its own principles, when it uses lying and dishonesty to enact its own justice system? That should happen?

THIEL asks Bukhari: I want to follow up on this idea that mistakes were made. Do you actually think big mistakes were made by these liberation movements in the early seventies?

Debate: Should We Grant Amnesty to America's Political Prisoners?

BUKHARI: Let me say this: In making decisions about when to do what, we may have, at different points, misconstrued where the people were at.

THIEL: So you were in the vanguard and the people weren't in the vanguard yet. Is that what the problem was?

BUKHARI: What I'm saying is the same thing I said to the parole board when I made parole. I don't condone violence for the sake of violence. But at the same time, I'm not opposed to using violence if violence is necessary. I would not go out and do the same thing now that I did then, because the timing is not right. But at some point in time if the situation requires it, I would. But I don't think the situation requires it.

[*Closing statements:*]

ROSE: I understand your position, and I think perhaps it is time to put this all behind us. On a case-by-case basis, I would have no problem with sitting down and reviewing these files, with one caveat. If the first thing the person I'm reviewing tells me is, "Let me out, because I believe in everything I believed in twenty years ago, and I would do the same things I did twenty years ago," that person's not entitled for any consideration whatsoever.

KUBY: One of the things I think this discussion shows is that one person's terrorist in some circumstances is another person's freedom fighter. The people in America's prisons who have committed these acts acted as part of an ongoing political struggle. And if we are ever going to resolve the problem of political violence in this country, it can only come through discussion, through dialogue, through amnesty, and hopefully through freedom.

Notes

1. The descriptions in quotes reflect the way the participants were identified on the show. Ron Kuby is an attorney in New York City. After years of practice in an office with renowned civil rights attorney William Kunstler, Ron formed his own law office following Kunstler's death in 1995. Ron has also been a TV and radio commentator, having appeared regularly on WABC and later on *Air America* and *Court TV*. His office website says, "The Law Office of Ronald L. Kuby has represented some of the most reviled and revered people in some of the most high-profile criminal and civil rights actions in the United States" (kubylaw.com).

   Alan Berkman, MD, died on June 5, 2009, after battling cancer, both in prison and after his release, for twenty-four years. He had been a progressive activist since the early 1960s, when he became active in the movements for civil rights and against the Vietnam War. After medical school he practiced community medicine in New York City and Lowndes County, Alabama. In 1971 he provided medical care to survivors of the Attica prison uprising; he also provided medical expertise for the legal cases arising from the uprising. In 1974 he crawled through gunfire to deliver medical care to the Native American resistance at Wounded Knee. He was a political prisoner in federal custody from 1985 to 1992, nearly dying of cancer because of maltreatment (as documented in the *New York Times* and on CBS-TV's *60 Minutes*). After his release he worked in the field of HIV/AIDS, first treating mentally ill, homeless men with HIV; then founding Health GAP/Global Access Project, an organization to bridge "the chasm between the resources available to the wealthy and the poor countries," in Alan's words. He also became an international AIDS expert. At the time of his death, Alan was vice chair of the Department of Epidemiology at Columbia University's Mailman School of Public Health. (For more, see "Alan Berkman, 63, Activist Doctor Dies," obituary, the *New York Times*, June 14, 2009, p. A-19.)

2. As a prosecutor, Charles Rose often faced Ron Kuby in court cases, prosecutor versus defense attorney. From 1979 to 1994, Rose worked in the office of the US attorney for the Eastern District of New York. According to an obituary in the *New York Times*, Rose "supervised the prosecution of cases developed by the Police Department and the Federal Bureau of Investigation in a joint task force on terrorism. In that role he was concerned mainly with a group seeking independence

for Puerto Rico and also with an anarchist group, the United Freedom Front." In December 1998, Rose died of a brain tumor.

At the time of the debate, R. Ted Cruz was an attorney with a Washington, DC, law firm. Cruz went on to become US solicitor general for Texas (2003–8). According to his résumé, Cruz served as "Department of Justice Coordinator for the Bush Transition Team. From June 1999 until December 2000, he served as Domestic Policy Advisor to President George W. Bush on the Bush-Cheney 2000 campaign, where he had primary responsibility for all legal policy." The résumé also highlights the following achievements:

"Successfully represented Texas before the US Supreme Court in Medellin v. Texas, which held in a landmark 6-3 decision that the World Court cannot bind the US justice system and the president cannot order the state courts to obey the World Court. [The case involved a Mexican man sentenced to death in Texas; he appealed based on the failure of the United States to allow him to communicate with the Mexican consulate. Medellin was executed on August 6, 2008. The case was a significant victory for states' rights: the Bush administration succeeded in getting a ruling that the president cannot order a state to follow international law.]

"Helped assemble the Bush legal team, devise strategy, and draft pleadings in the Florida and US Supreme Courts during the 2000 Florida presidential recounts, winning twice in the US Supreme Court."

The Independent Institute is a privately funded "libertarian" think tank with offices in Oakland, California, and Washington, DC. Its goals are "to transcend the all-too-common politicization and superficiality of public policy research and debate, redefine the debate over public issues, and foster new and effective directions for government reform" (independent.org). Thiel, a research fellow at the institute and a lawyer, is the founder, former chairman, and chief executive officer of PayPal and the author of *The Diversity Myth: Multiculturalism and Political Intolerance on Campus*, published by the institute.

3. FALN: Fuerzas Armadas de Liberacíon Nacional, a clandestine organization for Puerto Rican independence.

4. Fraunces Tavern is a restaurant in the financial district of New York City. See note 9 in this chapter.

5. Susan Rosenberg was released in January, 2001, under a commutation

order by President Bill Clinton.

6. In fact, Alan was convicted only of possession of explosives.

7. In other speeches and writings, Safiya says the attacks conducted under COINTELPRO were responsible for the lack of ultimate success of community organizing projects.

8. New York police officer Thomas Shea killed Clifford Glover in 1973; Eleanor Bumpurs was shot and killed by cops in 1984. Like the case of Amadou Diallo years later, these cases became flashpoints for community outrage over the killing of Black citizens by police.

9. The FALN took credit for a bombing of Fraunces Tavern, on January 24, 1975, in which four people were killed. The action became a focus of intense debate over armed struggle and the right of the Puerto Rican people to fight for independence.

22. Kamau Sadiki: Injustice Continues . . .

Dated 2002, this essay is one of the last texts Safiya wrote before her death. This is a slightly edited version of the essay; the original appears on various Internet sites and in the book *Let Freedom Ring.*[1]

Sitting in a cell in the Fulton County Jail in Atlanta, Georgia, under the name of Freddie Hilton, is Kamau Sadiki. Kamau is awaiting trial on a thirty-year-old murder case.[2] A Fulton County police officer was found shot to death in his car outside a service station in [1971]. A case that they refused to try thirty years ago because they didn't believe they could win it. The question is, Why him? Why now?

Kamau Sadiki is a former member of the Black Panther Party. At the age of seventeen he dedicated his life to the service of his people. He worked out of the Jamaica office of the Black Panther Party. Having internalized the Ten-Point Program and Platform, the Three Main Rules of Discipline, and the Eight Points of Attention, Kamau used his knowledge to guide his organizing efforts within the Black community.[3]

He worked in the Free Breakfast Program, getting up every morning, going to his designated assignment, and cooking and feeding hungry children before they went to school. When the Free Breakfast Program was over for that morning, he reported to the office, gathered his papers, received his assignment for the day, and went out into the community to sell his papers, the Black Panther Party newspapers. While selling his papers, he continued to educate the people, organizing tenants, welfare mothers—whomever he came in contact with. At the end of the day, he reported to the office. He wrote his daily report and attended political education classes.

Kamau Sadiki was one of the thousands of young Black men and women who made up the Black Panther Party—the rank-and-file members of the Party who made the Party the international political machine it was. While the media followed Huey Newton, Bobby Seale, and others, the day-to-day work of the Party was being carried out by these rank-and-file brothers and sisters, the backbone of the Black Panther Party. They were the nameless and faceless, the tireless workers who carried out the programs of the Party, without whom there would have been no one to do the work of the free health clinics, free clothing drive, liberation schools, and Free Breakfast for Children Program. It was to these brothers and sisters that the people in the Black community looked when they needed help and support.

It was because of this tireless work in the community that J. Edgar Hoover, the FBI director at that time, declared the Black Panther Party to be the greatest threat to national security and sought to destroy it. It was not because we advocated the use of the gun that the FBI considered the Black Panther Party a threat. It was because of the politics that guided the gun. We had been taught that politics guide the gun; therefore our politics had to be correct and constantly evolving. We had to study and read the newspapers to keep abreast of the constantly changing political situation. But this was not the image that the government wanted to portray of the Black Panther Party. It preferred the image of the ruthless gangster, the racist, gun-toting thug. Every opportunity that came up to talk or write about the Black Panther Party was used to portray this image.

When the opportunity didn't arise on its own, the government created situations and circumstances to make the claim.

An all-out propaganda war was waged on the Black Panther Party. Simultaneously, a psychological and military campaign was instituted. The government's war of terror against the Black Panther Party saw more than twenty-eight young Black men and women of the Black Panther Party killed over a period of less than four years, hundreds more in prison or underground, dozens in exile, and the Black Panther Party in disarray. Even though the Black Panther Party, as an entity, had been destroyed, the government never ceased observing those Panthers who were still alive. Whether or not others believed it, the government took seriously that aspect of the Black Panther Party's teaching that included the Ten-Ten-Ten Program: if one Panther organized ten people, those ten people organized ten people, and those ten people organized ten people, exponentially we would organize the world for revolution. The only way to stop that was to weed out the Panthers. Not only must the Black Panther Party be destroyed, but all the people who were exposed to the teachings must be weeded out and put on ice or destroyed.

During this turbulent time, Kamau had been among the members of the Party who had gone underground. He was subsequently captured and spent five years in prison.[4] While he was on parole, he legally changed his name from Fred Hilton to Kamau Sadiki.

About eighteen months ago, a story appeared in the *New York Daily News* about a former Panther being arrested and charged with child sexual abuse. The newspaper identified the former Panther as Freddie Hilton. The first thing that comes into the minds of most people when such an allegation is read in the newspaper is that it must be true. But we in the Black Panther Party have been taught the adage, "No investigation, no right to speak." In a case like this, a political case, it's extremely important to get to the bottom of such an allegation as quickly as possible. Part of the pattern of COINTELPRO has been to demonize individuals, destroy their credibility, and discredit their character, thereby making them vulnerable to the enemy because their base of support has been eroded.

It appears that the charge against Kamau was brought by the woman he had been living with for a number of years and that she brought it in order to get him out of the house. Kamau had been, and still is, very sick and suffering from sarcoidosis, cirrhosis of the liver, and hepatitis C. He had been out of work sick for an extended period. Everyone believed he was going to die. However, he didn't die. He went into remission, got better, and returned to work. The problem was, his woman friend had moved on with her life and wanted him out of the way. She told the police that he had abused her daughter three years earlier. When that didn't stand up to scrutiny, the police were told he had a gun in the house and where it could be found and that he was a former Black Panther, etc.

Even though the government did not initiate this arrest, they seized the opportunity, based on today's climate, to get Kamau off the street. A domestic dispute was handled in an incorrect manner and a man's reputation and character have been sullied and destroyed. Says Kamau, "All I have is my name and my honor. They can't be allowed to take that away from me." The molestation charge was dropped, and Kamau pled guilty to a disorderly conduct charge. While he was serving his sentence, the warrant from Georgia was issued.

The damage had already been done. A seed had been planted in the minds of the people. While the story of the charge being made had appeared in the newspaper, there was no story of the disposition of the case. Kamau Sadiki had never, at any time, molested any child. But people are more interested in the fact that this allegation was made than they are in the fact that he is going on trial for the murder of a police officer.

While the people who would normally come to his defense were still reeling from these charges and were being told not to make a big deal out of it, the state was using this time to put pressure on Kamau. Knowing that he suffers from hepatitis C, cirrhosis of the liver, and sarcoidosis, they told him that unless he helped them capture Assata Shakur he would "die in prison." They told him that if he worked with them and got Assata to leave Cuba and go to some other country where they could apprehend her, they would not prosecute him on the police killing. This seemed to be the right time to play this card. So many different forces were congealing in the world that had changed the mood of the country in favor of mania and fear. The conflict had heightened with 9/11. The USA PATRIOT Act had been passed, making it unpatriotic to disagree with or not go along with the policies of the government. Police and other uniformed personnel were heroes and heroines and above the law—untouchable. What could not have been prosecuted thirty years ago was now, in this climate, possible.

Then, too, Kamau has not been in the spotlight in the past twenty-five years. What people don't know is, he never was. After being released from prison [in 1981], he went to work. Having two daughters and himself to support, he went to work. He worked for the telephone company in New York for more than eighteen years. Both his daughters finished college and are now married with families of their own. No, Kamau wasn't out beating the drums; he was being the quiet warrior that he is. He is also a Muslim—another liability in these United States, where the term is almost synonymous with "terrorist" now.

There are many other lies and distortions that come to play in this case. The most glaring and insidious is that Freddie Hilton had been in hiding under the name Kamau Sadiki, making it hard for the government to find him and indict him—a bold-faced lie. During the entire five years Kamau spent in prison, he wrote and signed all his mail (which was always monitored) under the name Kamau Sadiki. When he was released from prison, he was on parole; while he was on parole he had his name legally changed to Kamau Sadiki. His parole officer was aware of this. When he went to work, he didn't obtain a new Social Security number under Kamau Sadiki, but his name was changed on his old card to Kamau Sadiki. There was never an attempt to hide from anything. How could he hide? One of his daughters was also the daughter of Assata Shakur, and he couldn't hide from that. He was always under the scrutiny of the federal government, if for this reason alone.

Kamau Sadiki did not "come to the attention" of the police because of the molestation charge, but the charge was a convenient way to arrest him and keep him in jail while they attempted to use him. They knew who he was and where he was all the time. What they didn't have was a convenient excuse to arrest him. Once he was in jail, they knew they didn't have a lot of time because the molestation charge would not hold up. So they placed the warrant from Georgia on him to give them additional time to put pressure on him.

New evidence?! No. No new evidence. The same old story that was not enough to indict at the time of the death of the police officer in [1971] is now enough to indict in 2002. Thirty years later, they are able to find independent witnesses to corroborate the story. It boggles the mind that they have found a way to make memories, which usually fade over time, reverse themselves and grow stronger.

We have long held that there is a diabolical scheme going on in the minds of those who run this government. It is not something that started yesterday or the day before. It is not something that will end tomorrow or the day after. This scheme is to rid the world of those who disagree with the politics of the United States. The Black Panther Party was such an entity, and it no longer exists. It was systematically and meticulously destroyed almost thirty years ago. But the effort to destroy the legacy of the Black Panther Party continues. Books are continually written attacking the Party. Daily, articles still appear in newspapers and periodicals redefining the work of the Black Panther Party. Panthers are still in prison and still going to prison from cases dating back to the sixties and seventies.

The further away we get from the sixties and seventies, the more likely it becomes that people will forget what happened and what we were really about. When issues are taken out of their historical place and placed into another day and time, people tend to get confused. The government banks on that. Historically, it has worked for them. In this new day and time, in the shadow of 9/11, in Atlanta, Georgia, one of the greatest historical figures of the civil rights/Black power era was convicted and sent to prison for life without the possibility of parole.[5] The response of the community was, "We told you we were capable of convicting him." This gave impetus to the government's plan to clean up the streets of dissent.

In 1967 it was disclosed that one of the goals of COINTEL-PRO was to "expose, disrupt, misdirect, discredit, or otherwise neutralize. . . . No opportunity must be missed to exploit through counterintelligence techniques . . . for maximum effectiveness. . . . Long-range goals are being set. . . . Prevent [them from] gaining respectability . . . and a final goal should be to prevent the long-range growth of militant black organizations, especially among youth."[6]

COINTELPRO didn't go away. It continues today. This case,

as well as those of Mumia Abu-Jamal and Imam Jamil Abdullah Al-Amin, are prime examples of the existence of COINTELPRO and its agenda. We have a tendency to forget, to think that things have changed. The enemy doesn't forget. They maintain files and lists. They maintain think tanks and, when it is convenient and at the proper time, they move. The movements of the sixties caught them by surprise. They rushed to catch up and won the first skirmish. We still have casualties. While we were busy they were preparing so they wouldn't be caught off guard again. This round of activity on the part of the state is their effort to clean up the books. We must not allow them to do this. We must defend Kamau Sadiki. We must push back the state. We must not allow them to use Kamau as a scapegoat. We must Free Kamau Sadiki and all political prisoners.

Notes

1. Matt Meyer, ed., *Let Freedom Ring: A Collection of Documents from the Movements to Free US Political Prisoners* (Oakland, CA: PM Press, 2008).

2. On October 13, 2003, a year after this article was written—and shortly after Safiya's death—Kamau Sadiki was convicted of the 1971 shooting death of Atlanta police officer James Greene. Police reports of the case include the admission that "there was very little in the way of physical evidence—no weapons and no witnesses." Yet, thirty-two years after the fact, Kamau Sadiki was convicted of the act based on evidence that seems shaky and unreliable at best. (Twymon Myers, shot to death by police in New York City in November 1973, was also named as a suspect in the case.) A hearing on an appeal in Kamau Sadiki's case was held in April 2009; a decision is awaited.

    In 2001, when a girlfriend accused Kamau of molesting her daughter, according to a police website, "The molestation allegations would later be dropped but the girl's mother told the detectives that Sadiki used to be in the Black Liberation Army and that he kept an illegal gun in the house. [A police officer] went into a storage room in his New

Jersey office to get whatever files he could find. In one stack of papers, he found a wiretap request for Sadiki, then still Hilton. The draft of the affidavit mentioned Hilton as a suspect in the murder of an Atlanta Police Officer (with no disposition)." Then the police and the Atlanta FBI "found six witnesses to re-interview. Several of those individuals were former BLA members who had 'moved on,' becoming everything from ministers to professors. But [police] tracked down a woman who said that she'd seen Hilton and Myers murder Officer Greene. More than 30 years after that homicide, the only witness to the crime saw a photo of Sadiki. 'That's him,' she said." The judge imposed the maximum sentence possible. At sentencing, according to an account in the *Atlanta Journal-Constitution* at the time, Kamau "told the judge he is no longer proud of some of the BLA's actions, but said armed resistance was needed to respond to 'the oppressive climate at that time.'"

Kamau Sadiki, now in his late fifties, remains in prison in Augusta, Georgia, State Medical Prison. According to one of his daughters, Ksisay Torres, he is gravely ill.

3. For information on these programs of the Black Panther Party, see introduction, note 5, p. xlii.

4. Kamau Sadiki had been released from a New York State prison in 1981. His conviction, according to state corrections department files, was for possession of a weapon.

5. The reference is to Jamil Al-Amin, formerly known as H. Rap Brown, who was convicted of the 2000 killing of a police officer and sentenced to life in prison. Jamil Al-Amin is now incarcerated in the notorious federal control and isolation unit at Florence, Colorado, despite the fact that his case was tried in the state of Georgia.

6. "Counterintelligence Program/Black Nationalist—Hate Groups/Internal Security," FBI memo ("From: Director FBI"), various dates, 1967 and 1968 (reprinted at whatreallyhappened.com/RANCHO/POLITICS/COINTELPRO/COINTELPRO-FBI.docs.html and many other sites and books).

Afterword

For me, reading the thoughts of Safiya Asya Bukhari is a bit-tersweet experience; for to read her is to hear her, and to recognize her brilliance, her acute intelligence, her self-depre-cating humor, her deep commitment—all that, but mostly, her searing honesty. Such thoughts evoke an almost ethereal aroma of sweetness, like passing by a sunlit garden in a spring breeze.

Thus, we must acknowledge the truth that she is no longer among us, and that many of us didn't take the time to let her know how brilliant, beautiful, intelligent, committed, and hon-est we knew she was. Why not? Because we wrongly assumed that we could do it tomorrow, that we would drop her a letter next week, after the present project was over.

We had time.

But she did not. That fierce, powerful, determined Panther woman expired like a supernova: quickly, abruptly, in a flash, lighting up the heavens like a morning star. Did she know? In her final, fevered hours, did she know how admired she was, how respected, how loved? Hence the bitterness.

My memory of Safiya actually predates her adoption of her Muslim name. To a young, bare-faced Panther transferred from Columbia Avenue's Philadelphia branch office to the Black Panther Party East Coast Ministry of Information office in the Bronx, she was Sister Bernice, a tough, salty-mouthed officer who ran the office with grit and will.

Those who are familiar with my *We Want Freedom: A Life in the Black Panther Party* (2004) may recall my recollections of

Panther women, and in particular Sister Bernice, who ran the Bronx BPP office "with all the tenderness of a drill sergeant." In describing this sister, I recalled:

> She could be mercurial. At one moment she could be whispering encouragement to you as you worked on a project, but in the next she would bark out, "drop down and give me twenty!" and stand there, her dark, bespectacled face an impassive mask of obsidian, as she counted out the pushups: "1, 2, . . . 17, 17½—give me a real pushup, nigga—18, 19, 20." The office was a beehive of Panther productivity, and she, Sister Bernice, was the undisputed queen.[1]

That Sister Bernice would later emerge as Safiya Asya Bukhari. Her studies and life experiences (of love and war) led her to become a deeply conscientious and religious woman. But as these things enriched and transformed her life, her speech, her dress, and her worldview, the iron will of her core self remained. So did her solid integrity.

When she and her Black Liberation Army squad got engaged in an unfortunate shoot-out in Norfolk, Virginia, she was urged to choose between the Black revolution and her newfound religion as a condition of support. As she described it:

> On the one hand, I was faced with revolutionaries who had problems with my being Muslim. On the other hand, I was being told by Muslims that in order to receive support from them I had to denounce the Black liberation movement and my codefendant who was not a Muslim. All this was happening while I was in jail awaiting trial on a capital case.
>
> I didn't denounce anything or anyone.[2]

Although Safiya faced the electric chair, upon her and her codefendant's conviction (in a one-day trial) they were sentenced to forty years in prison. In April 1975, Bukhari was shipped to Virginia Correctional Center for Women in Goochland, Virginia. The medical "treatment" (for want of a better word) was so poor that Safiya was forced to escape to get belated treatment for fibroid tumors.

Safiya in "Freedom"

After eight harrowing years in prison (almost half spent in solitary), Safiya returned to Harlem a stronger, more committed revolutionary, and plunged into political work to defend her People, and also to support political prisoners. She was instrumental in founding the Jericho Movement, which sought freedom and amnesty for political prisoners and prisoners of war.

She was utterly tireless and committed to her People's freedom from the time she was nineteen to the day she passed from this life into what she believed to be the next.

Only with her untimely passing did some of us recognize the sheer magnitude of our loss. While perhaps best known as a Panther woman, she was obviously much more. She was a working member of the Republic of New Afrika; she was a wife (for a time), a mother, and a grandmother. She was a key organizer in half a dozen Black and socialist movements. She was a deep thinker who rarely forgot the lessons learned in her life, whether they came from her college days, her sorority (Eta Alpha Mu), her parents, her readings (whether of Mao's "Red Book" or the Holy Qur'an), and the harrowing lessons echoing down the centuries from the lost ancestors, from Africa, from the bleak Middle Passage, to the struggles of captives who yearned for freedom.

And as she was a student of these many things, so she was also a teacher, not only of youth, but also of her contemporaries, some of whom seemed to forget early lessons that she was determined to remind and reteach them.

It comes down to *organizing*.

It comes down to the people.

Even after her death, I'd talk to people on the phone and I heard more than once the refrain, "I've gotta call Safiya—," and an embarrassed silence would follow, as realization slowly caught up to reality.

But her passing wasn't the only tragedy; the tragedy was that more people didn't know her, learn from her, or grow from her fund of hard-won wisdom.

For many (hopefully the younger folks), this collection of her essays, written almost on the fly (that is, written by Safiya as an activist, engaged daily in social and revolutionary movements, rather than as a writer), is the next best thing. For her heart is here. Besides her beloved daughter, she loved her people with the passion of a mother. She wanted her people free. She wanted her people independent. She wanted her people safe. She wanted her people to be a force for life and love in the world.

She wanted her people *free*.

May her words preserved here play a part in that long, continuing freedom struggle, and the necessary revolution to come.

Mumia Abu-Jamal
Death Row, Summer 2006

Notes

1. Mumia Abu-Jamal, *We Want Freedom: A Life in the Black Panther Party* (Cambridge, MA: South End Press, 2004), 181.
2. Safiya Bukhari, "'Islam and Revolution' Is Not a Contradiction." [That essay is published in this book; see chapter 7, p. 64.]

Index

MUMIA ABU-JAMAL is author of many books, including *Jailhouse Lawyers*, *Live From Death Row*, and *We Want Freedom*. He has been living on death row in a Pennsylvania prison since 1982.

Born in the Bronx, SAFIYA BUKHARI joined the Black Panther Party in 1969. Imprisoned for nine years on charges in a Black Liberation Army case, Bukhari was released in 1983 and went on to co-found the New York Free Mumia Abu-Jamal Coalition and other organizations advocating for the release of political prisoners. She died in 2003 at the age of fifty-three.

ANGELA Y. DAVIS has been advocating for social justice causes for over five decades. She is Professor Emerita of History of Consciousness and of Feminist Studies at the University of California at Santa Cruz. She has spoken out for the rights of political prisoners, and for the abolition of imprisonment as the dominant strategy for addressing social problems, and is the author of many books including *The Meaning of Freedom*, *Women, Race & Class*, and *Are Prisons Obsolete?*

WONDA JONES is the daughter of Safiya Bukhari and a creator of the Safiya Bukhari-Albert Nuh Washington Foundation, which raises funds for the families of US political prisoners.

LAURA WHITEHORN has been a political activist since the 1960s. She spent fourteen years in prison for political acts. Released in 1999, she lives in New York City.

Printed in the USA
CPSIA information can be obtained
at www.ICGtesting.com
JSHW061500041024
71098JS00004B/147

9 781558 616103